DATE DUE

DEMCO

DEVELOPING FACULTY
TO USE TECHNOLOGY

DEVELOPING FACULTY TO USE TECHNOLOGY

Programs and Strategies to Enhance Teaching

David G. Brown

EDITOR

International Center For Computer-Enhanced Learning
Wake Forest University

ANKER PUBLISHING COMPANY, INC.
Bolton, Massachusetts

Developing Faculty to Use Technology
Programs and Strategies to Enhance Teaching

ISBN 1-882982-62-2

Composition by Deerfoot Studios
Cover design by Jennifer Arbaiza Graphic Design

Anker Publishing Company, Inc.
176 Ballville Road
P.O. Box 249
Bolton, MA 01740-0249 USA

www.ankerpub.com

ABOUT THE EDITOR

David G. Brown, a vice president at Wake Forest University, is a professor of economics and the dean of the International Center for Computer-Enhanced Learning. He has served as president of Transylvania University, chancellor of the University of North Carolina at Asheville, provost at three universities (Wake Forest, Miami of Ohio, and Drake), and chaired several national groups including the American Association for Higher Education, Higher Education Colloquium, the American Council on Education's Council of Chief Academic Officers, and the National Association of State Universities and Land-Grant College's Academic Council. He is editor-in-chief of the *Gallery of Courses Taught With Technology* and a member of EDUCAUSE's teaching and learning committee. He founded the North Carolina Center for Creative Retirement, the Annual Conference on Ubiquitous Computing, and the Council of Public Liberal Arts Colleges.

As Wake Forest provost, Dr. Brown chaired the committee that brought ubiquitous laptop computing to the university. He has keynoted several conferences in the United States and at the EDUCAUSE Australasia 2001 in Brisbane, the International Conference on Improving Learning and Teaching in Johannesburg, and the NACU Conference in San Juan. In addition to several hundred presentations and papers, his books include *Ubiquitous Computing* (2003), *Using Technology in Learner-Centered Education* (2002), *Teaching with Technology* (2000), *Interactive Learning* (2000), *Always in Touch* (1999), *Electronically Enhanced Education* (1999), *Leadership Roles of Chief Academic Officers* (1984), *Leadership Vitality* (1979), and *The Mobile Professors* (1967).

An active user of technology in his own classroom, he has been recognized as an "inspirational teacher of undergraduates" by the University of North Carolina at Chapel Hill. His classes have been featured on the front page of the *New York Times,* as a special on British Broadcasting Worldwide Network, as well as in *The Chronicle of Higher Education, USA Today,* and *Business Week.* Trained at Denison and Princeton Universities, his most recent course has focused upon "The Economists' Way of Thinking About College Basketball." Dr. Brown has consulted with more than 300 colleges and universities regarding their use of technology in the classroom and administratively.

Dr. Brown's wife of 45 years, Lin Brown, is a gerontologist and community volunteer. Both children are married. Alison lives in Chicago (River Forest) and Dirk lives in Boone, North Carolina. More information is available at his web site, http://www.wfu.edu/~brown.

About the Contributors

ANNE L. ALLEN is an Instructional Designer and Manager of the Center for Instructional Technology and Training in Academic Technology at the University of Florida. In addition to project development, she teaches courses in usability and best practices for the web, and has taught accessibility for the web. She can be reached at alallen@ufl.edu.

SUSAN W. ALMAN is Coordinator of Professional Development and Distance Education in the University of Pittsburgh Department of Library and Information Science. Her research interests include asynchronous learning, change management, interpersonal communication, marketing, and social sciences. She received her BA from Washington and Jefferson College and her MLS and PhD from the University of Pittsburgh. She can be reached at salman@mail.sis.pitt.edu.

MARGARET S. ANDERSON is Assistant to the Director of Technology in the Office of Instructional Support and Development at the University of Georgia (UGA). She has taught statistics and computer applications in the Terry College of Business, and is interested in uses of instructional technology to enhance teaching and learning. She currently supports WebCT at UGA. She can be reached at manderso@uga.edu.

RESTIANI ANDRIATI is Manager of the Faculty Instructional Development Lab (FIDL) at the Center for Instructional Development & Distance Education at the University of Pittsburgh. She holds MS degrees in Computer Engineering and Information Sciences. As the FIDL manager, she maintains a state-of-the-art instructional technology facility for university faculty and supervises the staff support for that facility. She can be reached at andriati@pitt.edu.

MICHAEL ARENTH is Assistant Director for Instructional Media Services with the Center for Instructional Development & Distance Education at the University of Pittsburgh. He is responsible for coordinating classroom instructional support services, including traditional audiovisual support, notebook computer distribution, media-enhanced classroom management, satellite downlinking, and interactive television. He can be reached at arenth@cidde.pitt.edu.

CAROL BAKER is Director of the Office of Measurement and Evaluation of Teaching at the University of Pittsburgh. She also teaches courses in testing and statistical analysis in the School of Education and consults with faculty and staff who are involved in survey and experimental research. She can be reached at ceb@pitt.edu.

KEVIN BARRY is Assistant Director for the Kaneb Center for Teaching and Learning at the University of Notre Dame. He consults with faculty and teaching assistants to help them choose and implement pedagogical strategies and technology to enhance teaching and learning, develops technology-based curriculum resources, and teaches in the Computer Applications and Alliance for Catholic Education Programs. He can be reached at kbarry2@nd.edu.

HOWARD W. BECK is a Professor in the Department of Agricultural and Biological Engineering at the University of Florida. His research area involves combining database management with artificial intelligence techniques to build applications in the area of agricultural information technologies. He can be reached at hwb@ufl.edu.

DIANE BILLINGS is Chancellor's Professor and Associate Dean for Teaching, Learning, and Information Resources at Indiana University School of Nursing and the Center for Teaching and Lifelong Learning. She has written numerous books and articles about teaching and learning in web-based courses. She is a member of the Teaching Learning Technology Group Flashlight Project and conducts benchmarking research about best practices in web courses. She can be reached at dbillin@iupui.edu.

CAROL BURCH-BROWN is Professor of Art and Interdisciplinary Studies at Virginia Polytechnic Institute and State University. She teaches photography, visual arts, and women's studies. She has had solo and group exhibitions of drawings, paintings, and photographs at galleries in New York, Chicago, Los Angeles, and in the Eastern United States. A Diggs Teaching Scholar at Virginia Tech, her teaching emphasizes interdisciplinary processes, combining elements of studio, seminar, and digital environments. She can be reached at cbb@vt.edu.

JOHN K. BURTON is Professor of Educational Psychology and Instructional Technology at Virginia Polytechnic Institute and State University where he serves as Chair of the Department of Teaching and Learning. He also directs the Center for Instructional Technology Solutions which is the grants and contract arm of the Instructional Technology Program. He can be reached at jburton@vt.edu.

SUZANNE CADWELL is a Computing Consultant with the Center for Instructional Technology at the University of North Carolina at Chapel Hill. She develops online help documents and leads workshops for faculty, teaching assistants, and support staff who use Blackboard's course management system. She can be reached at scadwell@email.unc.edu.

CHRIS CLARK is a Consultant to Faculty at the Kaneb Center at the University of Notre Dame. He earned his BA at Cornell University and MA at the University of Rochester. He originally taught high school Spanish, but for over 20 years has been helping faculty use technology. He has presented at national conferences and published a number of articles on educational technology. He can be reached at Chris.G.Clark.96@nd.edu.

SHERRY CLOUSER CLARK is an Instructional Design and Technology Specialist in the Office of Instructional Support and Development at the University of Georgia. She provides support for faculty, staff, and teaching assistants in all areas related to teaching with technology, primarily WebCT. Her research interests include online classroom community and faculty development. She can be reached at sclark@uga.edu.

ELLEN R. COHN is Assistant Dean for Instruction, School of Health and Rehabilitation Sciences, and Associate Professor, Department of Communication Science and Disorders at the University of Pittsburgh. She also holds a secondary faculty appointment in the School of Pharmacy. Her teaching spans the areas of rehabilitation, rhetoric and communication, and pharmacy-based communication. She can be reached at ecohn@pitt.edu.

NANCY CROUCH is the Assistant Chief Information Officer at Wake Forest University. New to the technology field in 1997, she established the Student Technology Advisors (STARS) Program. The university's student programs initiative has expanded under her direction from two programs to six since 1997 and now employs over 100 students in the Information Systems department. She can be reached at crouch@wfu.edu.

DIANE J. DAVIS is Director of the Center for Instructional Development & Distance Education at the University of Pittsburgh, a position she has held since the center was established in 1995. She served as chair of the Learning Technology Consortium from 1998 to 2000 and continues to have an active role in that collaborative group. She can be reached at djdavis@pitt.edu.

CAROL DEARMENT is an Instructional Designer at the University of Pittsburgh's Center for Instructional Development & Distance Education where, in addition to working with faculty on diverse projects, she edits the *Teaching Times* newsletter. With more than a decade of experience teaching college

English and communication courses, she has researched such education-related topics as online dialogue and text-based messaging for teaching and learning. She can be reached at dearment@cidde.pitt.edu.

ARAYA DEBESSAY is a Professor in the Department of Accounting and Management Information Systems at the University of Delaware. He is the current Chair of the American Accounting Association's Pedgagogy Committee and has received several teaching awards: the Middle Atlantic Association of Colleges of Business Administration Award for Innovation in Business Education, the University of Delaware Excellence-in-Teaching Award, and Departmental Outstanding Teaching Awards. He can be reached at debessay@udel.edu.

JANET R. DE VRY is Manager of Instructional Services for IT/User Services at the University of Delaware. She is responsible for a teaching, learning, and technology site, promotes programs for faculty in effective use of technology, and oversees the computing instructional program for the university community. She enjoys learning and speaking about optimizing learning environments. She can be reached at janet@udel.edu.

MICHELE ESTES is the Coordinator of Creative Services at the University of Georgia's Office of Instructional Support and Development. She manages a group of full-time, part-time, and student staff who design and develop multimedia for faculty instruction on campus. Her research interests include both theoretical and practical models of instructional and universal design. She can be reached at mestes@uga.edu.

ELIZABETH A. EVANS is a Project Manager at the University of North Carolina at Chapel Hill and has led cross-campus teams to implement Blackboard and a campus-wide events calendar, among others. She also co-chaired the campus's Intellectual Climate Implementation Committee and is chairing a working group on the Internet and social sciences research. She can be reached at uevans@email.unc.edu.

SARA J. EXUM is the Technology Training Manager for the Office of Information Technologies at the University of Notre Dame. She administers the technology training programs for faculty, staff, and students. Prior to joining the training department, she was responsible for communications strategy and implementation for the Office of Information Technologies. She can be reached at exum.1@nd.edu.

CHRISTINE Y. FITZPATRICK is Deputy Communications Officer in the Indiana University Office of the Vice President for Information Technology. She oversees the University Information Technology Services (UITS) Communications and Planning Office and is responsible for IT-related communications and events. She is also an Adjunct Assistant Professor of Technical Communications at Indiana University–Purdue University Indianapolis. She can be reached at cfitzpat@iu.edu.

WILLIAM FRAWLEY is Dean of the Columbian College of Arts and Science and Professor of Anthropology and Psychology at George Washington University. From 1979 to 2002, he was at the University of Delaware. His recent books include *Vygotsky and Cognitive Science* (Harvard, 1998), and *Making Dictionaries: Preserving Indigenous Languages of the Americas* (University of California, 2002). He has been heavily involved in curricular redesign, thematic learning communities, and writing, mathematics, and informational literacy across the curriculum. He can be reached at frawley@gwu.edu.

BARBARA A. FREY is a Senior Instructional Designer in the Center for Instructional Development & Distance Education at the University of Pittsburgh. She also teaches as adjunct faculty in the Department of Adult Education, Instructional Systems, and Workforce Education for the Penn State World Campus. Her research interests include course design, program evaluation, and faculty development in web-based programs. She can be reached at baf30@pitt.edu.

STEVEN A. GAMBLE is retired from the University of Georgia where he was Coordinator of Instructional Resources and Classroom Support in the Office of Instructional Support and Development. He serves as media specialist/consultant at Athens Regional Medical Center in Athens, GA. He can be reached at sagamble@ix.netcom.com.

SUSAN P. GIANCOLA is the owner of Giancola Research Associates, an evaluation research company, and an adjunct professor of assessment, research methods, and evaluation with the University of Delaware's School of Education. She received her doctorate in educational research from the University of Pennsylvania and has nearly 15 years of experience in information technology and educational evaluation. She can be reached at giancola@comcast.net.

ROSS A. GRIFFITH, Director of Institutional Research and Academic Administration at Wake Forest University, has served Wake Forest since 1966 in a career including admissions, affirmative action, space management, planning, and institutional research. He has recently given national presentations on strategic planning and assessment and accreditation and has published about the assessment of ubiquitous computing as a part of the Wake Forest strategic plan. He can be reached at Griffith@wfu.edu.

VALERIE P. HANS is Professor of Sociology and Criminal Justice and Professor of Psychology at the University of Delaware. She is also a faculty leader in the University of Delaware's Institute for Transforming Undergraduate Education. She enjoys developing legal problem-based learning exercises and integrating technology into her courses on law and the courts. She can be reached at vhans@udel.edu.

JAY HARRIMAN is Associate Director of the Office of Instructional Support and Development and Adjunct Assistant Professor in the Department of Instructional Technology at the University of Georgia. He is also president (2003–2004) of the International Association for Educational Communications and Technology (AECT). He can be reached at harriman@uga.edu.

J. THOMAS HEAD is Director of Instructional Services at Virginia Polytechnic Institute and State University. He manages an academic support unit that provides multimedia imaging and production facilities, student computer labs, assistive technologies, and test scoring services for faculty and students. He is a workshop facilitator in the Faculty Development Institute that serves all faculty in the university on a four-year cycle. He can be reached at tom.head@vt.edu.

BOB HENSHAW is an Instructional Applications Consultant for the Center for Instructional Technology at the University of North Carolina–Chapel Hill. He has been supporting faculty use of technology and managing instructional technology projects since 1995. He has taught an information sciences course on campus several times that uses instructional technology. He can be reached at bhenshaw@email.unc.edu.

PAUL HYDE started developing and supporting educational applications of technology in the days of PLATO and the Apple IIe. More recently, he has returned to academe for an M.Ed. in educational technology and to work as an information resource consultant for Information Technologies at the University of Delaware. He teaches regularly. He can be reached at paulhyde@udel.edu.

WILLIAM K. JACKSON is Director of the Office of Instructional Support and Development at the University of Georgia (UGA), where he is responsible for a comprehensive array of faculty, teaching assistants, and instructional development programs. He is also a charter member of the UGA Teaching Academy and a Senior Fellow of the Institute of Higher Education. He holds graduate degrees in physics and educational administration (higher education). He can be reached at bjackson@uga.edu.

DOUGLAS F. JOHNSON is the Course Management Systems Administrator, an Instructional Designer, and a faculty trainer for the University of Florida (UF) Office of Academic Technology. He is an award-winning designer/instructor of online high school and advanced placement courses, now applying those skills supporting faculty at UF. He is currently a PhD candidate in education law and finance. He can be reached at wanderer@ufl.edu.

PATRICIA KALIVODA is currently an Associate Vice President for Public Service and Outreach at the University of Georgia. Prior to moving into this position, she spent two years as an Assistant Vice President for Academic Affairs in the Provost's Office. She co-directs two faculty development programs sponsored by the Office of Instructional Support and Development (OISD), and was a founding co-coordinator of the Governor's Teaching Fellows Program. She can be reached at tlk@uga.edu.

ANN KILKELLY is Professor of Theatre Arts and Women's Studies at Virginia Polytechnic Institute and State University. She has won two Smithsonian Senior Fellowships for Research and A National Endowment for the Humanities Collaborative Research Grant. She directed the Women's Studies Program at Virginia Tech for six years and has received the Diggs Teacher/Scholar Award at Virginia Tech. Her present teaching interests include the use of performance techniques to enhance community and diversity in and out of the classroom, script analysis, and women, culture, and the arts. She can be reached at akilkell@vt.edu.

DARIA C. KIRBY, an Assistant Professor of Business at the University of Pittsburgh, teaches courses in organizational behavior and international organizational behavior. She has also taught executive education courses in the United States and Europe, and earned the Golden Key National Society Teaching Award in 1996. Her research examines ethnic minority expatriates' work attitudes and their ability to succeed in the workplace despite barriers. She can be reached at Daria@katz.pitt.edu.

KAREN M. KRAL is the primary WebCT Administrator at the University of Delaware. She has been involved with technology training and consulting for over 17 years. She began supporting UNIX and VMS systems and more recently supported MS Word and MS Access. She enjoys the challenges of helping the ever increasing numbers of WebCT users to use the system effectively. She can be reached at karenk@udel.edu.

ANDREW LANG is Associate Director for Academic Technology in the College of Arts and Sciences at the University of North Carolina at Chapel Hill. His background includes degrees in physics, music, and educational research and psychology. Since 1996, he has collaborated with faculty from a wide variety of disciplines in exploring ways of integrating technology into instruction. He can be reached at alang@email.unc.edu.

NICK LAUDATO is the Associate Director for Instructional Technology with the Center for Instructional Development & Distance Education at the University of Pittsburgh. He teaches in the School of Information Systems and serves as Senior IT Executive and Instructional Technologist with CampusWorks, Inc., an information technology and operations management consultant to higher education. He can be reached at laudato@pitt.edu.

THOMAS C. LAUGHNER is Associate Director of Education Technologies Services in the Office of Information Technologies and a lecturer in the College of Arts and Letters at the University of Notre Dame. His work involves identifying appropriate technologies to assist in the teaching and learning process. His current research interests involve making learning spaces more effective and creating learning communities in online courses. He can be reached at thomas.c.laughner.1@nd.edu.

BARBARA B. LOCKEE is Associate Professor of Instructional Technology at Virginia Polytechnic Institute and State University. She teaches courses in distance education, training, and instructional design. Her research interests focus on instructional design and development issues within distributed learning environments, with a particular emphasis on evaluation design for distance education. She can be reached at lockeebb@vt.edu.

TIMOTHY W. LUKE manages a fully online Master of Arts Program in Political Science as well as co-directs the Center for Digital Discourse and Culture at Virginia Polytechnic Institute and State University. He also serves as University Distinguished Professor of Political Science and Associate Dean of the Division of Liberal Arts, College of Arts and Sciences. He writes about the politics of information economies and societies as well as environmental political issues. He can be reached at twluke@vt.edu.

LEILA LYONS is Director of User Services in the Information Technologies unit at the University of Delaware. She is responsible for the delivery of desktop computing support to the university's faculty, staff, and students; support for the integration of technology into teaching and learning; and support for research data management. She can be reached at leila@udel.edu.

LORI A. MATHIS is Instructional Applications Manager for the Center for Instructional Technology at the University of North Carolina at Chapel Hill (UNC–Chapel Hill). With a graduate background in rhetoric and composition, she has eight years of experience at The Ohio State University and

UNC–Chapel Hill supporting instructors who use computer and Internet technologies to implement their teaching goals in residential and distance education programs. She can be reached at mathis@email.unc.edu.

MARK MCCALLISTER is Assistant Director of the Office of Academic Technology at the University of Florida. His responsibilities include classroom technology support, video/collaboration services, operation of computer labs and classrooms, and support of workstation hardware and software. He is an Assistant Editor of the *Leader,* a publication of the Consortium of College and University Media Centers. He can be reached at markm@ufl.edu.

ANNE H. MOORE is Associate Vice President of Learning Technologies at Virginia Polytechnic Institute and State University where she provides leadership in university technology integration initiatives. A former staff director for two statewide commissions on higher education's future, she is also the founding chair of the Electronic Campus of Virginia. She has written numerous articles and speaks widely on topics related to change in higher education. She can be reached at ahmoore@vt.edu.

D. MICHAEL MOORE is Professor of Instructional Technology at Virginia Polytechnic Institute and State University and Program Area Leader of the Instructional Technology Graduate Program. He has published extensively in the area of visual learning and visual research. He can be reached at moorem@vt.edu.

JOHN F. MOORE is Director of Educational Technologies and the Faculty Development Institute at Virginia Polytechnic Institute and State University. A former instructional designer and television producer, he leads initiatives in faculty development, online learning systems, and e-portfolios. Past research involved the effects and value of mediated learning for students, faculty, and health consumers. He can be reached at john.moore@vt.edu.

TERRY MORROW is the University of Florida's Associate Director of the Office of Academic Technology, Director of the Center for Instructional Technology and Training, and Director of Media Services. He previously was a faculty member at Penn State University where he was also involved in design and support of technology-enhanced classrooms. He can be reached at ctm@ufl.edu.

JOANNE M. NICOLL is Associate Director in the Center for Instructional Development & Distance Education (CIDDE) at the University of Pittsburgh. She is responsible for the coordination of the instructional design area and faculty development services, focusing on teaching enhancement and course development/revision. She can be reached at nicoll@pitt.edu.

ROBERT F. PACK is Vice Provost for Academic Planning and Resource Management at the University of Pittsburgh. He is the university's primary representative to EDUCAUSE, the Coalition for Networked Information and the National Learning Infrastructure Initiative. He founded the Learning Technology Consortium, a group of nine universities that meet regularly to share best practices and develop common approaches to the use of technology for instruction. He has a particular interest in the impact of technology on higher education. He can reached at robert.pack@pitt.edu.

CORDAH ROBINSON PEARCE has been an Instructional Technologies Consultant and Developer at Indiana University–Bloomington's Teaching and Learning Technologies Centers since 1995. She served as Interim Director from March 2001to June 2002. Her academic background is in theatre, linguistics, art, and design. She specializes in outreach, faculty development activities, faculty user support, screen design, and illustration. She can be reached at cordah@indiana.edu.

RICK PETERSON is a Computer Science Engineering graduate of Northwestern University and received his MA in organization development and transformation from the California Institute of Integral Studies. He has over 20 years of experience working with information systems, and is currently Director of Information Technology for the College of Arts and Sciences at the University of North Carolina at Chapel Hill. He also assists educational and not-for-profit organizations in assessing and developing their information technology resources. He can be reached at rick_peterson@unc.edu.

SHANNON C. PHILLIPS is an Instructional Designer and Manager of the New Media Center at Virginia Polytechnic Institute and State University. She also acts as an instructor and track facilitator in the Faculty Development Institute. Her main focus is the support of the various campus populations encountering and using technology in the learning environment. She can be contacted at sphillips@vt.edu.

DAVID POTENZIANI is Director of Instructional and Information Systems (IIS) at the University of North Carolina at Chapel Hill School of Public Health. His group provides information systems for video and data networking, data processing, web development, and classroom instructional technology. IIS assists in the development of online materials for instruction in a variety of courses for academic credit, certification, and training. He can be reached at David_Potenziani@unc.edu.

KATHRYN B. PROPST has been a consultant and developer at the Teaching and Learning Technologies Centers at Indiana University–Bloomington for nearly ten years. Her academic background is in biological anthropology and she has taught courses in human and nonhuman primate evolution and basic human anatomy. She can be reached at kpropst@indiana.edu.

JENNIFER META ROBINSON is Director of Campus Instructional Consulting and the Scholarship of Teaching and Learning Program at Indiana University–Bloomington. Formerly associate director of technology services in Indiana University's Kelley School of Business, she helped professors use instructional technology. She now consults campus-wide on many teaching issues and aids professors' scholarly inquiry into disciplinary learning. She can be reached at jenmetar@indiana.edu.

JUDY L. ROBINSON works in Academic Technology at the University of Florida (UF). She has worked with numerous faculty creating interactive multimedia for online courses and CD-ROMs and taught software applications to UF faculty. Prior to earning her PhD in communications at the University of Florida, she taught high school English and media studies in Canada. She can be reached at kayaker@ufl.edu.

ELIZABETH RUBENS is Instructional Systems Project Manager at Indiana University–Purdue University Indianapolis (IUPUI) in the Office for Professional Development. She has been instrumental in implementing many faculty development programs in instructional design and development at IUPUI's Center for Teaching and Learning. Currently she is working on assessment initiatives and gathering examples of "good practice" in online instruction. She can be reached at erubens@iupui.edu.

ANN RUCINSKI is a registered dietitian and holds a masters degree in nutrition education from Immaculata University. She currently is the Dietetic Internship Supervisor for the Distance Dietetic Internship Program at the University of Delaware. The internship utilizes various technologies in the management of the program. She can be reached at rucinski@udel.edu.

ED SCHWARTZ is an Instructional Designer, Director of the New Media Center, and Manager of the Faculty Development Institute at Virginia Polytechnic Institute and State University. He has authored several books on interactive videodiscs in education and was the instructional developer for the University of Delaware Videodisc Music Series. His focus is to provide support for the use of technology in instruction. He can be reached at ed.schwartz@vt.edu.

ERIN F. SICURANZA is an Instructional Designer in Information Technologies/User Services at the University of Delaware. She serves as a consultant for faculty and teaching assistants who want to incorporate instructional technologies into their courses. Her main area of focus is on web-enhanced hybrid courses, which contain both face-to-face and online components. She can be reached at esicuran@udel.edu.

KATHLEEN S. SMITH is a Senior Academic Professional at the University of Georgia and has directed the Teaching Assistant (TA) Program for the Office of Instructional Support and Development since 1990. Her research interests include the development of international teaching assistants as successful instructors in the North American classroom and a longitudinal study of the career path of participants in the TA Mentor Program, a preparing future faculty initiative. She can be reached at ktsmith@arches.uga.edu.

ROSALIND TEDFORD is Manager of the Information Technology Center of the Z. Smith Reynolds Library at Wake Forest University (WFU). With an MA in English and an MLIS, she has spent the last five years planning and implementing Wake Forest's faculty and student training programs. As WFU's Blackboard specialist, she is especially interested in online pedagogy and course management systems. She can be reached at tedforrl@wfu.edu.

KATHLEEN THOMAS is Manager of the Information Technology Services Center for Instructional Technology, the central instructional technology support organization at the University of North Carolina at Chapel Hill. She has been supporting use of instructional technology since 1995. She can be reached at Kathy_Thomas@unc.edu.

ROBERT VIDRINE is an Instructional Technology Specialist with the Departments of Anthropology and Education at Wake Forest University. His foremost duties are to promote and encourage the successful integration of new technology into classroom instruction and academic research by demystifying these new tools and introducing new ways of implementing them. He can be reached at vidrinmr@wfu.edu.

GEORGE H. WATSON is Unidel Professor of Physics and Astronomy and an Associate Dean in the College of Arts and Science at the University of Delaware. He was the principal investigator on the grant from the National Science Foundation's Program on Institution-Wide Reform of Undergraduate Education that led to the creation of the Institute for Transforming Undergraduate Education. Currently he is leading a project to develop problem-based learning curricula for physics as well as a project to reform science and math education in Perú. He can be reached at ghw@udel.edu.

SHANNON O. WILDER is Instructional Design and Technology Specialist with the Office of Instructional Support and Development at the University of Georgia. She teaches faculty development workshops and consults with instructors, exploring ways of integrating technology into their teaching. An artist as well as an educator, she is co-author of several books on design with web and multimedia software. She can be reached at swilder@uga.edu.

TERRY M. WILDMAN is Professor of Educational Psychology and Director of the Center for Excellence in Undergraduate Teaching at Virginia Polytechnic Institute and State University. His teaching and scholarship focuses on applications of learning research to instructional practice and more generally on teacher learning and development. He can be reached at wiley@vt.edu.

DENNIS WILLIAMS is Associate Director of University Media Services at the University of Delaware. He has worked in educational media in higher education for more than 30 years. Since 1993, his efforts have focused on the design and installation of technology in more than 150 classrooms, laboratories, and conference rooms at the university. He can be reached at williams@udel.edu.

MICHAEL WILLIAMS is Associate Professor of Mathematics and Director of the Math Emporium at Virginia Polytechnic Institute and State University. A former vice president for information systems, he has been on the cutting edge of technology initiatives in academia for the past 20 years. Besides probability and applied mathematics, his current interests include how we learn mathematics. He can be reached at williams@vt.edu.

DANIEL WILSON is an Instructional Technologist in the Faculty Instructional Development Lab (FIDL) at the University of Pittsburgh's Center for Instructional Development & Distance Education. He holds a masters degree in information science. His primary responsibilities include teaching faculty about instructional technology, system administration, and system development. He can be reached at wilson@cidde.pitt.edu.

JIANNONG XIN is a faculty member in the Institute of Food and Agricultural Sciences/Office of Information Technology at the University of Florida. He has been actively involved in the development of information technology (IT) applications in agriculture. He has co-edited three books and published numerous articles on IT applications. He can be reached at xin@ufl.edu.

FEDRO S. ZAZUETA is Professor and Director of the Office of Academic Technology at the University of Florida. He has published numerous articles on agroinformatics, including software for engineering design. He received from the US Department of Agriculture the Award for Superior Service for outstanding achievements in the use of computer technologies to improve competitiveness and efficiency. He can be reached at fsz@ufl.edu.

TABLE OF CONTENTS

PART II: COMMUNICATION

PART III: STAFFING AND SUPPORT STRATEGIES

xxiv

Part VI: Assessment of Student Programs

Part VII: Assessing the Effect of Technology on Learning

PREFACE

This book is about faculty development programs, university-sponsored initiatives. In fact, programming faculty development is an oxymoron. Faculty are independent professionals responsible for their own development. Hospitals don't "develop" their medical doctors. Universities don't "develop" their professors. Hospitals and universities facilitate development. They provide opportunities. They make time, facilities, and sometimes stipends available. Ultimately, however, the professionals strategize and implement their own development plans. This book chronicles how nine universities are helping individual faculty members pursue their desires for self-development.

Our intent is to provide "thought starters" for the architects of faculty development programs—for directors of teaching and learning centers, chief information officers and other information technology (IT) personnel, deans and provosts, pedagogical consultants and course designers, members of faculty committees, and individual faculty members.

The programs detailed here are diverse, some are even mutually exclusive. Since faculty development programs must reflect the intention, history, experience, and personalities of each university, it is foolish to seek out one program that is best for all. By getting to know how very different programs at very different universities pursue successful faculty development, we hope the reader will become better able to craft the program that is uniquely best for his or her own university.

For six years, leaders from our nine universities have met semiannually, always on a campus. Typically, we tour facilities, share knowledge, trade experiences, talk about challenges, and work through problems presented by group members. Although our strategies for faculty development differ greatly, there are a few universals.

All face the reality that the IT and faculty cultures are grounded in very different primary values. All universities have to determine how responsibilities will be divided between central resources and college-based development. All must determine the role of their teaching and learning center. All must accommodate the fact that different disciplines use technology in very different ways.

All faculty development programs must be grounded in an understanding of the independence of each professor. The classic tension between priorities given to teaching versus research is common to all universities. And, everywhere, there is never enough time.

Each of the universities represented in this volume takes pride in its faculty development program. Each program aspect highlighted here is working locally (and each of us undoubtedly has dropped programs that weren't working). We recognize, however, that our enthusiasm for a particular program may be misplaced in another setting. The intent of this volume is not to advance the single model that is right for all times and all universities. Instead, our intent is to stimulate thought, to offer specific ideas, to broaden horizons. Through this volume we hope to bring more people into the conversations that have been so productive at our semiannual meetings.

Readers can approach this volume by topic or university, or both. Each essay is meant to stand on its own. Readers are encouraged to skip around, to read first the essays that interest them the most.

Essays are grouped in broad topic areas but there is some overlap. For example, the description of a summer faculty grant program may be preceded by a statement of the philosophy of the program and followed by an assessment of its effectiveness. Alternately, an essay that is in the philosophy section may include a description of the classroom design that reflects the philosophy. In other words, the groups are loose ones and should not be taken too seriously.

Readers who would prefer to read all that has been written about the faculty development program at a particular university can consult the table of contents, which lists each author's university affiliation.

Faculty development in technology is a developing art. We very much hope that you will take the opportunity to email individual authors, even to make suggestions about how their programs might be further improved. If you know of a faculty development program model that would benefit us (and others), email brown@wfu.edu. Your citation will be shared with our group and may become part of a follow-up publication.

David G. Brown

PART I
PHILOSOPHY

1

PHILOSOPHY: FACULTY AS EAGER ADOPTERS

David G. Brown
Wake Forest University

Several universities have been stunned by faculty resistance to mandates that all courses must have a web site, or all classes must use a listserv, or all faculty must enroll in how-to-teach-with-technology workshops. Administrators often misinterpret this resistance as resistance to using technology with teaching. That's wrong. It's resistance to mandates, not technology.

Most faculty are eager to try anything that might help students learn better, more, faster, or more efficiently. Contrary to popular profiling, the vast majority of faculty members love new ideas, relish debate among alternatives, play frequently with fresh techniques, and are more open than most professionals to changing their ways. Whether it's new subject matter such as molecular biology, new students as evidenced by the aging of college populations, new ideas as reflected in current journal articles, new types of institutions (e.g., junior colleges after World War II), new pedagogy (e.g., textbooks and books of readings), or new programs (e.g., distance learning degrees), colleges and their faculties are quick to try out the new. This should surprise no one: Colleges, after all, are in the business of preparing leaders for the future. Always one eye must be cast upon what is becoming, even as another keeps clearly in sight the lessons of history.

Faculty motivation and desire is not a barrier to innovation! An inadequate library may discourage faculty from library-dependent assignments, just as faculty will not insist upon computer-based work from students until there is a reasonable assurance that all class members have access to the Internet and that the computer network won't break down. The high risks associated with any innovation may lead faculty to incremental adoptions, just as gardeners resist changing all variables at once in fear of losing an entire year's crop. Also, the time appropriately demanded by current students and current research will make more difficult the finding of fresh hours for creating duplicative assignments, just as road constructors delay project completion when they build transition detours in order to keep traffic flowing through the construction period. Availability, risk, and time are problems. Motivation and desire are not.

Moreover, faculty peer culture is now working for technology. Few academic departments would even consider hiring a new faculty member without certifying capacities to use computers. As methods of assessment improve, teaching effectiveness is becoming an ever stronger determinant of promotion and tenure. The worldwide respect for teaching and technology is driving all disciplines to honor their members who perform well in these areas.

In spite of the understandable impatience of computer center directors and financial officers who put out megabucks for computer instrumentation, faculty must be privileged to adopt technology to the extent and at the pace that is comfortable for them. Computer technology is infrastructure for the using, if desired. We don't have rules that every faculty member must use the library, and we shouldn't require any faculty member to use the Internet or computers. From the technology zealots, patience may be required.

Exhortations and mandates will only delay faculty experimentation with technology. Almost all faculty would like to be moving faster and farther. They know the problems. The opportunity for faculty leaders, and their administrators, is to emphasize the positive. A gentle, voluntary approach is best. Emphasis should be placed upon the faculty inclination toward experimentation. Even small first ventures into technology (e.g., the use of email with classes) should be highlighted and praised. Robust computer networks and the universal availability of appropriate software and hardware should be assured. With reinforcement from a generous administrative attitude, the quality of teaching will constantly improve. Positive strokes work best, especially when they are deserved.

SUGGESTED READINGS

An interview with David G. Brown, *The Technology Source*, July 2002. Read this and a number of other interesting articles on faculty development at http://ts.mivu.org/default.asp?show=section&id=9.

Best Practices in Faculty Development (with Elson Floyd), *Multiversity*, Winter, 1998–99. Available electronically at http://www.wfu.edu/~brown /MultiversityBestPracticeBrown_Floyd.htm.

Brown, D. G., & Jackson, S. (2001). Creating a context for consensus. In C. A. Barone & P. R. Hagner (Eds.), *Technology-enhanced teaching and learning: Leading and supporting the transformation of your campus* (pp. 13–24). San Francisco, CA: Jossey-Bass.

2

PHILOSOPHY OF FACULTY DEVELOPMENT AT VIRGINIA TECH

Anne H. Moore and J. Thomas Head
Virginia Polytechnic Institute and State University

INTRODUCTION

From the start, the primary goals of Virginia Tech's Faculty Development Institute (FDI) have been to invest in faculty creativity and ingenuity and to support calculated risks to improve teaching and learning. In the early 1990s, the university faced a state mandate to submit a restructuring plan to serve more students without an increase in resources. University leadership responded by reallocating internal resources and committing comprehensive support to systematically integrating technology in teaching and learning activities over time. Then as now, Virginia Tech aimed to invest in learning innovations and, as a byproduct, to build institutional capacity for discovery and serving modern needs for advanced education.

PLANNING AND PRINCIPLES

Planning for the comprehensive faculty development effort began in the fall of 1992. From its inception, the program was driven by faculty who helped to design the workshops' format, identified outside experts who could describe their pioneering efforts, and ensured that the integration of technology was based on curricular goals. Early in the planning process, designers determined that the program would be scalable and based on a model of continuous improvement. It was also deemed essential that the program be integral to the university's strategic plan.

The initiative has evolved, based on the following principles:

- Faculty will not be interested in technology for its own sake. They must perceive that it benefits their students' learning environment.

- Faculty must have the training to integrate technology that can facilitate their teaching. The training must be ongoing and designed specifically for their campus environment.

- Faculty must be provided hardware and software continuously and consistently.

- Faculty must feel confident that their students will have the access to technology to complete their assignments and projects.

- Faculty pioneers must have the release time and funding to risk developing their courses. Virginia Tech has a successful grants program through the Center for Innovation in Learning and the Center for Excellence in Undergraduate Teaching.

- Faculty must perceive that adequate technical staff will support their efforts over the long run.

- Department chairs, deans, and the chief academic officer must endorse the goal of technology integration.

IMPLEMENTATION

The FDI began during the summer of 1993 with three pilot faculty workshops that were designed to support curricular reform in mathematics, English, and the humanities. Extensive planning involving faculty focus groups was critical to ensure that these workshops met the faculty's needs. Great care was taken to ensure that faculty could see the connection between integrating technology and student learning. Since faculty sophistication regarding instructional technology has changed dramatically over the past decade, it was critical that the program evolve. The early years focused on software tools to enhance teaching and learning, while current options for faculty include instructional design and specialized curriculum activities. FDI is now considered a year-round experience with continuing seminars and online training.

Survey results show strong support for these new approaches to learning among students and faculty involved in classes that have been restructured as a result of this initiative. Active learning has been facilitated both in and out of the classroom, and constructive collaboration among students has been encouraged. Technology is promoting communication outside the classroom via electronic mail, threaded discussions, and chat rooms. These efforts have shown a positive impact on students' understanding of, and interest in, the course material, while promoting better class attendance. In addition, students believe they have more opportunities to develop skills that transcend the subject matter, including problem solving and critical thinking.

3

PROGRAM PHILOSOPHY: KEEPING SIGHT OF WHAT'S IMPORTANT

Thomas C. Laughner
University of Notre Dame

In 1992, the University of Notre Dame opened DeBartolo Hall, a state-of-the-art building with technology available in each of its 82 classrooms. This building symbolized a new era at the university, one in which technology was to play an integral role in teaching and learning. It marked the start of a cultural shift that finds every student now using email, 95% of students owning computers, and 90% using WebCT in at least one course.

When DeBartolo Hall opened, there was a concerted effort to provide an infrastructure that would make technology accessible to faculty, creating little or no obstacles to their success. Our programs and services for faculty support are based on several underlying philosophies that guide us as we plan and consult on technology projects.

No faculty member has to use technology. While most faculty use technology in their day-to-day lives, research, or teaching, they do so out of choice. By adopting this laissez-faire philosophy, we know that our job is to remove as many barriers as possible so that faculty will choose the appropriate technology use for their classes.

Technology is only part of the equation. Before the correct technology can be selected for a course, the pedagogical consequences must be considered. We encourage faculty to consider their learning objectives, what research implies about how students best learn, the major assignments that will fulfill the learning objectives, and how best to use student and faculty time and space. In addition, the availability and dependability of campus resources, both infrastructure and support, must be considered. After the technology is selected, attention should be paid to how it is implemented and the consequences, positive and negative, it has on student learning.

Chalk is a perfectly acceptable technology. A colleague said, "Many people believe that technology is only those things that were invented after they were born." For our program, chalk, overhead transparencies, and slide projectors are acceptable technologies if they meet the instructor's pedagogical objectives. Technology is one of many tools that can help faculty achieve their teaching objectives. Our goal is to find the right set of tools to help meet those objectives. As often as possible, we steer faculty in the direction of low-threshold applications—those tools that are quick to learn and to implement but most benefit student learning.

Faculty and student time are precious resources. Everyone is familiar with the time constraints on faculty. In addition to their teaching load, they have research deadlines, administrative tasks, and countless other responsibilities. Students, too, have full course schedules, families, jobs, extracurricular activities, and studying. Our goal is to minimize the time faculty and students have to spend thinking about technology. Specifically:

- The Office of Information Technologies gives classroom support very high priority. If ten minutes of class time are lost, an entire lecture can be lost. Support staff strive to be in a classroom within two minutes to solve any problems that may arise. I've been the recipient of this service, when support staff swooped into the classroom, fixed the problem, stood by to make sure everything was working, and then just as quickly left the room.

- Training sessions are intentionally limited to two hours or less. The sessions focus on meeting only the specific pedagogical needs of a course. For example, one of Notre Dame's WebCT courses is titled Increasing Student Communication with WebCT. The workshop focuses solely on those WebCT components used for communication: chat, bulletin board, and email.

Even if faculty decide to use technology, they often don't want to be computer experts. When we work with faculty on complex projects, they become the development team's content expert. While they tell us how the project is progressing, the programming is left to consultants.

One of the most successful programs to take advantage of this philosophy is the Educational Technology Jump-Start Program. Implemented in 1992, this grant program funds faculty and teaching assistant technology projects. Although the time of full-time consulting staff is free, implementing technology for a course involves numerous other expenses. The money can buy student time, software, assistance with copyright clearances, or other project-related expenses. Student time is the resource most often requested. Grants average $1,000 and can be given more than once. They cannot pay for computer hardware, because the computer center has a separate fund for this, nor can they go directly to the applicant.

As our campus culture continues to evolve, underlying philosophies become increasingly important. New technologies continue to change our work environment, and new campus initiatives continue to be implemented. While faculty are dedicated to ensuring that students have access to the best education possible, they also want to make sure that their time will be used most effectively. Our goal is to provide that efficiency.

RESOURCES

Kaneb Center for Teaching and Learning
Teaching Well Using Technology: http://twut.nd.edu
Kaneb Center for Teaching and Learning: http://kaneb.nd.edu
Learning Technology Lab: http://www.nd.edu/~learning

Office of Information Technologies
Educational Technology Program: http://www.nd.edu/~edtech
Education Services: http://www.nd.edu/~training

4

TOWARD A PHILOSOPHY OF ONLINE EDUCATION

Douglas F. Johnson
University of Florida

For every societal advance, there are trade-offs. In one of my favorite movie scenes, from *Inherit the Wind*, about the famous 1925 Scopes trial (*Tennessee v. John Scopes*) in which the propriety of teaching evolution was debated, the teacher's defense attorney, Henry Drummond (Spencer Tracy), argues before the jury:

> Progress has never been a bargain; you have to pay for it. Sometimes I think there's a man who sits behind a counter and says, "All right, you can have a telephone; but you lose privacy, and the charm of distance. Madam, you may vote, but at a price; you lose the right to retreat behind the powder-puff or your petticoat. Mister, you may conquer the air; but the birds will lose their wonder, and the clouds will smell of gasoline.

Many would argue that online education is currently exacting such a price. Critics are already lamenting what is lost, particularly from interpersonal relations in the classroom, but the real test of online education will be what is on balance gained.

At its heart, the debate over online teaching and learning is about the meaning and purpose of education. According to Aristotle, education's purpose was to make people virtuous. He asserted that all seek what they believe to be good. Evil, then, is the result of ignorance, as people choose what they mistake for good. The solution to evil is education, because only through proper knowledge and understanding can people identify and choose what is truly good. Because of its integral relationship to virtue, Aristotle argued, education was the state's highest duty, a duty that the modern United States has enshrined in every state constitution. Likewise, Aristotle's conception of the critical importance of education supports all subsequent philosophies of education.

Over the centuries, scholars have adapted and reinterpreted Aristotle's articulation of the purpose and philosophy of education. Medieval theologians, such as Augustine, Anselm, and Aquinas, saw education as critical to purifying the soul. Renaissance scholars, such as Galileo, Newton, and Kepler, saw education as the cornerstone of understanding the world we inhabit, and their theological contemporaries, Erasmus and Luther, viewed education as a tool to critique, to refine, and to improve social institutions. Descartes, Locke, Rousseau, and the Enlightenment rationalists asserted the primacy of reason for understanding self and society. In the 19th and 20th centuries, these assertions bore fruit in the universal education movement and the development of public school systems. In the 21st century, the newest refinement of education is technological, and because of this development, a new dialogue must begin to articulate the underlying value and purposes of education in a technologically driven world. This essay does not aim to present a fully developed philosophy of online education but to sketch the framework for such a philosophy.

A philosophy of online education must recognize and incorporate a number of critical constructs, which include:

- *an understanding of cognition and how people learn:* What, for example, does information processing research indicate about how the mind works and how to maximize learning?

- *an understanding of learning theory and learning styles:* In this active field, much of the work remains hypothetical and unresearched; still, Sternberg's triarchic theory of intelligence and Gardner's multiple intelligences, among others, offer fruitful material for examining teaching and learning.

- *an articulation of the types and value of interaction:* For example, three types of interactions are often identified as critical to the learning process: learner/content, learner/instructor, and learner/learner.

- *an examination of what elements of human interaction might be lost and how that loss might be mitigated:* Part of the traditional conception of academia asserts the value of the learning community; how can a learning community be created and fostered in an online environment?

- *an identification of the critical elements of traditional pedagogy and how they might be preserved in an online context:* Often-raised concerns about the content of online courses along with the fear that lone courses may be dumbed down perhaps to compensate for the absence of direct student support must be addressed and mitigated; the effective equivalence of online and face-to-face courses must be asserted as a desired and measured goal.

- *a discussion of what valued ends might be gained:* The philosophy of traditional education often asserts its role in citizenship and preparing students for democratic participation; so, too, online education must articulate its own explicit and implicit outcomes, not least the preparation of students to be active participants in, rather than passive recipients of, an increasingly technology-driven world.

A philosophy of online education must also recognize the fundamental factors that are spreading technology throughout society, which include:

- the expansion of reach and market
- the advantages of convenience
- the necessity for lifelong learning and the development of just-in-time skills
- the movement away from long-term careers to frequent job changes
- the increasing migration of corporations, jobs, and workers around the world

As Internet use increases within the realm of business communication, marketing, and sales, so does its emphasis in online teaching and learning. As technology impels business and society to be more international, more flexible, and more carefully targeted to specific needs, education must follow. Creating a flexible learning process and an environment that incorporates online technologies can attract more students and improve their access to learning opportunities while enhancing their understanding and retention of new information about both the process and the content of education. Such a learning environment can best target specific and rapidly changing educational needs.

These changes do not mitigate the rationale for the traditional liberal arts curriculum, as many fear. In fact, they reinforce it, for what can be of greater value in a just-in-time, needs-driven world than a broad base of understanding, a demonstrated ability to learn a wide variety of subjects, and a proven track record of learning how to learn? Online education presents important opportunities to reach a mobile population, but it must be structured on clearly conceived concepts so that the cherished and time-tested educational purposes of the past may continue to add value to the learning needs of the present.

5

FITTING WORKSHOPS TO FACULTY MORES

David G. Brown
Wake Forest University

At Wake Forest University, a group of technology-savvy faculty from six different liberal arts disciplines (CELI) has been responsible for advocating that their colleagues explore the use of technology in their teaching. The group has secured foundation grants, allocated project funds, sponsored speakers from off-campus, held focus groups, and created numerous seminars and workshops. Importantly, CELI is part of the faculty, not the administration. Even so, the group quickly learned that when their workshops were sponsored by our Teaching and Learning Center, an office committed to the improvement of teaching not only via technology, they drew more and more diverse participants than when the identical workshops were sponsored only by CELI.

This lesson leads to a general principle: Whenever possible, introduce faculty to technology through agencies that they know and trust. Special-purpose advocacy groups have their place but not in motivating faculty to get involved.

A number of faculty development strategies grow from this philosophy. As is the case at many other universities, at Wake Forest, the group of administrators that liberal arts faculty trust most is the librarians. Therefore, we cross-trained our librarians to train faculty and student groups in computer use. This training is a natural fulfillment of the librarians' professional commitments to providing information access and service.

Faculty are primarily loyal to their departments and disciplines. By funding instructional technology specialists, selected and supervised by department chairs and housed within the departments, advice and advocacy are given by a trusted source, someone who speaks the language and knows the concepts of the discipline. (Robert Vidrine describes this program in Chapter 25.)

By offering workshops and special help from central advisors to *clusters* of faculty from a single department, rather than to individual faculty members sprinkled throughout campus, training can be focused on the topics of greatest interest to the discipline. Even more important is the reinforcement and creative energy that proximate faculty provide each other. Many of the issues that might otherwise require the attention of a central computer staff are solved within the faculty before they even contact their Instructional Technology Specialist!

Outside speakers invited by CELI tend to attract the same faces, almost regardless of topic. When these funds are allocated to departments, more and different people join "the same old crowd," and the impact is greater.

Several years ago, a generous foundation grant allowed us to buy released time (a one-course reduction in teaching load) during regular semesters for individual faculty to redesign their courses by adding computer-supported enhancements. Competitive proposals were submitted to CELI, and those projects promising the greatest impact were funded. When several years of experience with the program were evaluated, we decided to shift the remaining funds to a program of summer grants. During a project-month during the summer, faculty could focus exclusively upon course development. They didn't have to lock current students out of their office or decline a student invitation to a poetry reading. More importantly, during the summer, all the grantees could gather several times each week to support each other in their developmental endeavors. They could become a community, mutually dedicated to teaching enhanced by technology.

If technology is to be used in teaching and research, it must become inseparable from these endeavors. Add-ons are ineffective. Adding the use of technology to promotion and tenure criteria, especially when mandated from central administration, is ineffective. Urging each department to consider the role of technology in keeping up with the discipline, with colleagues, students and alumni, and with modern research is the way to go. Knowledge of how and where to use technology has to be equated with how and where to use the library, how and where to use an electronic microscope, how and where to keep up with the literature in the field.

There are no shortcuts. The most successful faculty development programs are ones that use existing channels, value systems, and networks of trusted colleagues.

SUGGESTED READINGS

Brown, D. G., & Jackson, S. (2001). Creating a context for consensus. In C.
   A. Barone & P. Hagner (Eds.), *Technology-enhanced teaching and learning*
   (pp. 13–14). San Francisco, CA Jossey-Bass.

Jackson, S., & Brown, D. G. (2002). *Discipline specific teaching support.*
   Annual Meeting of National Learning Infrastructure Initiative, San
   Diego, January 2002. Available: http://www.wfu.edu/~brown

6

FACULTY DEVELOPMENT IN THE LARGE RESEARCH UNIVERSITY

Joanne M. Nicoll and Diane J. Davis
University of Pittsburgh

Large research universities face special challenges in the area of faculty development because of their size, their missions, and their diversity. This article describes one approach to these challenges and the three specific strategies that it entails.

The University of Pittsburgh is a public, urban, Research I university. It has a student enrollment of more than 26,000 at its main Pittsburgh campus and an additional 6,000 at four regional campuses. The main campus has about 3,700 full- and part-time faculty, and another 400 teach at regional campuses. There are 16 undergraduate, graduate, and professional schools at the University of Pittsburgh.

In 1995, Pitt merged several existing units to form the Center for Instructional Development & Distance Education. CIDDE's four primary functions are instructional development, faculty development, instructional support, and university service. Instructional design and development are cornerstones of CIDDE's mission, both because of institutional priorities and because of the unit's particular strengths in this area. CIDDE's five instructional designers and three of its four senior administrators are experienced instructional design professionals.

Prior to 1995, the University of Pittsburgh had a very small office of faculty development with a very broad mission that encompassed three major components: developing faculty as teachers, developing courses and curricula, and developing the organization to better support teaching and learning. CIDDE's charge was to rethink the faculty development mission and create strategies to enhance the existing capabilities.

STRATEGY 1: FOCUS AND THEME

A critical review of the university's faculty development program prior to 1995 identified the need for a clearer focus. Trying to address all three areas of faculty development in such a large institution resulted in lack of cohesion and clear direction.

CIDDE determined that it would capitalize on its instructional development strengths to support the academic community. While emphasizing services for course and curriculum development, CIDDE found that it still was able to advance in other areas of faculty development: helping faculty to improve their teaching and strengthening the organizational climate for teaching and learning.

CIDDE also recognized the need for a pedagogical theme. In dealing with such a large and diverse faculty, we needed a strong, unifying approach to instructional enhancement. After a great deal of thought and discussion, we selected "active learning" as the pedagogical theme that would drive our agenda, in the belief that, if just one thing would have a significant impact on student success, it was active learning. The theme has proven particularly appropriate for a large research university. It neither prescribes nor proscribes particular teaching and learning activities; it is meaningful across all disciplines and levels of instruction; and it acknowledges both the role of the professor and the role of the student in the learning process. Active learning is a concept broad enough to accommodate a variety of discipline-specific teaching strategies yet focused enough to provide a meaningful and measurable pedagogical goal.

Having a focus and a theme has given cohesion to the University's faculty development activities. Discussions about active learning have become commonplace at the University of Pittsburgh, and our theme has easily accommodated new interests, such as service learning.

STRATEGY 2: INTEGRATION OF FACULTY DEVELOPMENT SERVICES

A second important strategy for faculty development in a large and diverse climate is integration of services. CIDDE, as a new unit comprised of several previously autonomous groups, had to be well-integrated in order to assist integration of faculty development across the institution.

Integration Within the Unit

CIDDE's four functions—instructional development, faculty development, instructional support, and university-wide support—are not allocated to specific individuals or roles within the unit. Instead, all CIDDE staff are responsible for all four functions. In the case of faculty development, CIDDE has an associate director who oversees the general direction and focus for this function, and a faculty development coordinator, who plans and manages specific activities. However, nearly everyone in the unit is engaged in faculty development work.

Media services staff and instructional technologists, for example, train faculty on the use of specialized classroom media and technologies, while instructional designers lead teaching-related workshops and provide individual course design consultation. Administrative staff prepare materials, compile evaluation data, and manage the logistics of each event.

By integrating faculty development as a unit-wide function, we have been able to increase the resources and talent devoted to this important activity. Instead of a small group of individuals attempting to accomplish the many facets of an impossibly large mission, integration of services has enabled CIDDE to distribute the work over a larger number of staff, each of whom has expertise appropriate to the task. Integration of services also benefits staff development. The teamwork that occurs through this process is rewarding to all staff, and recognition for success is more widely shared.

CIDDE's structure as a unit with multiple functions is what makes this integration possible. Prior to its creation, faculty development was the responsibility of a very small, specialized unit, like those at many universities across the country. These units typically are staffed by a few highly dedicated and competent individuals whose accomplishments are impressive. For large universities that have the option of developing a more comprehensive faculty support unit, the benefits from integration of services can be equally significant.

Institutional Integration

Regardless of the size and scope of the responsible unit, close integration with other academic and administrative services is essential to achieving any faculty development mission. No one entity can independently carry out faculty development in a large research institution. At the University of Pittsburgh, many individual schools have their own faculty development practices, and CIDDE augments them as appropriate. For example, CIDDE helps to design faculty development activities led by schools and departments as well as by staff from the library, the office of university counsel, the information technology group, and the learning-skills center. The following are mechanisms we have found particularly helpful in achieving integration:

Meetings with deans. Every two years, the director of CIDDE meets individually with each academic dean to discuss the needs and priorities of that school related to CIDDE's mission. These discussions include the dean's perspective on appropriate faculty development services that will complement departmental initiatives. Information from these discussions is used to plan future programs and strategies.

Advisory committees. The Provost's Advisory Council on Instructional Excellence is responsible for providing information and advice on faculty development and for administering an instructional grants program. Since CIDDE's primary focus is on instructional development, the grants program and faculty development agenda are complementary. The Council is composed of faculty who are recognized for excellence in both teaching and research. A subcommittee of the group collaborates with our unit to select topics and strategies, which then are discussed and approved by the entire Council before being forwarded to the provost.

CIDDE also has an advisory board that reviews and makes recommendations on all its functions, including faculty development. This group includes members from key administrative units, such as the library, the registrar's office, and information technology, as well as faculty from a variety of schools and departments.

School liaisons. One or two individuals from each school are identified to serve as liaisons with CIDDE. School liaisons notify CIDDE of relevant faculty development needs among their colleagues, and they notify faculty about professional development opportunities and services that CIDDE provides. An email list facilitates regular communication between CIDDE and the school liaisons, while annual meetings provide opportunities for face-to-face feedback and discussion.

School-based programs. CIDDE has worked with several schools to design customized faculty development programs. These programs typically include workshops that are held in school facilities so that they are convenient for faculty. While other university faculty are often invited to attend these workshops, they are designed to meet the specific needs of one particular school. In some cases, a faculty development program already exists within a school or department, and CIDDE is called upon to provide some specialized assistance, such as course design workshops. School-based programs not only have better faculty participation, but also can serve as a vehicle for engaging faculty in the other kinds of professional development activities.

STRATEGY 3: COMPREHENSIVE SERVICES

Over the last seven years, CIDDE has come to appreciate the significance of providing comprehensive services at a large research university. With the multiple roles that faculty assume and the resulting time commitments, the ability for one unit to meet a range of teaching-related needs is advantageous. Current faculty expectations are for a more holistic approach to course-development services. Instead of struggling to arrange meetings with several different offices for assistance in revising their courses and incorporating instructional technology, instructors can tap into the comprehensive services of one unit.

The benefits of comprehensive service extend far beyond one-stop shopping. Additional benefits include:

Ensures common support-service goals. Instructional designers, with background in learning theory and instructional theory, focus on the importance of instructional goals when helping faculty incorporate technology into a course. Their decision making is instruction-driven as opposed to being based on a particular technology capability, and technology is chosen based on its potential to achieve an instructional goal. For example, an instructional designer may recommend the use of asynchronous discussions if the instructional goal is for students to provide well-reasoned responses that synthesize course concepts. Asynchronous discussion allows students the time to formulate responses that reflect higher-level thinking and analysis.

Takes advantage of interest in technology to enhance instruction. Faculty's interest in using instructional technology has been a motivating force for their involvement in course development and revision. Faculty who seek Blackboard training, for example, learn not only the mechanics of the software but also some procedures for redesigning their courses to make best use of the technology. CIDDE's instructional technology training incorporates principles of course design to encourage faculty to focus on using the software to help address specific course goals. Faculty also learn about the instructional design assistance that is available to them in CIDDE as they participate in training and raise questions that involve pedagogical principles.

Establishes an accessible front door for assistance. With comprehensive services available within one unit, faculty have become familiar with an established location for needed resources. The instructor who may have been unwilling to take the time to find help in the past now knows that one call to an instructional designer offers the needed direction. Ease of access to support services is especially important in a large university where such resources typically are dispersed.

SUMMARY

Providing effective faculty development services in a large research university is particularly challenging because of size and diversity. This article has described three core components of an approach used successfully at one such institution, where substantive faculty development goals were achieved through 1) establishing a focus and theme to unify faculty development efforts, 2) integrating services within the teaching support unit and throughout the university, and 3) providing comprehensive, easily accessible support services.

7

PHILOSOPHY: AGILE TECHNOLOGY SUPPORT

Jay Harriman and Michele Estes
University of Georgia

A key to faculty adoption and effective use of any media and technology for learning is the academic institution's support philosophy and organization. At the University of Georgia, the Office of Instructional Support and Development (OISD) employs organizational agility to serve all of its faculty and augment the activities of similar support units at the college and departmental level.

As technology and faculty needs change constantly, stimulating new challenges and opportunities, OISD embraces change through flexible management, staffing, services, and programs. A university-wide strategic planning effort in the late 1990s sparked the philosophy and related strategies, which were already under way. Webster defines *agile* as moving with speed, ease, and elegance. The agile organization thrives in a continuously changing and often unpredictable environment that requires being flexible, timely, cooperative and collaborative, communicative, and committed to mission. These principles have guided planning and services and enhanced the recognition of OISD as a leader in technology and learning at the University of Georgia. These principles also help us to create benchmarks for assessment and goals for improvement.

For example, if a faculty request is outside the specific responsibility of one staff member or even the whole office, every effort is made to secure appropriate in-house resources or other campus services. Faculty may seek guidance in preparing grant applications, and after receiving the award, employ the services of the office in development, implementation, and evaluation of the project. Others involved in year-long faculty development programs or one-time demonstrations may learn about new techniques and technologies, receive assistance in acquiring them for their departments, and get additional training through workshops and consultation.

While we follow some specific procedures, responsiveness is facilitated more by the service attitude and creativity of the staff. For example, faculty participation in what for many years were successful open workshops and seminars had dropped off. The office began taking the workshops and consultations on-site to the faculty in specific departments, which was viewed as both convenient and effective. We also implemented an instructional development lab as a central resource for faculty and their TAs. Instructional designers provide timely and meaningful consultation using up-to-date hardware and software solutions that may otherwise be unavailable to the faculty.

STAFFING

Agility in staffing applies not only to full-time, permanent hires, who should exhibit flexible traits and skills as well as tolerance for change, but also to a rethinking of what kind of staff can fill future needs, including part-time, temporary, and student staff. For instance, OISD's planning called for revised job descriptions and staff development for existing creative media personnel, who were based primarily in traditional video, photography, and graphics services. As demand for slides, posters, and photo prints had been declining, while use of digital media and web-based course development projects increased, these staff members assumed responsibilities for video streaming, virtual-reality media, interactive DVD, and other applications in addition to the traditional media still important for faculty use.

Jobs were described so that each shared skills and responsibilities (create a web page, edit digital video, burn a CD, etc.) and specialized in an area of digital media. This process was guided by references, such as Aquent Technologies' guide to technology jobs, including required skills and typical salaries. As internal job descriptions were enhanced, learning opportunities were provided through training, classes, and project assignments involving media applications new to the staff.

To augment the core of full-time staff in a cost-effective manner, the strategic plan called for greater reliance on part-time staff, especially talented undergraduate and graduate students from campus academic programs, such as Instructional Technology, New Media, and Mass Communications, who would bring the most up-to-date skill set in media and technology. Rather than fill a vacant, full-time, video producer position, two senior/graduate student telecommunications positions were created. The students gained up to a year of authentic experience and responsibility as they transitioned from college to full-time careers. In addition, a graduate assistantship exclusively for a Department of Instructional Technology student was established as part of a collaborative partnership agreement between OISD and that department. Students who have held the assistantship possess many needed web skills, using programs like Flash, Fireworks, and Dreamweaver that have enabled the design of an online portfolio for the office. It highlights the services now available because of the new staffing plan.

Rounding out staffing in the creative media area are two unpaid graduate student interns, who do receive course credit. Expectations for the student internships are established at the beginning of each semester and provide genuine work/learning experiences and opportunities to contribute to specific office projects, such as an online workflow database and a faculty tutorial for streaming media. We discovered during the first appointments that expectations, especially involving product development, have to be limited in scope, as significant reliance on these students can be unrealistic. We also learned that while flexible work schedules and locations can be established for interns who are also taking other classes, they must be on-site at least 25% of the time to maintain continuity and communications beyond email.

All of the student and temporary staff attend regular meetings that include project updates and showcase staff-developed learning materials and new media designed to meet specific objectives. Because of the staffing plan and the background of the instructional technology students, the unit has been able to establish a more effective instructional development process, particularly for long-term, grant-supported projects. It has also led to shared leadership of services and projects. In fact, the addition of the student staffing has catalyzed growth and change among the existing full-time staff.

Other examples of OISD's agility in staffing are shown here.

- OISD contracts with the central computing services organization, Enterprise Information Technology Services (EITS), for office-specific network and computer support. This arrangement requires an EITS staff member to reside in the OISD office for quick response time, while allowing for continued communication from the support person to the EITS office via phone, listserv, and regularly scheduled meetings. This dynamic relationship would not be possible with a permanent staff member.

- OISD engages in joint staffing arrangements with administrators and faculty who spend a percentage of their appointment dedicated to our programs. For example, an OISD staff member teaches a course for the Department of Instructional Technology, which, in exchange, funds an instructional technology graduate assistant position within OISD. The assistant contributes to the production needs of our office through application of multimedia expertise.

- Rather than hiring permanent full- or part-time staff in all areas, income and remaining budget monies may be applied to multiple graduate and other student positions instead.

Cooperation and Collaboration

"We're stronger together" could well be the slogan for some of the partnerships that have evolved among OISD, academic departments, and other support services on campus. EITS and OISD provide campus-wide support for the online course tool, WebCT. A television studio once controlled exclusively by OISD is now shared with three colleges: Arts and Sciences, Education, and Mass Communications. Classes, productions, and enhanced-learning experiences are conducted for the students, and OISD gains a TV crew of student support. In collaboration, the Institute of Higher Education and the vice-president for instruction support a Teaching Academy that explores learning technologies. The creative media unit often partners with departmental technology centers on project development rather than carrying out the projects totally in-house.

Agility means not only adding to or enhancing existing services but also giving up some activities and resources that may not fit the evolving mission of the unit and may be better served by others. The office at one time initiated and managed the campus cable television system. When central information technology and networking services became a CIO organization (EITS), we determined that bringing telephone, data, and video infrastructure services together would be desirable. OISD had created a new position to coordinate cable TV technical operations. This extended OISD's collaboration with EITS for installation of cable modems for dorm rooms, and facilitated the transfer of the entire technical cable service to EITS. Fulfilling its own mission to design and develop content, however, OISD has continued to program the two instructional channels on the university cable system and, in cooperation with mass communications, continuing education, and public affairs programs, operates the university's educational access channel on the separate citywide cable system.

Leadership

Agile organizations have a dynamic reporting structure. Staff at any level may suggest change, identify new services, explore better methods and organization, and take on new responsibilities. OISD attempts to reward initiative and growth as deemed appropriate.

Leaders in one area of OISD may become leaders in another area as well. In one instance, an AV-services specialist who dealt primarily with equipment and film/video checkout and delivery assumed direct responsibility for the office videoconferencing services. In another, instructional design and technology specialists hired primarily to assist faculty with online course tools have assumed new responsibilities, like leading a discussion group on distance learning, managing the office web site, and assisting the Teaching Academy and a technology and learning group that recommends allocation of student technology fees and Learning Technologies Grants. Another specialist headed the redefined creative media unit. At this writing, the office was poised to move classroom support staff to a new classroom/electronic library building, necessitating a new organizational structure that demands agility and creativity in developing and implementing those changes.

Management at different levels must be willing to make quick decisions when opportunities that cannot wait for consensus building or top-down signoff arise. Therefore, management is given discretion to make decisions without necessarily awaiting time-consuming hierarchical reviews. In the event that top management implements sweeping or radical change, it must communicate quickly and clearly the changes and rationale. If the organization's management values agility, it should model such behavior and recognize staff who exhibit it.

COMMUNICATION

Effective communication is extremely important for support organizations working with diverse faculty who often have varying expectations, expertise, and experience with technology and campus services. Staff must truly listen and respond effectively to requests. "No, we can't or don't do that" should never the be the answer, rather, "I'm not sure, but let's see what we *can* do." Clearly, sticky areas concerning copyright and intellectual property as well as challenges to institutional and departmental policies and unreasonable demands must be handled carefully and diplomatically. Faculty should learn the appropriate ways to access resources and services to improve the instructional process.

The agile organization promotes good communication, which encourages input and feedback at all levels. The office sometimes falls short in ensuring fast-track innovative activities or in communicating problems throughout the office or to key individuals quickly; nevertheless, as a guiding principle of agility, reliable and efficient communication remains a goal. A number of staff use electronic distribution lists to ensure campus problems are communicated throughout the office.

In an effort to promote awareness, the office web site changes to reflect input from users and clients. Faculty listservs, web postings, cable television, and in-house publications announce and present activities and recognize faculty and office initiatives.

BUDGET AND OTHER RESOURCES

Budget, specifically the availability of funds for special needs or unforeseen opportunities, is central to a truly agile organization. The willingness to collaborate and to piece together unique or unconventional resources significantly enhances possibilities for meeting staffing or equipment needs.

By partnering with the university's higher education institute on a statewide university faculty development program, the office was able to acquire PDAs for the participants and office support staff and to purchase other program equipment needs. Another partnership with a college in the university sponsored a technology-specialist position devoted half-time to serving the college faculty and the remainder to serving all clients. A joint video equipment proposal between the College of Journalism and OISD resulted in a partnership with a national company, significantly reducing costs, and providing continuity and shared support for the equipment.

As the office relies on income revenue for part of its budget, spending must be monitored carefully and limited in the early part of the fiscal year. This approach has provided funds for changing priorities later in the year. The question might arise about charges for services. The office has extended flexibility to its cost-recovery needs as well as the provision of services to faculty with minimal resources or grant funding by developing classroom instruction categories that are free or reduced in price. Internal mini-grants are supported both by in-kind service and by funds from the income budgets.

SUMMARY

By acknowledging change in both technology and faculty needs, the office has established a philosophy of agility for its strategic planning and operations. Key principles include flexibility, rapid response, good communication, collaboration, shared leadership, and creativity that influence staffing, budgeting, management, programs, and services. They all effectively assist faculty in their mission to enhance teaching and improve student learning.

RESOURCES

OISD Home Page: http://www.oisd.uga.edu/

OISD Strategic Plan: http://www.uga.edu/strategicplanning/part4/support.
html

Aquent Technolgies Inc.: http://www.aquent.com/

8

THE ETHICS OF TEACHING IN AN ONLINE ENVIRONMENT

Douglas F. Johnson
University of Florida

Francis Bacon's "Knowledge is power," is one of the most famous adages about power. Perhaps equally famous is Lord Acton's dictum, "Power tends to corrupt; and absolute power corrupts absolutely." While it can be argued that juxtaposing these statements is illegitimate, this pairing has the benefit of reminding us that education, the inculcation of knowledge, is never neutral of value, that all education communicates a set or many sets of values, and that, because of its utility, knowledge is a powerful and, hence, value-laden commodity.

If we accept these premises:

- that knowledge gives a certain kind of power

- that power makes possible certain kinds of actions that are otherwise impossible

- that actions are rarely value-neutral

then it becomes clear that those who engage in instruction and communicate knowledge must consider the ethical implications of their teaching.

The word *ethics* derives from the Greek *ethos*. Ethics is commonly considered synonymous with morals; however, *ethos* refers more broadly to presenting a positive character. In the first chapter of *Rhetoric*, Aristotle asserts that persuasion is profoundly influenced by the perception of a person's character and concludes that character/*ethos* "may almost be called the most effective means of persuasion." Therefore, for any instructor who seeks to communicate important information, being perceived as "ethical" is important.

In traditional settings, faculty have a variety of means for presenting character. These include face-to-face interactions, personal habits, and information about professional and personal relations gleaned by students through observation, gossip, etc. Students frequently use this information to make registration decisions about the value of a given class or instructor. Of course, other factors may outweigh a negative perception of an instructor, in which case students use these perceptions of *ethos* to fashion their dealings with the instructor. As important as ethical teaching may be in a traditional context, for online instructors who operate at a distance from their students, an ethical approach to teaching may be absolutely critical, because students often do not have other measures of the *ethos* and credibility of the instructor than their experiences in a particular course.

In discussing the ethics of online teaching, we must acknowledge that important questions about the ethics of teaching in the traditional context remain. However, the failure to resolve questions in one domain does not obviate the legitimacy of raising them in another. Likewise, it is important to recognize that students bring an ethical responsibility to each course and to their studies. However, that issue is beyond the purview of this discussion.

What, then, constitutes ethical online teaching? It is frequently asserted that the Golden Rule as paraphrased from Jesus of Nazareth best encapsulates the core of ethics: "Do unto others as you would have done unto you" (Matt 7:21). Similar formulations exist in many religions and philosophies; see, for example, *Analects* 15.23 (Confucian), *Sutrakritanga 1.11.33* (Jain), *Talmud, Shabbat 31a* (Jewish), or the philosopher Isocrates (436–338 BCE): "Do not do unto others what angers you if done to you by others." Regardless of its origin, this principle provides an excellent point of entry for considering ethical online teaching: If I were a student in an online class, what would I expect? What would I want? What would engender my enthusiasm about the people and the process with which I am engaged? If we can place ourselves in our students' position, envision their needs and desires, and consciously and systematically attempt to meet their needs and consider their desires, then we are engaged in ethical online teaching.

Of course, we all know that students sometimes take courses not to increase knowledge or expand horizons, but simply to get a high grade with minimal effort. In considering students' needs, it is important to recognize that they may not always properly understand their needs. Ethical teaching asks us also to recognize the demands of our profession and the purposes of our instruction in preparing students for future careers and lives. Hence, ethical teaching frequently requires us to guide students toward a more mature understanding of the purposes of education.

Ethical online teaching also asks us to consider such pragmatic concerns as the purpose and value of assignments, how we respond to email and discussion postings, how much and what kind of work we assign, how quickly and how well we respond to and grade submitted work, the mechanisms we use to communicate course content, the quality of our interactions with and assessment of students, and what steps we take to facilitate student interactions with the content, the instructor, and other students.

Ethical online teaching may also require us to consider learning styles and personality types. A growing body of research examines how learning styles affect student interaction with, and retention of, course content. Research on personality types suggests that pedagogical practices that are effective for one type of student may be ineffective for another. If our instruction is to meet the needs of all our clients, we must constantly seek ways to allow diverse personalities to grasp the content. The industrial model of education, where one size fits all, is rapidly being replaced by what might be considered a service-economy model, where learning is tailored to the learner. At the same time, the purpose of education is ultimately to tailor the learner to a discipline or a profession. So there can be a dynamic tension between meeting the needs of the learner while also meeting the purposes of the learning.

Ethical online instruction should also consider how to replicate what is most valued in face-to-face instruction. Online education is often chided for diminishing the interaction between student and teacher and among students. The extent to which this complaint is accurate is debatable; it is not, however, debatable that such interaction is highly valued by individuals and society and, therefore, that ethical online instruction must maximize opportunities for interpersonal interaction.

The ethics of online teaching also require that we make ourselves aware of other similarities and differences between face-to-face instruction and teaching at a distance. For example, in every classroom, students must master various skills: learning the content, figuring out the assignments, and discerning how the instructor wants the work to be completed. In an online class, students must master these learning curves without the visual cues and body language that might help them interpret their meaning. Online students face additional learning curves: how to learn at a distance; how to function independently, with self-initiation; how to communicate effectively without the cues of proximity; and how to use the necessary technologies.

With substantial increases in learning curves, many instructors and programs are tempted to dumb down their online curricula. However, that means face-to-face students and online students take courses that are supposed to be the same but offer substantially different depth or coverage and, hence, different value for their investment of time, money, and effort—an ethically questionable proposition. Instead of dumbing down, instructors must actively develop online strategies and practices that mitigate the challenges and enhance the opportunities so that all students receive fundamentally equivalent value for their commitment.

Ethical online teaching also requires us to consider the stakeholders in our instruction. What knowledge and skills do society and the institution expect us to inculcate in our students? What does our discipline expect? Whether our course is traditional college subject matter or part of a training certificate, assumptions are made about how our teaching contributes to the completion of a program. We must accommodate those assumptions, or we risk failing our students and the program by sending out unprepared graduates. At the same time, we must articulate to program directors how our teaching may not fulfill certain expectations so that curricula may be expanded in other courses, or new courses may be developed to ensure that the required knowledge and skills are inculcated as expected.

We should also recognize that ethical online teaching is not limited to the list of students on the class roster. I want to suggest that the ethics of teaching in an online environment require us—society, educational institutions, instructors, and students—to grapple with some serious broader issues regarding online education. As the Internet increases the availability of education, we must consider those whose access may be hindered; for example, the poor and the disabled.

As online education increases its reach, we must consider its impact on cultures different from our own. Online education could easily become the vehicle for a new imperialism. Indigenous educational systems could be undermined by online alternatives. The middle classes of a third-world nation might abandon local educational systems for online programs, withdrawing their support for the education and opportunities available to the poor. Many elites in less-developed countries already send their children overseas. Distance education could easily exacerbate this problem. Conversely, steps could be taken to make online offerings available to the poor, and to build programs that would encourage elites to remain at home and engaged in local educational systems, but such steps would require careful planning and implementation.

Finally, we must ask perhaps the ultimate ethical question: How does our online instruction increase the search and the potential for achieving the good life? If no knowledge and no teaching is value-neutral, we must seek to articulate honest answers to questions about how the content of our teaching and the instructional methods we employ empower individuals for the betterment of humanity.

In the end, the most critical element to ethical online teaching may well be self-awareness. The 12th-century scholar Peter Abelard highlighted this connection between ethics and self-awareness when he subtitled his work, *Ethics,* "Know Yourself" [*scito teipsum*]. The connection between ethics and self-awareness requires us to examine ourselves and our curricula in the light of ethical thinking to make sure that we present them as credible sources of knowledge. To return to ancient Greece, Socrates is often quoted: "An unexamined life is not worth living." For our purposes, I would suggest that unexamined teaching is not worth delivering. This axiom is true in any context; it is particularly true online.

9

Motivating Faculty: Five Strategies

William Frawley
University of Delaware

At perhaps the most crucial point in the action of *Casablanca,* where Victor departs to freedom and Rick stays behind, the ambivalent head of the French-Moroccan police responds to the demands of the occupying German forces to stop subterfuge and sabotage by instructing his subordinates matter-of-factly: "Round up the usual suspects." This phrase often characterizes recruitment strategies in development programs designed to induce faculty involvement in instructional technology. No matter how much money you have to award, at crucial points in the institution's future, you find yourself rounding up the usual suspects. It is not that the usual suspects are somehow undeserving, but they constitute an increasingly small and, sometimes unfortunately, encapsulated group at universities, especially research universities, where those dedicating time to instructional technology can be either invisible to the dominant forces of the institution or, in extreme cases, marginalized.

From 2000 to 2002 at the University of Delaware, the Center for Teaching Effectiveness (CTE) has awarded some $200,000 in faculty development grants for projects using advanced and emerging technology in instruction (see www.udel.edu/cte). What is striking about this program is less the amount of money awarded (which was in part generated *because of* faculty motivation: The provost added funds because of wide faculty interest), than the fact that those who have submitted grants come from all across the institution, even partnering across unlikely partnering units, and include senior researchers from the university's most respected and visible departments. CTE awarded grants to chemical engineers, musicians, cognitive neuroscientists, management specialists, English professors, artists, physicists, nutritionists, and marine scientists.

How did CTE manage to cast the Request for Proposal (RFP) net out beyond the usual suspects? Here are five strategies. In and of themselves, these strategies are not anything new. What was innovative about the CTE program is the way they came together to guide faculty interest.

Speak Their Language

Faculty are motivated when they see that their ideas and potential efforts have launching and landing sites in a grant program. CTE staff and advisory groups worked to make the parameters of the development grants analogous to items that faculty recognize as valuable parts of their intellectual life. We structured the grant program so that they recognized it as something like the grant programs to which they regularly submit—NSF, NEH, NIH—where interested principle investigators (PI) first approach a program director with an idea and then work with the agency to develop the proposal. We awarded larger sums of money ($20,000) to a few projects, and so made the program more visibly competitive. In that way, those who received the awards were able to demonstrate that they had emerged at the top of a rigorously peer-reviewed competition. One unfortunate consequence of extensive, small-award development grants is that the support cannot match the depth needed to see a project through in all its implications, and so such programs can inadvertently reinforce modest efforts.

We also worked with faculty to encourage them to describe their research in instructional terms and then helped them to convert their research questions into instructional problems. This process appealed to faculty in an unusual way: Rather than asking faculty what pedagogical issues they thought they could address, we sought first to uncover issues in their disciplinary inquiry that could be refined into teaching matters—we let research drive instruction. Thus, one chemical engineer needed to design an interface to bring images from his electron microscope to the classroom. This research problem of transmitting high-resolution images emerged as an instructional problem after several discussions, and it quickly became the basis of a focused proposal for improving the educational experiences of chemical engineering students.

Finally, we worked within the system of yearly awards for faculty by persuading department chairs and deans to recognize that these funded instructional activities were as meritorious as any other aspect of faculty performance, especially because the grants generated substantial funds for the department.

Unabashedly Exploit the Goodwill of Others

Faculty are impressed by their peers. When a chaired professor explains how she changed her mind about something because of her involvement in a grant program, more than one ear perks up. We used the power of peer influence by asking respected faculty to work with those interested in the grant program and, frankly, by dropping their names at critical points in conversations. When the cognitive neuroscientists came to me to ask if their idea—to bring

ERP data from their brain-imaging laboratory into the classroom—was a candidate for the grant program, we immediately mentioned the work of a chemical engineering professor who had done much the same from his lab, although with different kinds of images. This struck a ready chord with the psychologists, and they then attended a workshop where the engineer presented his work. The cognitive neuroscientists thus saw that their instructional idea had broader currency and was entirely analogous to a problem that occupied faculty in one of the most prominent departments on campus. This small but timely act was enough to produce a very interesting, funded proposal on the remote delivery of high-resolution brain images to the undergraduate psychology classroom.

Be Instrumental

Ideas have power and potential when they are seen as means of solving larger problems, not just as ends in themselves. We required interested participants to articulate how their proposals could be models for others and how their solutions might be generalized to other problems. In this way, high technology solutions could be seen as critical contributions to the overall institutional effort. For example, we recently funded a proposal to develop interactive, web-based problems for bioresources engineering. This project offered a unique solution to interactivity that was unavailable in the university's other courseware packages. As a consequence, this project promises to generate a genuinely new alternative for science faculty who want a more flexible suite of problems for their introductory classes. And the PI gains visibility and respect among his peers for having been the source of imagination and innovation behind the products.

Take Risks

Not only do development grant programs round up the usual suspects, but they also often fail to push the boundaries of innovation very far, if at all. That is why development grant programs often go to great pains to be explicit about what constitutes curricular development beyond normal expectations. We learned a great lesson from two members of our planning committee, a chemical engineer and the head of the biotechnology center, who wanted to fund *proof of concept proposals,* which provide seed money for budding ideas that might be interesting risks. This approach resonates well with faculty, who often have the germ of an idea about instructional technology and would see it through if given the resources to explore. So we decided that we would also use the fund as venture capital and advertised the RFP as such.

This explicit risk-taking generated enormous interest since faculty saw it as an invitation to run their ideas by us—which, of course, led to many conversations and brainstorming sessions. Could we deliver satellite images from our submarine? Could we digitize our historical costume collection and have hot links on parts of clothing that lead students through history via the costumes? Could we equip nutritionists in the field with PDAs and have them conduct interventions with an intelligent assistant? Can we develop 3-D images of proteins so that students can actually visualize molecular structure? The answer to all these questions is: "Why not? Let's give it a go!" There is much less risk in these budding ideas than might be imagined because even if grants that support them fail to produce a complete, working instructional technology, the lessons learned along the way will be enormously valuable. The risk of not taking these risks exceeds the risks of taking them.

Never Give Anything Away for Free

Perhaps the greatest disincentive to faculty development is the mere awarding of funds without asking for a return. When this situation develops, development programs take on the image of cash cows and faculty begin to see the funds as a ready source of easy revenue, rather than as an opportunity to contribute. We used an old principle of business negotiation. Never give a client everything he asks for, even if you can afford it. Give a little, and ask for something back; when you get that, give a little more, and then ask for something back. Motivation can be perpetuated by involvement and connection. We made every PI work with us from the beginning, so that we could generate a personal, bilateral relationship from the start. All faculty who are funded must participate in workshops, public forums, and our General Education Institute. We tell them how impressed we are by their work and ask them to display their successes to others. We also ask for interim and final reports, as most grant programs do, but we give faculty a web-based template on which they can submit their report and email them notification of its availability. In this way, we make it easy for them to give back. The model proposals we have posted on our web site have turned out to be motivators for others.

Faculty are motivated when they see themselves as an essential part of an intellectual community, with recognizable and meaningful rewards. In such an environment, everyone becomes the usual suspects, and when that happens, it's much easier to round them up.

RESOURCE

For downloadable materials accompanying conference presentations on this subject visit www.udel.edu/billf/~frawley.html.

Part II
COMMUNICATION

10

COMMUNICATION ACROSS INSTITUTIONAL BOUNDARIES

Diane J. Davis and Robert F. Pack
University of Pittsburgh

What are benefits of collaboration across institutional boundaries for faculty development? Is a consortium effective as a mechanism for interinstitutional communication? This chapter briefly describes a university consortium focused on learning technology and faculty development and explains how it has evolved to support collaboration and communication across nine campuses.

The University of Pittsburgh is a founding member of the Learning Technology Consortium (LTC), a group initiated in 1997 as a collaboration of institutions with common interests and challenges in the area of teaching and learning with technology. The nine members are Indiana University, University of Notre Dame, University of Delaware, University of Florida, University of Georgia, University of Pittsburgh, University of North Carolina at Chapel Hill, Virginia Polytechnic Institute and State University, and Wake Forest University. Members were invited to join the LTC on the basis of having similar instructional goals, strong technology and faculty support programs, and an interest in collaboration. LTC's mission is "to support university teaching and learning through collaboration focused on the effective use of instructional technologies." (See http://www.ltc.ufl.edu, and select Organizational Materials for the LTC's mission and goals.)

One important goal of the LTC was to institute a forum for conversation. All of the member institutions are active in regional and national conferences on faculty development and instructional technology. Many are leaders in these areas. But the sheer number of participants at most conferences limits opportunities for meaningful dialogue. These institutions were seeking an extended roundtable where ideas and challenges could be analyzed and explored in greater depth. About 20 individuals from the nine campuses attend a day-and-a-half meeting each spring and fall. The location of the meetings rotates from school to school, so that participants have the added advantage of visiting all nine campuses and seeing firsthand some of their most notable initiatives.

Campus Updates are among the most valued items on the LTC agenda. Representatives from each campus report on new initiatives, identifying successes as well as problems they want to discuss. Everyone in the group learns about strategies that they may adapt for their own institutions, and everyone has an opportunity to benefit from the experiences of others. At Pitt, for example, we are always eager to acknowledge how advice from Virginia Tech has contributed to the success of our summer institute for faculty and how Wake Forest gave us a model for developing a good departmental liaison program. Our instructional development lab at Pitt, completed in early 2002, reflects some of the best thinking and experiences of our LTC colleagues. Similarly, the University of Delaware recently completed a specialized classroom facility using the design from a similar facility at the University of Pittsburgh.

In addition to its program development benefits, the LTC provides its members with an opportunity for informal benchmarking in the areas of faculty development and instructional technology. Learning about successful initiatives at other campuses offers an incentive to reassess our own programs, thereby motivating improvement within each participating institution. Fortunately, communication among the members of the consortium is not limited to the biannual meetings. As we implement new ideas, we have easy access to a network of individuals at eight other universities who are eager and able to respond to questions as often as we ask.

A common challenge in instructional technology is keeping up with new and evolving technologies. The LTC allows us to share our experiences with new applications. At its earliest meetings—and before support groups for this purpose were initiated—LTC members who had adopted course-management systems openly discussed the benefits and problems of these new technologies. The consortium enabled members to collaborate on new installations and on the design of faculty training programs. Sharing information and experience about emerging technologies helps member institutions reduce the time and cost of individual assessment. It also facilitates their ability to keep up with newer developments.

The LTC is interested in classroom design as a way to ensure that educational facilities can accommodate new technologies and teaching methods. Members from the University of Notre Dame have taken the lead in developing web pages on classroom design resources that have been incorporated into the LTC web site (http://www.ltc.ufl.edu). Consortium members have a strong commitment to the design of classroom configurations that can support the instructional technologies and strategies that faculty prefer.

Formal collaboration on specific projects is a goal that the consortium hopes to expand. Our initial efforts have focused on conference presentations. Consortium members have had at least six collaborative proposals accepted for presentation at various national conferences, including papers on faculty development strategies, course-management systems, teaching with technology, and assessment. This volume of articles on faculty development and instructional technology is the second book involving LTC collaborations. (The first is *Teaching with Technology,* also edited by David G. Brown.) In addition, the consortium has undertaken a study involving member campuses on how the use of online instruction in traditional courses changes what happens in the classroom (Davis, Wingard, & Lockee, 2002).

Collaboration on specific instructional development projects is the next goal. Members recognize the potential benefits of cooperation in developing course materials and applications, and they recognize the need for effective strategies to overcome practical and logistical barriers presented by inter-institutional development teams. Since all of the LTC member institutions have faculty grants programs and technology training activities, we are exploring those common elements as a pathway toward collaboration on instructional development.

Overall, our experience with the LTC has been positive and productive. Here are some things we've learned over the first five formative years of the organization that may be helpful to others who are considering similar alliances:

- A consortium like the LTC is extremely effective for developing and maintaining communication with a network of colleagues at other institutions. Its most immediate benefits are in the design of effective strategies and programs and the ability to avoid or to resolve problems related to common activities.

- Institutional as well as individual commitment facilitates the continuation and stability of the consortium. In the LTC, commitment to membership first comes from the chief academic officer of the institution, who then identifies the individuals on that campus who are most appropriate to participate.

- Continuity in membership and participation in the consortium is important to its viability and vitality. While others often participate in meetings, each LTC institution has two designated representatives who try to attend every meeting in order to provide continuity.

- Holding consortium meetings at each campus on a rotating basis enables participants to see specialized facilities as well as the environment in which each member functions. Hosting a meeting every few years is a commitment of each LTC institution. This contribution, along with the travel and lodging expenses of the school's participants at all other meetings, has enabled the organization to avoid creating a dues structure.

- Collaboration evolves over time. While establishing goals and selecting specific projects is important, it is useful to allow adequate time for discussion. Members need the opportunity to help shape the priorities of the organization as they learn about each other's strengths and interests—and this takes time. While the LTC began in 1997, its statement of mission and goals was not formalized until 2000.

REFERENCES

Brown, D. G. (Ed.). (2000). *Teaching with technology: Seventy-five professors from eight universities tell their stories.* Bolton, MA: Anker.

Davis, D. J., Wingard, R. G., & Lockee, B. B. (2002). *Changes in the classroom: Practice and predictions.* Presentation at the annual meeting of Educause, Atlanta, GA.

11

CROSS-CAMPUS COLLABORATION: EVERYBODY WINS

Elizabeth A. Evans and Kathleen Thomas
University of North Carolina at Chapel Hill

The implementation of a course-management system depends on many segments of the campus community. When we began implementing Blackboard's enterprise product, version 5 level 3, for the University of North Carolina at Chapel Hill's fall 2001 semester, we invited participation from many groups. Although managing a large project team had its own challenges, the efforts paid off. With two exceptions (described below), the implementation went smoothly, and the project was completed on time and under budget. Without participation from groups affected by the implementation, we feel sure the project would have floundered.

Implementing Blackboard 5 would require contributions from many staff in our academic and administrative computing centers. In addition to the technical work, we also had to be sure that the user interface was customized as much as possible. Faculty and students had a vested interest in the user interface, the way courses and users were created from administrative data, and the way support for the application was managed. We wanted input from the campus libraries. The Center for Teaching and Learning, which on our campus is a separate entity from the Center for Instructional Technology (CIT), was an important piece of the project puzzle. Our registrar's participation helped ensure our compliance with university, state, and federal laws and policies and also helped us to understand the student data better. Our project team ended up with thirty members, each of whom was enthusiastic about participating in the implementation.

Thus, we developed two goals for the implementation process: 1) to involve technical staff, user support staff, administrators, faculty, and students in the project; and 2) to manage the large project team as efficiently as possible so its size didn't slow the project's schedule.

Our first step was to hold a telephone conference with Blackboard to define the project's initial scope. At that conference, we included the executive directors of academic and administrative computing, appropriate middle managers from both groups, and the staff members who would actually perform the work—in all, seventeen people. We decided that our Blackboard technical team would not stand alone but include staff with existing responsibilities in areas the Blackboard implementation would need. For example, our academic computing Oracle database administrator (DBA) is the DBA for Blackboard, and our academic-computing, web-systems administrator is responsible for the production Blackboard server. Other staff included the programmer responsible for the application itself, the authentication/security staff, student information services representatives, members of the CIT who would provide user support for the application, and members of the Instructional Technology Development group (ITDev).

After the initial telephone conference, Blackboard began sending materials that would be reviewed with their staff during a two-day site visit, including several workbooks that would be completed during the visit. We wanted each of our 30 team members to have input into the process, and we wanted to be sure we heard and addressed any concerns, but we also wanted to make the process efficient. Blackboard identified key areas for the project, and we added a few that we felt were important for our situation. The full project team was divided into subteams for each area. Before the Blackboard site visit, teams associated with a workbook met to discuss and complete it. In addition, a meeting of approximately 15 team members representing end users met to discuss and to resolve concerns.

By the time the Blackboard staff arrived on campus for our implementation site visit, our project team members were apprised of their roles and responsibilities. We had completed each workbook, and we had a good idea what questions we wanted to ask the Blackboard representatives. Blackboard set the agenda for the two-day site visit. Because we were very well prepared, we were able to stop early the first day and start later the second day, which boosted morale, especially among the subteam scheduled to meet early on the second day.

Although the Blackboard staff expressed some reservations about the size of our project team, we were convinced that participation by all technical staff and representation from every group affected were necessary for a successful project. We had only one complaint from a group that felt excluded. It was resolved when we compiled our records, including notes inviting the group to join and indicating what meetings they had attended. The problem, as it turned out, was in the group's internal communication process.

The second problem didn't surface until we had successfully brought the Blackboard system up a day earlier than scheduled. Although we had some data errors to clean up, they were relatively simple. The much larger problem was discovered when off-campus users started reporting severe performance problems. Technical staff, user-support staff, and affected users were all involved in the intensive time commitment to diagnose and to correct the problem. Nevertheless, it persisted long enough that we allowed several courses in one professional school to move back to our existing CourseInfo server for the fall semester. As a result, we were reminded of a valuable lesson: We should have done more off-campus testing to make sure we thoroughly included yet another constituency: our students and faculty at a distance.

The problem with remote access prevents us from calling our Blackboard implementation a total success. However, most of our faculty and students saw only a smooth transition. Because of the superb technical support from our academic and administrative computing staff, we were able to do most of the work ourselves. Because we planned carefully and early to involve appropriate team members, we were well prepared for our meetings and communications with Blackboard staff, thereby using fewer of their fee-based professional services than budgeted. Based on our experience with this project, our belief that project teams should be as inclusive as possible has been reinforced. Cross-campus collaboration really does result in a winning project.

12

TIPS ON COMMUNICATING EFFECTIVELY WITH FACULTY

Sara J. Exum
University of Notre Dame

Finding methods to communicate with faculty effectively and consistently is the challenge at every college or university. What captures the interest of faculty? What is the best way to get faculty to hear what we are saying? What should we avoid? These questions have no short, easy answers, since what works in one circumstance doesn't work in others.

Over the past several years, the need of the Office of Information Technologies to tell faculty about its services, particularly those that relate to teaching, learning, and research, has grown. How do we get the word out? The following are some methods that were found effective or ineffective.

EFFECTIVE METHODS

First and foremost, in order to communicate successfully to faculty, no single method works. Your message must be distributed in multiple ways. Messages that everyone must hear should be distributed electronically by email and/or on the Internet, on paper, and even through multimedia presentations. Being part of a technology organization, we can easily suppose that everyone has an email account, and, therefore, everyone must read email! For example, at Notre Dame, we once sent an email message to faculty about training opportunities available to them. For budgetary and experimental reasons, email was the only way we distributed this information. Ultimately, registration in the higher level courses was good, but the introductory courses were unsubscribed. We learned quickly that one method of communication didn't work well with faculty, especially when we had to reach those who might not even know how to use email.

Targeting groups of faculty who have a special interest in the service or event your message describes helps it to be successfully received. If you can discern what faculty members are interested in, you can tailor your messages to that particular audience. Such specificity saves you the headache of writing messages for everyone, whether or not they are interested. Gathering and maintaining data on faculty interests may be challenging but worth the time investment. At Notre Dame, we have a listserv specifically for faculty who are interested in technology, so when we have to distribute technology-related information that may be above and beyond the interest of the average instructor, we distribute the message to this list.

When a message is particularly important and needs the immediate attention of, or response from, the faculty, you increase your chances of success by distributing endorsed communications. If the provost, the dean, or any other individual respected by the faculty endorses the message, it is more likely to be well received. The endorsement works best if the provost or dean sends it in his or her name, but a joint communication is also effective. For example, at one time, we were seeking faculty feedback and asked them to attend public forums at which the feedback would be gathered. We distributed the information to all faculty, requesting their attendance. Deans then redistributed the message to attend the forums to their faculty with an endorsement. Consequently, attendance to the forums was good.

Similarly, if you want the faculty to learn more about a given technology, send a message to pique the students' interest. They are likely to share their enthusiasm with their instructors, and when you communicate directly to faculty about the service, a foundation has already been laid by their most influential constituency. Communicating to the dean of a college about an exciting program or sharing a new service with the provost may also transmit to faculty. The goal is to get others interested and talking so that when you communicate with the intended audience, they are already primed for listening. We use this method frequently when we have to communicate messages of a delicate nature or messages for which we need buy-in before we distribute them to campus. In these cases, we send our draft messages to various influential constituents for their feedback. Not only does this sample draft procedure plant the seed, but it also helps us work out the kinks in our communications. Another influence on successful communication is proper formatting, particularly in email. People receive many email messages every day, some of which are long and difficult to read. To assist faculty in picking out the pertinent information in a message, break it into chunks with headers (for example, "How does this change affect me?") so that readers can quickly browse your communication for the critical information. Intelligent headers and other formatting devices increase the chances that faculty will find and retain the information.

INEFFECTIVE METHODS

Using only one medium to communicate to faculty could lead to the slow death of your communication strategy. Different people like to receive their information in different ways. You will probably use only one medium to communicate a given message, but your overall communication strategy should include electronic, paper, multimedia, and even face-to-face communication. Don't make assumptions about how your audience likes to receive information. Always analyze the results of your communication strategies. We learned the need for reflective analysis quickly when we sent our training opportunities communication only via email.

No one likes to be spammed or to receive junk mail. If you're going to communicate with faculty regularly, do not send too many email messages or too many paper communiqués. If you overwhelm people with information, you may eventually be tuned out. Your strategy should include regular intervals of consistent communication and no extraneous messages.

When faculty aren't reading, they are often writing, so the last thing that they need is a long-winded message. While it's important to include all of the relevant information in your communications, it's equally important not to overcommunicate. Be brief and to the point and include details only where relevant.

In the end, finding an effective mix of communication media that meets faculty needs can be challenging. Don't be afraid to try something new, something nontraditional, since you never know when you might uncover a method that really works for your campus!

13

BUILDING A COMMUNITY ACROSS CAMPUS: THE DISTANCE EDUCATION INTEREST GROUP

Sherry Clouser Clark
University of Georgia

DESCRIPTION

The purpose of the Distance Education Interest Group (DEIG) at the University of Georgia is to provide networking opportunities for faculty and staff working on distance courses or programs. Some members are involved in developing or delivering courses or programs at a distance, some support distance education efforts, and others are simply curious about distance education and what is happening in this area around campus. The DEIG is sponsored by the Office of Instructional Support and Development and co-facilitated by an OISD staff member and a distance education specialist from the College of Agriculture and Environmental Sciences.

The DEIG meets monthly for a variety of programs. To date, topics have included roundtable discussions about course and program details, services available from the University System of Georgia as well as the university, brainstorming on how to improve distance education, vendor demonstrations of products with the potential to facilitate distance education development and delivery, and an asynchronous web-based course on online teaching and learning. The first meeting was formative and allowed for input from faculty and staff attendees regarding the group's purpose and objectives. Based on the outcome of that first meeting and re-negotiation since then, a listserv is maintained by the DEIG coordinators. All subscribers are welcome to post discussion topics, comments, and questions. In addition, the group coordinators post a weekly message called "DEIG Shorts." Meeting announcements, requests for information, conference announcements, and news briefs are among the short items included in the post.

Response and Outcomes

DEIG meetings are regularly attended by a core membership. The most successful events have been those with important guest speakers; for example, when the vice-president for instruction talked about his experiences with distance education. The vice-president's attendance validated the efforts of the DEIG members and allowed their voices to be heard by university administration.

A future outcome of the DEIG is a Frequently Asked Questions web site for anyone at UGA who is interested in teaching or developing courses for distance delivery. The FAQ is currently under construction and would not be possible without the combined efforts of the participating DEIG members.

Another future outcome of the group, in conjunction with the Office of Instructional Support and Development, is a Teaching Success Stories web site. This site will highlight the experiences of DEIG members and others who are developing courses and teaching at a distance. Interested faculty and staff will have the opportunity to learn what works in distance education directly from their peers. Again, this site would not be possible without the help of the DEIG members.

Finally, the DEIG has been successful in creating a sense of community and shared purpose among the participants. They talk to one another about such issues as intellectual property and accessibility and exchange ideas about meeting student and instructor needs online. DEIG members can turn to the group with a variety of questions and find myriad suggestions from their peers right here on campus. The DEIG has become an important resource for members as well as campus administrators looking for input on distance education issues.

Lessons Learned

There has been just one change in group operations over the past year. Based on discussion during the first meeting, a WebCT site intended to facilitate community building among group members between meetings was developed. The attendees of the meeting felt that a WebCT site would provide better tools for communication than a listserv. The listserv was originally created for announcements only, while the WebCT site would be open to everyone. The group members were asked to take some time to create a home page within the site that would inform others about their efforts in distance education. Also, the discussions tool was implemented as a way to allow online conversations on various topics related to distance education. The WebCT site was not successful. A handful of members checked in regularly for new information, but others rarely logged in. The coordinators reminded members every now and again to log in and post comments and questions, but the discussion area went mostly unused. Members addressed this problem twice in DEIG meetings. The first time, the group decided to give the WebCT site another try. The site remained unsuccessful, so the second time this issue came up, the group decided to open up the listserv and allow discussions to take place there. The weekly "DEIG Shorts" message remains a tool to keep group members informed about distance education endeavors and advancements at UGA and elsewhere.

You Can Do It, Too!

An interest group is an excellent way to bring together faculty and staff as well as students, in some instances, to learn and to discuss any current topic or issue on campus. Some other technology topics that may lend themselves well to an interest group include using technology with large classes, technology in research, and wireless technology. A major factor in the success of the DEIG has been the input and participation of key faculty and staff. They are interested in sharing and learning more, and their enthusiasm is contagious. If you can find a topic that sparks enthusiasm on your campus, you have a great foundation for an interest group.

Resource

http://www.isd.uga.edu/deig

14

PARTICIPATORY COMMUNICATION PLANNING AND IMPLEMENTATION

Christine Y. Fitzpatrick
Indiana University

Communication and user support are integral to the successful adoption and diffusion of any innovation, yet support staff in technology organizations often hear too little too late when large projects are planned. Shining exceptions exist whenever technical project leaders bring all parties on board early. Oncourse, Indiana University's (IU's) locally developed course management system, was created with extensive input from many quarters. This participatory, user-centered approach is also reflected in the development of its user support strategies and is a model for consideration.

Oncourse is IU's online environment for teaching and learning. Developed at Indiana University–Purdue University Indianapolis (IUPUI) in 1998, Oncourse is a key component of IU's strategic plan, particularly in support of distributed education. Like other online course management applications, Oncourse allows faculty and students to create, integrate, use, and maintain web-based teaching and learning resources. Distinctively, however, Oncourse was from the very beginning an enterprise environment (i.e., course data is linked to administrative data), automatically creating class sections from registrar data and populating the course spaces with enrolled students and faculty.

Early enthusiasm for Oncourse suggested potential for widespread adoption by faculty and especially by students across IU's eight campuses. In order to enable rapid acceptance and effective use of the innovation, however, the project had to move from a promising local experiment to a robust, system-wide application that is complemented by user support, training, and education programs.

Accordingly, in spring 1999, an implementation team was formed within University Information Technology Services (UITS), IU's central technology organization, to make Oncourse available to more than 90,000 students and nearly 5,000 faculty university-wide by July. Team members were drawn from divisions and offices across the organization, including representatives from two key divisions, University Information Systems (system administration, database administration, and development) and Teaching and Learning Information Technologies (frontline support and training). Also essential to the team's success were faculty development specialists from teaching and learning centers on the core campuses of IU (Bloomington and Indianapolis) and representatives of the UITS Communications and Planning Office (CPO).

The UITS CPO, part of the Office of the Vice President for Information Technology, is responsible for internal and external communications for UITS. CPO staff contribute expertise in audience analysis, reporting, message design, and visual communication. They deemed it important for communications and user support information for Oncourse to be developed with input from project stakeholders, including members of the target audiences. Ideally, CPO staff would also increase accuracy, consistency, and standard terminology. Therefore, to coordinate the implementation of Oncourse, a cross-functional team was established for communications and support.

Twenty-four members of The Oncourse Communications and Support Group first convened on April 7, 1999. From this large assembly, three smaller working groups of three to seven members were quickly established for communications, documentation, and education. Members not volunteering for, nor appointed to, working groups participated as a larger review community.

Weekly meetings were held for the full group, through videoconferencing between IU Bloomington and IUPUI. Early discussions identified core values and goals to guide effective practice. For example, the group determined that faculty and technology support providers were the most important audience for information about Oncourse, especially in the first year of service. Without faculty interest and subsequent successful adoption of the technology or the availability of informed local support, students would not be able to realize the potential of Oncourse. Another critical goal the group identified was to reduce duplication of effort, using computer-mediated communication, including Oncourse itself, for planning, document sharing, and review. A listserv became the platform for much of this sharing and thrives today.

While Oncourse developers worked on the application and its scalability, the communications and support working groups developed materials to support the production rollout of Oncourse. Specific deliverables achieved that summer include:

- A redesigned university entry path (via the web) to Oncourse and redesigned campus login pages established the application as a university resource, available on each campus. Other information included instructions for logging on to Oncourse.

- News and information pages developed for Oncourse stored announcements, the history of Oncourse, and guest information.

- A Getting Help with Oncourse page posted documentation, frequently asked questions, and a quick tour of the site.

- Faculty and student "Getting Started Guides" assisted in accessing, logging in, and using Oncourse's basic features. HTML and PDF versions of these guides were linked to Oncourse.

- Online help included context sensitivity.

- Knowledge Base documents detailed how to access and use Oncourse.

- Education classes in Oncourse basics, including materials, were developed and ready for delivery to faculty and students in late summer and fall.

- Announcements for online media and campus/university publications were designed.

- Discussions via the teaching and learning centers allowed faculty to share their Oncourse experiences and ideas with their colleagues.

Since Oncourse was launched as a university resource in 1999, its Communications and Support Group has been extended to include the entire development team and faculty development staff from other IU campuses. The group remains active in development, consistent with the user-centered practices that have been established for Oncourse. Members actively test new features and raise questions about user support.

While the group was formed to support the launch of Oncourse, its work is far from over. Membership has changed a bit, but the core activities of communication, education, support, and faculty development continue to be the group's charge. Members meet monthly via videoconference and maintain an active listserv. Working in support of Oncourse development as well as the community of users, the group has also helped to improve accessibility and user interface. Most recently, it has developed a fully integrated, context-sensitive help system that includes advice for making effective use of particular features and instructions for using Oncourse. This successful participatory strategy has helped to build and to support a diverse community that has grown from several hundred beta testers in 1999 to 70,000 by fall 2002.

RESOURCES

Oncourse: http://oncourse.iu.edu
See especially "News and Information" and "Getting Help with Oncourse" to review the materials developed by the Oncourse Communications and Support Working Groups.

Communications and Planning Office: http://www.indiana.edu/~uits/cpo

IU Knowledge Base: http://kb.iu.edu. Enter the search term: Oncourse

University Information Technology Services: http://www.indiana.edu/~uits

Indiana University: http://www.indiana.edu

15

COMMUNICATION TOOLS TO SUPPORT FACULTY USE OF WEbCT

Douglas F. Johnson
University of Florida

INTRODUCTION

Many researchers in the field of online education assert that one of the most critical elements in the success of an online course is frequent, effective communication (Coldeway, MacRury, & Spencer 1980; Creed, 1996; Threlkeld & Brzoska, 1994). Given that much support for faculty engaged in distance education is also delivered at a distance, good communication is also a requisite of good support. At the University of Florida, a variety of communication tools are actively employed to facilitate communication between faculty and WebCT support.

TELEPHONE AND EMAIL

The most familiar starting points for faculty support communication are the telephone and email. Because they are both handled immediately, they are essentially identical communication mechanisms. To facilitate faculty access, the WebCT administrator's phone number and email address are published on all UF WebCT web pages as well as at other locations faculty might go seeking assistance, including various faculty support centers around campus and help desk locations.

Phone calls and voicemail messages are processed according to the fundamental principles of Customer Service Management: "Customers Know What They Want," "Customers' Needs Are Paramount," and "Communication Is Key to Our Success" (NIH, 2001). According to these principles, the WebCT administrator takes notes on each call, identifying the caller, contact information, and the request for assistance. The administrator also frequently asks questions to clarify the problem and to learn how the client has attempted to solve it. When possible, immediate assistance is provided. When not, the caller is given an assessment of what the problem is likely to be and how long it may take to resolve. When the problem is resolved, the WebCT administrator calls the client to confirm the solution, and the service is only then considered completed. A similar process is employed with email.

WebCT Users Listserv

> Here's a nifty little utility I learned about at a conference for those of you who use the chat feature of WebCT, particularly if you grade students based on participation: ChatStat...

> Sorry to inundate you with messages, but I just received notice that the servers running WebCT versions 2.2 and 3.1 will be down for roughly three hours from 1 to 4 a.m. tomorrow morning (5/10) and possibly again on Friday morning (5/11).

> I am having problems with students posting responses to discussion questions in the wrong location. Does anyone have some suggestions of good ways to organize/manage discussions to keep threaded topics together?

These three messages are taken from the UF WebCT users' list archives and illustrate some of the opportunities gained by using a listserv to get information to, and enhance communication among, faculty users of WebCT. The first message is from a user, sharing information about a tool learned about at a conference. The second message from the WebCT administrator lets users know of an impending server outage. The final message is from a user seeking best-practice suggestions from other users.

A listserv allows you to create, manage, and control electronic mailing lists on a network or over the Internet. When a user sends an email to the list, the software sends a copy of it to all other members. Hence, they can be effective tools for getting information to, and facilitating communication among, a group sharing an interest. They have been around almost as long as email, and as a result, a significant body of research and writing has emerged regarding their use to "create vital, energetic and occasional communities for professional development activities, building curriculum and information resource libraries and facilitating informal communicative networks, serving the social, professional and personal needs of teachers" (Wild, 1999). Theoretical frameworks and models of listserv use have been articulated (Rojo, 1995).

At UF, a listserv account has been established for users of WebCT. Membership is voluntary, but roughly 90% of all faculty with WebCT course accounts participate. The WebCT users' list at UF is unmoderated and self-censoring, meaning that messages are not screened before they are sent, and anyone who chooses can sign up. Administrative overhead is thus kept to a minimum, though the potential is raised for problems with unsolicited commercial email (spam), anonymous members, and the vituperative commentary referred to as *flaming* (see Collins, 1992, and Kiesler, Siegel, & McGuire, 1984, for some interesting studies on flaming). So far, none of these problems have emerged at UF.

WebCT Announcements Feature

The WebCT course-management system provides an announcements feature that is an excellent tool for effective communication. It allows the WebCT administrator to post critical information to every user or to selected subgroups. The announcements are prominently marked on the users' entry portal page and can range from short statements to lengthy descriptions. HTML code can be used to format the font for emphasis, and URLs can be embedded to take readers to other sources of information.

The announcements feature can easily be overused, in which case users may well cease to notice changes to that section of their course portal. However, judicious use of this feature can be an effective communication mechanism, because it is one of the few tools for reaching every user of WebCT. The ability to link to other sources of information can also be invaluable.

WebCT Institutional Bookmarks Feature

Another useful feature of WebCT is the institutional bookmarks section of the portal. As its name suggests, the bookmarks section allows the WebCT administrator to post a hyperlinked list of resources for users. At the University of Florida, this list includes links to the WebCT@UF home page; support resources for both faculty and student users; the UF home page; the UF library system; the UF computer-use policy; and ISIS, the UF student information and registration system. By making these links easy to locate and access, the portal page becomes a full-featured communication center, providing support for WebCT at UF.

The WebCT@UF Web Page

A final powerful tool for communication and faculty support is the WebCT@UF web site. This site constantly grows and changes in response to WebCT users' needs. It serves as the authoritative point of access to WebCT at UF and links the various WebCT servers. By advertising this site as the authoritative point of access, the dislocation that can occur as a result of a server move, for example, is minimized.

The WebCT@UF web site is also the most comprehensive source of information about WebCT at UF. While announcements may be posted at other locations, this web site is noted as the source of details and additional information. When major changes are implemented, it allows the posting of lengthy articles that describe those changes and identify their benefits. White papers detailing the vision and planning for WebCT at UF are posted at the WebCT@UF web site to generate comment and to solicit input from both faculty and student users.

The WebCT@UF web site also contains a variety of information links; for example, to downloadable manuals that vary from beginner to advanced, so users can enhance their grasp of WebCT. A section for student users provides advice as well as manuals and tutorials for various WebCT tools and features. The section for faculty provides information on WebCT policies, both general and at UF; how to get new course accounts; information that can be provided to students; commonly sought online resources, such as links to compatible browsers and plug-ins; and a reading list of online resources that have been recommended by other UF faculty as particularly interesting or helpful for supporting the use of WebCT specifically and online learning in general.

The key to a successful web site is to make it useful, informative, and responsive to the changing needs of its users. The UF WebCT administrator constantly asks faculty what they could use or would like to see on that web site, and those suggestions are the heart of changes. Maintaining an active web site can be time- and labor-intensive but pays off by reducing the number of calls seeking information about WebCT.

CONCLUSION

Building a sense of community among a scattered group of people communicating largely, if not entirely, at a distance requires a wide variety of tools to facilitate and to enhance communication. Employing such a variety of tools can be both challenging and time-consuming. At the University of Florida, use of WebCT course accounts is growing at a rate of roughly 125% per year. Such success bears witness to the effective communication and technical support that has made WebCT a popular option for University of Florida faculty. Providing effective support is well worth the investment of time and resources.

REFERENCES

Coldeway, D. O., MacRury, K., & Spencer, R. (1980). *Distance education from the learner's perspective: The results of individual learner tracking at Athabasca University.* Edmonton, Alberta: Athabasca University. (ERIC Document Reproduction Service No. ED 259228)

Collins, M. (1992). *Flaming: The relationship between social context cues and uninhibited verbal behavior in computer-mediated communication.* Retrieved May 3, 2002, from http://www.emoderators.com/papers/flames.html

Creed, T. (1996). *Extending the classroom walls electronically.* Retrieved May 2, 2002, from http://www.employees.csbsju.edu/tcreed/techno3.html

Kiesler, S., Siegel, J., & McGuire, T. (1984). Social psychological aspects of computer-mediated communication. *American Psychologist, 39* (10), 1123–1134.

National Institutes of Health. (2001). *NIH customer service plan.* Retrieved May 2, 2002, from http://oma.od.nih.gov/ma/customer/customerserviceplan/

Rojo, A. (1995). *Participation in scholarly electronic forums.* Retrieved May 3, 2002, from http://www.emoderators.com/moderators/rojochap2.html

Threlkeld, R., & Brzoska, K. (1994). Research in distance education. In B. Willis (Ed.), *Distance education: Strategies and tools.* Englewood Cliffs, NJ: Educational Technology Publications, Inc.

Wild, M. (1999). The anatomy of practice in the use of mailing lists: A case study. *Australian Journal of Educational Technology, 15* (2), 117–135.

16

THE LISTSERV AS A COMMUNICATION TOOL: KEEPING BLACKBOARD USERS TALKING

Rosalind Tedford
Wake Forest University

At Wake Forest University, primary technology support for faculty falls on the instructional technology specialists, who reside in each department. While this model allows the hiring of support personnel with more discipline-specific knowledge and background, it can limit the communication between different departments on technology-related issues. Wake Forest has found a way to close this communication gap to some degree with its support model for Blackboard. This simple, relatively low-tech and low-cost approach has been an unqualified success for us, and we are happy to share it with others.

In 1998, Wake Forest chose to pilot what was then CourseInfo (now Blackboard) as a potential course-management system for the campus. Through selection, volunteerism, and a bit of prodding, 25 faculty, with a broad range of computer skills and classroom technology experience, participated in the pilot. They came to one four-hour training session during which their pilot course was created and populated with material. All picked up the technology quickly, but many were very anxious about confronting it on their own back in their offices. The challenge of how to best support them during the semester had to be met.

There seemed little sense in getting our entire information systems help desk up to speed on a product that was serving only 25 faculty and that might not even be adopted. We decided instead to form a listserv, where pilot participants could post their questions and we could post responses for all to see. I monitored the listserv along with the other primary CourseInfo trainer, our system administrator, and all of the faculty and support staff who had been on the committee charged with finding a course-management system. A few of our help-desk personnel also asked to be on the list, as did the instructional technology specialists who were supporting the pilot participants.

The list was a busy one, and we used it to get our participants through network problems, server upgrades, student enrollment, data uploading, and many other difficult moments. Because it was a learning experience for us all, the list was an invaluable way to get information out to all the right people quickly. Even after technical matters were ironed out, message volume continued to grow, as faculty were more and more adventurous in their use of CourseInfo and began to seek input from each other about how best to use the product. For those of us monitoring the list, we often felt as if we had let a tiger out of its cage, but as you will see, it was worth it in the long run.

At the end of the semester, we had a meeting with the pilot faculty, and they all said the listserv had been the best thing about the experience. They praised the support they had received and encouraged us to keep up the listserv once the product was in general use. Although we had not originally intended to do so, faculty vehemence led us to keep the listserv. We began having faculty subscribe to the list as the last task in the training sessions they started to attend during the summer of 1998. Membership in the list was not and is not mandatory, but we highly recommend it to anyone using the product.

I am proud to say that the list is entering its fifth year and is just as successful today as it was in 1998. We currently have nearly 200 faculty and support personnel on it, and that number continues to grow. The first year or so of the project, list traffic was heavy, especially in August and January, as faculty were setting up new classes. Once the bulk of our faculty had used the product for a while, however, we found that they began to support each other. Often, other faculty answered the questions posted to the list rather than the support personnel. This process was wonderful, because it limited the amount of time we spent answering questions and let us get back to the other parts of our jobs.

Today, the list is used primarily to announce server downtime, alert the users about impending upgrades and new features, post training dates, and keep communication about instructional technology flowing among the faculty. It is still used to answer how-to questions from newer users, but as that population is small each semester, the percentage of these questions is lower than in the past. The list also shows signs of broadening its horizons to include more pedagogical questions about the use of a course-management system, something I find very encouraging and hope to foster in the years to come. I now spend very little time each week answering questions from the list. When I do post, it is mostly to disseminate information relevant to Blackboard users.

What can other schools take away from our experience? First, if you have limited support resources for a technology initiative, a listserv is a wonderful way to concentrate what resources you do have. It is far easier to answer a question one time on a listserv than to field 20 phone calls about it. Second, if you want your faculty talking to each other about instructional technology, listservs are a great way to start. We all know how difficult it can be to get faculty into the same physical space for workshops or seminars, but getting them in the same virtual space is easy and effective. Our faculty love knowing what others are doing with Blackboard, whether they are in the same department or not. As primary support staff, I love hearing what is going on across campus, so I can match up faculty with similar concerns.

Finally, the public relations boost from something this easy is worth the difficulties in getting it off the ground. Our listserv is consistently referred to by faculty as a best practice in technology support on campus, and we have offered several presentations about it at national conferences. Although we couldn't have predicted this, it has become a true success story, one that rose out of a need to offer support with limited resources and that developed into a model support and communication tool.

17

SHOWCASING FACULTY WORK: A JOINT EFFORT

Janet R. de Vry
University of Delaware

Faculty are the best evangelists for transforming learning through appropriate use of technology and rely on IT professionals to assist them in publicizing their efforts to the broader campus community. At the University of Delaware (UD), we are committed to publicizing faculty efforts wherever and whenever we can. For example, we showcase faculty work in the campus newspaper and on our faculty technology web site. We offer live faculty showcases at our biannual collaborative faculty institute and, increasingly, teach classes together. A number of IT staff make joint presentations with faculty at local and national conferences and co-author journal articles.

SHOWCASES: IN PRINT AND ONLINE

The IT technical writing staff writes articles and inserts that highlight faculty work for the campus newspaper. The most recent article (*Update*, 2002) focuses on how four UD faculty are using technology to make more effective and efficient use of class time.

We promote faculty efforts in three distinct ways on our faculty technology development web site. We profile different individual faculty members every two months, then collect those profiles and list them in one web page. In addition, we offer a searchable online database that provides quick access to an overview of what all faculty who have made appointments with our staff are doing with instructional technology. The web page and database link to each other. Additional links provide opportunities for more in-depth exploration. The database can be sorted and searched by discipline or affiliation, such as grants received or participation in the Institute for Transforming Undergraduate Education. We promote faculty accomplishments to demonstrate inspirational teaching experiences from every discipline.

We struggled to accommodate searchable categories for pedagogy and technology into our showcase, but several experiments failed. Although the concept of sorting by learning principle seems useful, in reality, these proved too unwieldy. "Many teaching applications seemed to defy easy labeling by principle—usually because successful strategies use a variety of sound pedagogical principles," said Paul Hyde, educational technology consultant. Similarly, technology categories did not prove helpful. Hyde stated, "We found that categorizing entries by technology used could be a distraction, since many projects could achieve the same success with a number of alternate technologies."

We are now working to minimize the time required to present faculty experiences online. Even with easy-to-use forms, experience has proven that entries are usually made with the help of IT staff and some editing by a technical writer. Future plans include linking to digitized testimonials and presentations in the showcase entries.

SHOWCASES: IN PERSON

While faculty development literature stresses that faculty want to hear from those in their own discipline, such sectarianism is not the only or best way to reach them. Faculty frequently work in isolation from their colleagues in other departments. They have commented that gatherings where they have interacted with a more diverse group have been energizing and led to collaborations that would not otherwise have developed. Ralph Begleiter, the Edward F. and Elizabeth Goodman Rosenberg Professor of Communication, teamed up with faculty members from the College of Agriculture to narrate an animation on RNA after one such encounter. "As a new faculty member, I was at a meeting of all those who had received student technology assistant grants and heard Sherry and Lesa say they were considering having a voice narrate an animation project they were working on. After the session, I whispered to them that I had been making a career out of radio and TV narration and would be glad to do their narration if they went ahead with their project. The rest is history" (McAdams, 2001).

While faculty make some of the best advocates for applying technology to learning, those promoting events and showcasing their work need to be somewhat savvy about their attitudes and audience. Early adopters and innovators can actually scare off mainstream faculty who are not interested in bells and whistles and want to spend their time on teaching and research. One faculty member commented, "No one listens to Professor X when he advocates using technology, because he spends so much time experimenting with it. Since I do not spend all my time with technology, they will believe me when I say something is easy to do and makes a difference in learning." We also try to approach new faculty in new departments so that the message remains fresh.

It's a good idea to encourage faculty presenters to openly discuss lessons learned. Glib advertising is not the best approach with this audience. In answering the question, "What aspect of the program was most valuable," on a faculty showcase evaluation form, Sandra Millard, assistant director, Morris Library, noted "the demonstration and frank descriptions by faculty and User Services staff of the work and the time that went into the designs and the thinking behind the decisions." Kathy Denhardt, policy scientist, wrote, "It was very important to *see* what others had developed and to get a realistic estimation of the time it took to create. The variety in types of courses and applications was also very useful."

In communicating with faculty about faculty technology development efforts, we take advantage of all opportunities that present themselves. We make choices about the best presenter for a specific audience, and we try to open frank discussions about learning strategies, time, and potential pitfalls. We must encourage faculty to come together both within their own disciplines and in interdisciplinary settings. We provide a rich online array of profiles and a searchable showcase of faculty work. We collaborate with faculty on projects and in promoting them at conferences and in journals. Increasingly, we will explore new ways to use technology to showcase faculty teaching with technology.

REFERENCES

McAdams, P. (2001, April 5). Animation project helps explain genetic engineering, *Update, 3*. Available: http://www.udel.edu/PR/UpDate/01/13/animation.html

Technology transforms teaching and learning. (2002, April/May). *Update, 24.*

RESOURCES

Geoghegan, W. H. (1994). *Whatever happened to instructional technology? Reaching mainstream faculty.* Norwalk, CT: International Business Schools Computing Association.

University of Delaware Faculty Showcase: http://present.smith.udel.edu/showcase/

18

WHEN POPULAR SOFTWARE GOES AWAY: HELPING FACULTY TRANSITION TO NEW PRODUCTS

Jennifer Meta Robinson
Indiana University

Early technology adopters are eager to try the latest product, but many faculty remain committed to a particular instructional technology, both hardware and software, long after that tool has been improved upon and effectively replaced. Time is often the key factor: A faculty member who devotes substantial time to learning to use a particular technology may not have the additional time, energy, and interest in continually updating those skills. At Indiana University, many faculty have embraced the educational possibilities of new technologies, including web enhancements of on-campus courses, but they also can become discouraged at the additional time necessary to keep up with new developments. In my experience, instructional support staff can help minimize faculty frustration by following a few guidelines.

During the late 1990s, a small, innovative, and ambitious group of instructional technology developers at Indiana University put their heads together on their own time to design a web-based teaching environment built on the platform of a proprietary software package. After extensive beta testing of the new environment, which included in-class email service, threaded discussion, team communication, anonymous feedback, and quizzing, the instructional and technology services staff demonstrated the program's features and potential in a series of programs and training sessions held for the faculty. The reception for this product was especially enthusiastic because many faculty had been struggling to code their own web sites from scratch. In 1999, when the environment was rolled out, dozens of faculty invested themselves in learning the software, moving their course materials to that software, tediously enrolling their students, adapting their lessons, and otherwise integrating this technological tool into their teaching.

What these developers and the faculty did not know, however, was that the licensing fees for the commercial software package, on which the new teaching environment was based, would skyrocket in January 2000, immediately after many professors had committed to it and in the middle of the academic year when free time is negligible. In fact, the increase in fees made continued licensing prohibitively expensive. When the administration decided that the entire program would have to be discontinued, staff promises to help faculty take their teaching to the cutting edge now felt like a betrayal.

Instructional and technology consultants found themselves facing difficult strategic questions: What were the best alternative web environments for the faculty? Which ones offered comparable functions, the easiest transition, and the longest-term stability? Which would make teaching easier? How would we break the bad news to the professors who had invested time and effort in an untenable product?

STEP 1: EVALUATING THE OPTIONS

Collaborating with technical staff, instructional consultants made detailed comparisons of the features offered by the in-house package and other commercial and university-sponsored software. The comparisons included the following four areas:

- *Support:* How many project-dedicated developers are there? Is there funding for outside contract developers in crunch times? Will training personnel come on site? Is a trained help desk staff available at least 40 hours a week?

- *Cost:* Is licensing per user? Per site? Is licensing cost likely to remain stable?

- *Commitment:* Has the developing agency/company committed to fund, upgrade, and otherwise maintain the product? For how long? Has it committed to making upgrades and other transitions easy on the user?

- *Functions:* What functions will be available at the time of adoption? Are other functions planned? What is the schedule of improvement? How much influence can we, as users, have on development processes and priorities?

The question of functionality was of most interest to the users, so the comparison of the flexibility, intuitiveness, automation, and potential for modification by users became crucial (see Table 18.1).

Table 18.1

Evaluation of Options

Function	Considerations
Access	Are there different levels of access for students, graduate assistants, and professors? Are off-campus visitors permitted access? Is course creation automatic, or must it be requested?
Announcements	Are they in a place where students will definitely see them?
Archiving	How long will courses remain active?
Assignment hand-in	Can they be sorted (by author, date, assignment)? Can the professor comment on assignments?
Attachments	Are multiple attachments possible?
Authentication	Is there pass-through authentication to and from other college resources?
Calendar/schedule	Does it look like a calendar? Can active links be included? Can attachments be included? Is it collapsible? Does it automatically provide dates and days of the week?
Chat	Available?
Course feedback	Is it anonymous?
Course policies	Are they easy to update?
Course resources	Can active links be included? Can documents be attached for download?
Course statistics	Are statistics compiled by student and activity?
Development	Is there an online form for development suggestions and trouble reports?
Discussion	Can entries be sorted (by author, date, subject)? Can student teams have private discussions? Can the instructor make private comments?

(continued)

Documentation	Online? On paper?
Export/import	Can course settings and content be exported to, or imported from, another course?
File and data management	How much storage is allowed? Are increases granted in special cases?
Grade book	Are grades from quizzes, tests, and assignments automatically added to grade book? Are comments possible? Are grades tallied? Are grades exportable (e.g., to a spreadsheet)?
Links to other online courses	Can a student access all online courses from a single web page? Both current and previous semesters?
Messaging	Is it internal or sent to an outside email address? Can groups be mailed?
Modification	Can professors modify low-level course environment variables to more closely own the course? Can functions be hidden if not used or redirected if the professor prefers another product?
Passwords	Are they linked to the university network account? Can they be changed by the user, or do new account names and passwords have to be created and distributed?
Rostering	Is it dynamic and connected to the registrar's latest data, or do students or faculty have to request it?
Quizzing and testing	Are statistics compiled (e.g., reliability, validity, averages, raw scores)? Are multiple attempts possible? Can the highest score be submitted? Is scoring automatic? Are comments on particular answers possible?
Web accessibility	Is web access possible, or must a user be on campus?

STEP 2: INTRODUCING FACULTY TO CHANGE IN INSTRUCTIONAL TECHNOLOGY

One of the primary questions in helping faculty transition to a new software or hardware product is how to minimize their sense of futility in exploring innovations in instructional technologies that may disappear. Using evidence and allowing choice are critical answers. Also, people with appropriate authority, technical proficiency, and interpersonal communication skills should be involved in introducing a clientele to change.

After comparing the current product with the alternatives, the next step requires deciding on the most *significant* and persuasive similarities and differences and their ramifications. These must be presented in a readable form so that faculty members can make informed decisions. For example, the most significant differences in the Indiana University case involved the level of familiarity with the basic software platforms and the automatic integration of university registrar data into the web-enabled courses.

With the data for making decisions outlined and with the backing of the school's administration, several open demonstrations of the most viable alternative product(s) can be productive. These sessions are likely to go more smoothly if they are not overly didactic and allow the faculty members areas in which to exercise their discretion. A few guidelines for these sessions include:

- Don't over-promise or oversell a product.

- If possible, get product developers to give the demo, and ask high-level administrators to attend. Allow in-house technical staff to appear slightly removed from particular products.

- Encourage faculty to ask questions.

- Ask faculty and staff to submit suggestions and priorities for future development.

- Provide test accounts for faculty and staff.

- Allow faculty members to make some choices; for example, about which product to adopt, when to adopt it, how much assistance they will receive.

STEP 3: SUPPORTING THE TRANSITION

Once the individual professors or the administration have chosen a new software product, adequate support for that transition is critical. Training should:

- be held in a computer lab where professors and staff can work hands-on on actual courses.
- be led by experts who can anticipate questions and problems.
- be tailored to the particular audience's concerns and needs.

Continuing support should:

- be available 24 hours a day, seven days a week, at least through the transition period.
- be available online, although paper documentation is especially important for less technically advanced users.
- include sound pedagogical methods for integrating the instructional technology into class activities.

When the popular course software "went away," the instructional consulting and technology services staff fairly quickly determined the best alternative to recommend to faculty. The university had put its full commitment into the funding, development, training, and support of Oncourse, another home-grown product with strong potential to develop into a flexible, functional package that faculty could reasonably consider and administrators could honestly endorse. Throughout the transition process, instructional consultants were never in the business of selling any particular software or hardware; instead, we helped faculty to make the most informed judgments they could, based on what they determined to be their needs and goals. This service orientation allows instructional consulting staff to make ethical and sound decisions in recommending instructional technology and to maintain a level of trust with clients that is crucial to our work.

19

COORDINATION AND COLLABORATION IN FACULTY SUPPORT

Terry M. Wildman
Virginia Polytechnic Institute and State University

Bringing faculty together to enhance instruction has been an integral part of Virginia Tech's strategic plan since the early 1990s. The investments in technology and faculty development related to technology have been enormous, and the impact on the culture of the institution has been remarkable, as indicated in some of the related articles. But investments in technology itself were not the only strategic responses to the need for a more responsive and effective instructional system. Here's a brief look at other parts of the story at Virginia Tech, showing that technology use actually occurs within a complex matrix of organizational structures and challenges.

Following a yearlong planning effort during 1992–1993, Virginia Tech launched its first teaching center, the Center for Excellence in Undergraduate Teaching (CEUT). Developed simultaneously with the Faculty Development Initiative (FDI; see Chapter 2), the center was given the more general mission of providing broad-based support for teaching and of serving as the institutional advocate for teaching excellence. Other initiatives begun at the same time included a Faculty Roles and Rewards project and a new core curriculum.

Out of these efforts, CEUT was given administrative responsibility for a newly established University Writing Program and budgetary responsibility for the Exemplary Departments Award Program and two teaching recognition programs, the Academy of Teaching Excellence and the Diggs Teaching Scholar Program. Several years later, in 1997, the university's Learning Communities Initiative was established and that effort also was located within the Center for Excellence in Undergraduate Teaching.

On the surface, the connection between the teaching center and the technology centers may be difficult to see. CEUT and FDI have quite different missions, and even the administrative connections are different—one reporting to the provost and the other to the vice president for information systems. However, they both serve the same faculty. While their development and support needs with respect to technology are extensive and continuing, the faculty are also involved in curriculum development, student advising, and maintaining safe and supportive classrooms. They develop tests and assign grades, serve on promotion and tenure committees, participate in faculty governance, and generally carry out myriad responsibilities.

These responsibilities and associated support needs cannot be neatly divided between technology and everything else. Our university's strategic goals with respect to the role of instructional technology use are carried out in a quite complex environment with regard to faculty concerns, development needs, and ways of interacting across departmental and college lines. Because programs and centers with less-than-obvious technology connections are still intimately involved, understanding the whole structure is necessary to really appreciate the institution's response to its evolving mission.

ADVANCEMENTS IN PEDAGOGY

We recognize that most teaching faculty come to their positions with little, if any, formal preparation in teaching methodology. Consequently, the teaching center offers a continuing range of opportunities for faculty to learn about various topics:

- the research on learning
- teaching strategies that include more active roles for students
- implementation of cooperative learning and problem-based learning
- design and use of classroom assessment procedures
- specific strategies for sections with enrollments ranging from 200 to 600
- strategies for small groups of students who may be involved in community projects

A particular concern in recent years has been to recognize that students must not only acquire content and skills related to their disciplines and professions but also advance in their intellectual development. By participating in workshops, many faculty are learning how to encourage students to think on their own. Thanks to continuing visits to Virginia Tech by Marcia Baxter Magolda, author of *Knowing and Reasoning in College* (1992) and *Creating Contexts for Learning and Self-Authorship* (1999), the contemporary research on student intellectual development is beginning to play a major role in how faculty think about and are rethinking their instructional responsibilities.

ENVIRONMENT AND CULTURE

The environment in which we work has major effects on thinking. Therefore, we've given a great deal of thought not only to the physical setting for instruction but the social context as well. When the entire context for learning and instruction is opened for consideration, a range of new partners who have not always worked together are brought into play. At Virginia Tech, the relationship between student affairs and academic affairs has grown increasingly intimate, and topics like diversity and academic integrity are no longer viewed in isolation. With support from CEUT and the Learning Communities Initiative, Virginia Tech's strategic goal of educating the whole person is becoming a real problem for consideration and not just a slogan. Even the operations of the university architect and registrar are brought more fully into the educational discussion when impact of the environment on learning is considered.

REFLECTION AND SCHOLARSHIP

Faculty members require time and opportunities for collaboration to make headway on the dilemmas that confront them daily. One of our more successful innovations has been a study group program, sponsored by the CEUT. Faculty are invited to form small groups that commit to a yearlong collaboration on teaching. The participants set the agenda, with the teaching center offering tips for effective group dynamics, space for meetings, research assistance, and a $300 professional development stipend for each participant. Begun in 1997, the program has grown from about 6 groups and 35–40 participants to a much larger effort in 2001–2002, involving 17 groups and 93 faculty participants. Groups now routinely stay together for more than one year, and several groups have worked together for two to four years. We've concluded from this program that faculty recognize that teaching itself is an activity requiring reflection and scholarship; they are drawn to it because of its inherent complexity, but they also see that the traditional departmental cultures may not support the opportunities necessary for social engagement in this most fundamental aspect of faculty responsibility. Faculty development centers can play a key role in bringing faculty together around problems of mutual concern. Interestingly, faculty seem to find the groups more compelling when the members represent different colleges, departments, and disciplines.

FUNDING FOR INNOVATION

One additional piece of the puzzle related to ongoing faculty support for innovation is funding. CEUT offers an ongoing grants program that provides summer fellowships, academic-year course-release options, and operational funds for projects that may not have departmental support. This university program is one of several from which faculty can obtain financial support. The Center for Innovation in Learning offers significant funding for larger-scale technology projects; the University Writing Program supports course enhancements to improve writing and speaking; and specific colleges provide funding for instructional enhancement, such as the engineering department's support for teaching during their recent move to the new ABET accreditation system.

The point is that in large institutions, a whole complex of funding and support services may be available to faculty. Some of these internal funding sources may have no explicit or necessary technology focus. However, in the past seven years, more than half of CEUT's funded projects involved a significant technology component. Indeed, many of the faculty who have eventually acquired internal funding for large-scale technology projects began with smaller grants from CEUT, and most of the faculty who have won the University Xcaliber Award for technological innovation began their exploratory work with funding from the teaching center.

A COORDINATED ACADEMIC COMMUNITY

The story related here begins to show that the programs and units formed to advance technology are not the only ones involved in the movement. At Virginia Tech, the goals of faculty support units overlap whether or not they have a specific technology focus built into their mission statement. One of the things I believe we do very well is to help faculty make rather seamless connections across units that have different formal missions but common underlying goals. As we have matured in our work with technology, we now understand that our common ground is the fundamental question of how to engage students with interesting problems, their faculty, and each other, with the growth of the whole person in mind.

20

THE VIRGINIA TECH CYBERSCHOOL AND THE ONLINE MASTER OF ARTS IN POLITICAL SCIENCE

Timothy W. Luke
Virginia Polytechnic Institute and State University

In this brief chapter, I want to discuss two programs that have worked well for distance learning at Virginia Tech: cyberschool and the Online Master of Arts in Political Science (OLMA/PSCI). These projects had their origins in the university's College of Arts and Sciences, but they drew backing from all across campus, including support from the dean of Arts and Sciences, Robert C. Bates, from the educational technologies office in Virginia Tech's information systems division, and from the provost's office with the Center for Innovation in Learning (CIL). The development of Virginia Tech Online (VTO), the university's one-stop center for distance learning information and services, and the Institute for Distance and Distributed Learning (IDDL), the university's main policy-setting and support operation for distance and distributed learning, grew out of the university's initial successes with cyberschool and the OLMA/PSCI program. Both of these new organizations, in turn, have been supported financially and institutionally since their inception by the provost's office, the vice-president for information systems, and the College of Arts and Sciences.

The College of Arts and Sciences has been a leading player in distance education at Virginia Tech since the creation of the cyberschool. After its start in 1994, cyberschool (http://www.cyber.vt.edu) laid the groundwork for new institutional responses to increased financial pressures and administrative demands that were caused by level or declining state financial support. A small group of faculty, mostly based in the humanities, arts, and social sciences departments, pushed the cyberschool project forward after finishing their computer instruction in the university's Faculty Development Institute in 1993 and 1994.

The idea behind cyberschool was quite simple. Students in the mid-1990s were having considerable trouble getting into face-to-face, on-campus classes, making it difficult to graduate in four years. At the same time, the university recognized that about 70% of all undergraduate students came to school with their own personal computer and that a high percentage of them had Internet access at their parents' home. For a small cadre of technology-oriented faculty in the arts, humanities, and social sciences, building a virtual summer school, or cyberschool, to present courses online made a great deal of sense. Taking courses taught from Blacksburg, Virginia, at home over the summer, students could finish their university education on schedule, while still working at locations closer to their families during the summer months. In 1995, three courses were presented online in Blacksburg; in 1996, seven were available, and by 1998, around 20 were accessible online. By 2000, the university had over 200 courses in its distance and distributed learning inventory, and almost half were fully online. In 2002, more than 300 courses are available online, and students can fulfill most of the university's core requirements entirely online. Cyberschool faculty have worked tirelessly with many other offices around campus to help the entire university prepare to conduct research, teaching, and service missions in the digital environments being built on the World Wide Web. Cyberschool emphasized making student learning and faculty teaching as easy and convenient online as in the traditional, face-to-face campus environment. Consequently, the cyberschool faculty lobbied the administration very hard to establish VTO (http://www.vto.vt.edu) and IDDL (http://www.iddl.vt.edu) so that a high level of service could be realized. Cyberschool faculty also pushed for a campus-wide student computer requirement, a new technology fee structure, and several other policy changes meant to reduce the barriers to distance and distributed learning.

Given its cyberschool experience with online undergraduate instruction, the department of political science began to develop a fully online Master's degree program in political science (http://www.cyber.vt.edu/psci/olma/olma.html) during 1997, and courses were being taught by summer 1998. The College of Arts and Sciences was being asked at that time to expand its teaching presence in the urban areas across northern Virginia, and this approach seemed like a relatively cost-effective strategy for providing the MA in political science to nontraditional students residing in the Washington, DC, area. Of course, the site is available to anyone anytime anywhere in the world, so nearly 50 students are now taking courses in the program from all over the United States as well as Europe and Asia. Most of the online MA students are serving with the US military, working for international agencies and state governments, or teaching in secondary schools and community colleges.

The decisions taken by the university at large to put much more emphasis on digitized library resources, to provide an excellent support structure for registration, enrollment, and records-management with VTO, and to push for a campus-wide electronic thesis and dissertation requirement made it possible to produce an excellent graduate educational experience online. The first student finished writing his MA thesis during fall 2001 and orally defended it to his committee members in Blacksburg and DC from his place of work near Frankfurt, Germany, during an extended video conference in December 2001.

Most political science faculty at all ranks were eager to participate in the online MA program, and this excitement continues today. The common caricature of university faculty members as neo-Luddite opponents to technological innovation simply is not true. Once faculty are shown the utility of new digital teaching tools, which enable them to communicate more effectively, while students learn more flexibly, they readily adopt them. While many faculty will remain wary of administrative dictates from above, they will enthusiastically join challenging new projects, like cyberschool or OLMA/PSCI, that afford them fresh opportunities to try out new approaches, to learn different educational techniques, and to use better communication methods.

Cyberschool and OLMA/PSCI were launched by individual faculty members working with their colleagues to leverage the potential of new digital technologies for teaching. Supportive administrators at Virginia Tech gave them the release time and material resources to make these experiments successful, but the faculty's curiosity and enthusiasm really carried this work forward. Left to themselves with exciting new electronic technologies, most faculties can come up with innovative solutions to present-day institutional challenges, especially if they are not hobbled by misdirected central administrative expectations. These two successful projects strongly underscore the potential for great success that can be realized by any university's central administration. All they have to do is give their faculty the resources and freedom to excel, while setting some basic targets for excellent performance. Virginia Tech discovered that the faculty will not only come up with new approaches to teaching and learning, but they can also develop important new basic policies and organizational frameworks for answering the challenges of learning online.

PART III

STAFFING AND SUPPORT STRATEGIES

21

SUPPORT OF TECHNOLOGY-ENHANCED CLASSROOMS AT THE UNIVERSITY OF GEORGIA

Steven A. Gamble
University of Georgia

Through the early 1990s, the University of Georgia enhanced its largest lecture halls and classrooms with integrated video/data/audio presentation systems. The systems were designed and installed by varying equipment vendors with little input from the university community. Emphasis was on acquiring the technology. The belief was that "if you build it, they will use it." It quickly became evident that this was not the case. A few early technology converts worked to use the classroom systems, but most instructors preferred to stay with chalk and overhead transparency projectors. Faculty reasons for not using the systems included: "I don't know what the technology can do"; "I don't know how to use the equipment"; "The systems are too complicated to operate"; "The equipment is unreliable"; "What happens if I have a problem in the middle of class?"; "Who is going to help me?"

In 1996, the Office of Instructional Support and Development (OISD) redirected the responsibilities of several existing staff to the support of classroom technology. Today, OISD Classroom Support Services (CSS) provides comprehensive support to address faculty classroom concerns. Through practice, CSS has developed several support strategies that have made it the central point of contact for instructors in all matters regarding campus classrooms.

CSS PROVIDES PERSONAL SUPPORT FOR TECHNOLOGY-ENHANCED CLASSROOMS

In strategic areas of campus, CSS maintains zone offices staffed by classroom technology specialists who are responsible for support of technology-enhanced classrooms in their zone. Zone specialists are proactive in learning the special needs of their faculty and serve as liaisons between CSS and the schools, departments, and faculty. Zone specialists provide faculty with personal contact for support.

CSS zone specialists provide training for users of instructional facilities.
Zone specialists provide introductory training sessions on the function and operation of newly installed systems and follow up with one-on-one training in each specific function for faculty teaching in technology-enhanced classrooms. Training takes place in the room where the instructor is teaching. Zone specialists repeat training sessions as often as requested by users.

CSS zone specialists provide access to equipment installed in the classroom. Keys to the room's equipment console are checked out for the semester to each instructor teaching in a technology-enhanced classroom. Zone specialists provide an operational overview to users who have not taught in the room before providing them a key. This process provides users with knowledge of the room's systems and ensures that they know whom to call for assistance when required.

CSS zone specialists provide specialized setup services. They will assist with the connection of a visiting speaker's laptop to the data network and the projection system or integrate special equipment into the room's presentation system when needed.

CSS zone specialists monitor classrooms on a daily basis. Room monitoring includes operational checks of all installed equipment, review of trouble reports, and observation of climate, seating, lighting, and supplies. Problems are reported to the appropriate support agency for correction.

CSS zone specialists provide rapid response to reported problems. Each technology-enhanced classroom is equipped with a hotline to contact the central CSS office. CSS technical support personnel resolve the instructor's problem over the phone or connect the instructor to the zone specialist via cell phone for immediate assistance. Classroom technology specialists usually provide in-classroom response to emergency calls within ten minutes. Malfunctioning equipment is routinely replaced, and the classroom put back in operation by the next class period. Classroom equipment trouble report forms are placed in all technology classrooms for instructors to notify OISD of nonemergency classroom problems.

CSS zone specialists provide assistance with room scheduling. They serve as liaisons between individual faculty and the classroom reservations office to ensure that instructors are assigned to appropriate classrooms.

OISD CLASSROOM SUPPORT IN THE DESIGN, INSTALLATION, MAINTENANCE, AND REPAIR OF INSTRUCTIONAL TECHNOLOGY SYSTEMS

Technical support provided by OISD Classroom Services includes:

Consultation and planning for instructional technology implementation in campus classrooms and other instructional facilities. CSS is the central contact point for the design of instructional technology systems in campus facilities. It works closely with the Office of Campus Architects in the design of new instructional facilities; Physical Plant Services in the renovation of existing facilities; and schools, colleges, and departments planning for instructional technology. CSS participation in the planning ensures that faculty desires are taken into consideration and that sound pedagogical practices are followed in the design, including layout, lighting, acoustics, and seating.

Design of video/data/audio presentation systems and other instructional technology systems. In-house design ensures consistent function and a common instructor interface in all technology-enhanced classrooms and promotes easier maintenance and quicker repairs. It allows CSS to customize systems for a specific set of users without sacrificing the common instructor interface used across campus and quick response to faculty requests for changes.

Installation of instructional technology systems. In-house installation allows more flexibility to work around room-use schedules. Intimate knowledge of all parts of the system makes maintenance and repair easier.

Maintenance and repair of instructional technology systems. CSS technical support staff perform all system maintenance and repair, which allows more flexibility to work around room-use schedules, and because the staff designed and installed the systems, they can be put back into service sooner. OISD classroom support will usually have a malfunctioning system up and running by the next class session.

Consultation on instructional technology equipment specifications. CSS technical support staff recommendations are based on experience and evaluation of products. They can temper the claims of equipment vendors and ensure that the equipment will provide the functions expected by the faculty. CSS participation in equipment selection and acquisition makes it easier for CSS to maintain a common stock of replacement equipment.

OTHER OISD CLASSROOM SUPPORT SERVICES

OISD classroom support maintains a loan pool of AV and other presentation equipment for use in campus classrooms without permanent presentation systems and an extensive collection of instructional media.

BACKGROUND INFORMATION

OISD Classroom Support Services

Staff: 9 EFT

One coordinator (administration/classroom/system design)
Two classroom support engineers
   (design/install/touch panel programming)
Three classroom technology specialists (support zones)
One AV manager (equipment/media loan/delivery)
Two resource specialists (equipment/media scheduling/help desk)

Technology-Enhanced Classrooms Supported

111   general assignment classrooms
88   departmental classrooms
22   special presentation rooms

RESOURCES

Classroom Support, Office of Instructional Support & Development, University of Georgia: http://www.isd.uga.edu/classroom/index.html

Typical UGA technology-enhanced classroom: http://ntchem.chem.uga.edu/DoC/AcaInsMEC2.html

OISD homepage: http://www.isd.uga.edu

22

SUPPORTING FACULTY WITH A WEB-DEVELOPMENT TEAM

Anne L. Allen
University of Florida

INTRODUCTION

Very often, supplying faculty with tools and training in web-development software is not enough. Many will not be able to develop the skills they need due to time constraints or other limitations. Their audiences are, on the whole, extremely web-savvy and expect more than static web pages or simple text on a page. To hold their attention and to relay information in a meaningful manner, advanced techniques are frequently needed. For example, complicated concepts or processes can often be demonstrated simply by using a Macromedia Flash animation. Interactivity can be gained through scripting. Video and audio are sometimes necessary or an appropriate enhancement but must be in a format and size that is easily deliverable over the Internet. Some courses need a companion CD, but it must be deliverable to a variety of platforms and easily used by students. Perhaps the most important factor is transferring an existing course to the web or a CD in a way that is appropriate to the media, not simply placing text online.

A web-development team can assist faculty with the more advanced aspects of course creation, while helping them to increase their skill level. Participating in a collaborative project will hold faculty interest and fire their desire to learn far more than examples in a class. Faculty will vary greatly in the level of involvement they feel comfortable with beyond supplying the subject matter. It may also take several projects for them to gain the skills necessary for maintaining and even developing their own projects. Faculty members returning for second, third, or more projects will increasingly present more sophisticated and creative ideas, and their success has a cascading effect. Once a proud professor has shown successful results to colleagues, they may wish to do the same in their subject matter. The bar for quality is raised, and student needs and expectations are usually better met. If the services are available, faculty will use them, and all involved will benefit, especially the students.

What are the components of a web-development team? Teams can vary widely, depending on the resources available and the projects anticipated. We will define members of the team and their roles and then explore variations for specific purposes or limited resources.

ROLES AND RESPONSIBILITIES

Subject-matter experts are the faculty members who initiate the project and provide all content material throughout the development project. They:

- produce written or electronically mediated instructional materials

- review content at various stages for accuracy

- give feedback to the interactive designer

Project manager/leaders are responsible for developing the project's scope and plan, creating a budget, scheduling, allocating resources, managing the team, and interfacing with the faculty member. They:

- manage the project, including staff, resources, and processes

- estimate project costs

- keep the project on track and on schedule through regular team meetings

- ensure the team has sufficient resources and tools

- set goals, motivate, and define the roles and responsibilities of team members

- support group work and link it with the total organization

- resolve conflicts among team members and various departments, functions, and managers

- ensure recognition of team members

- keep the faculty member informed of all decisions

- maintain records

- support evaluation, measurement for success, and benchmarking

Interactive designers/instructional designers are most responsible for creating a final product that is developed for, and appropriate to, the media used. They prevent the team from merely transferring text or the course as it exists on paper or in the classroom to a web page and instead help to create an interactive experience. They:

- prepare objectives as part of the project team
- define content, working with the faculty subject-matter expert
- select and sequence activities
- develop instructional materials, working with the subject-matter expert
- develop multimedia instructional design
- develop interactive design; for example, interactions within the project, how they work, and how students interact with the project materials
- work with the technical lead to design flow diagrams to support the instructional and interactive design
- create storyboards with the graphic designer and video and audio producers
- have working knowledge of the authoring tool(s)
- bear responsibility for the overall quality of the project's instruction and interactivity

Technical/leads oversee the project from a technical point of view. They assist the project manager in ensuring the technical strategy is sound, manage the programmers, and choose specialized team members, such as security experts, database programmers, and other system integrators. Technical leads, depending on the skills and resources available, may also perform the functions of the specialized team members. They:

- design how the product works from a technical standpoint
- decide what development tools will be used
- work with the instructional or interactive designer to design flow diagrams for the project
- conduct technical reviews of the project

Programmers develop applications for the project, which could be simple server-side scripts, database applications, Java applets, or Shockwave applets. Depending on the project, their skills could include an understanding of the object-oriented programming, Java, JavaScript, Visual Basic, VBScript, SQL, C/C++.

Graphic web designers create the look and feel of the site. Adobe Photoshop is often the main tool of choice. Web designers should have a good understanding of design principles, including information design and interaction design, and a print designer will not easily adapt to this role. Understanding how images should be made for the web is a vital skill. They:

- design and produce graphics for instructional materials
- design the overall look of the product
- work with the instructional designer to conceptualize the main interface and content graphics
- design the main interface as well as the typography and buttons for all the screens
- create content art, illustrations, and animation
- identify opportunities to use existing artwork
- work with the instructional designer to determine all graphic standards

Web-productions specialists integrate the site, using HTML or JavaScript. They code the HTML pages and integrate Java or Shockwave applications, images and animations. They are also responsible for creating a guide that documents the project's production. They must have:

- expertise in HTML
- excellent skills in development software, most often including Dreamweaver or other web editing software and Flash
- familiarity with accessibility standards

Information architects understand how to display information so that users see how to interact with the site and find the information they need. They are responsible for navigation, search and data retrieval, and interaction design. The instructional designer, web-production specialist, or project manager most often carries out this function, rather than a separate team member.

Audio producers or technicians design sounds or record narration. Sounds can range from music to noises that signal a user's action. In smaller teams, the instructional designer, web specialist, or project manager may fulfill this role. They:

- produce all audio
- generate final audio scripts

- cast talent

- schedule recording sessions

- mix edits and digitized video

- find sources of music and sound effects

- identify existing media

- control and archive audio libraries

- arrange licensing of existing audio material

- review the project from an audio perspective

Video editors or technicians create video images or digitize existing video images and deliver them in digital format to the web-production specialist. In smaller teams, the instructional designer or web specialist may fulfill this role. They:

- digitize and edit all video

- integrate video elements into the final product

- have extensive knowledge of the editing tool and working knowledge of the authoring tool

Quality evaluators or reviewers make sure the final product meets the criteria specified in the original scope of the project. They must be objective and therefore not among the developers but should interact with the developers to ensure that all bugs are addressed and resolved. The project manager working with the faculty member often fulfills this role. They:

- review the project from an educational and quality perspective

- identify ideal and actual performance conditions

- determine the cause of any discrepancy and recommend solution(s) and an evaluation strategy

SUMMARY

Having all this talent on your web-development team would be ideal, and it is often found in the private sector, but in education, resources are usually wanting. All too often, individuals with multiple skill sets are needed, which means recruiting for the team is much more difficult. Which skills are vital to success?

A team must have some core skills in order to plan, design, build, and deploy any project. Some projects will also require more specialized team members. When putting a team together, the following skills must be available:

Project management skills: the ability to see and to communicate the big picture to the team and the faculty member and make sure the project is built according to specification, on time, and on budget

Information design/architecture skills: the ability to design a usable and useful user interface, including interaction and navigation mechanisms

Web production and design skills: the ability to transform the information into visual design

Graphic production skills: the ability to create web graphics that are fast loading and look great on all browsers

Instructional or interactive design skills: the ability to develop interactive content for projects, including copyediting, video, audio, animation, and anything that is not part of the user interface

Programming skills: the ability to create web pages using HTML, web editing software, JavaScript, and other client/server scripting languages

Technical/network infrastructure skills: the ability to understand the requirements for serving a web site on the Internet and to recommend the best strategy based on the faculty member's needs.

One member of the team may have two or more of the skill sets described above, and the number of projects that can be juggled concurrently also varies according to role. The project manager and the technical expert can handle the most projects at once; the instructional designer, programmer, and graphic artist must have fewer. The web-production specialist should have no more than one or two projects at any time.

While team members with multiple skill sets streamline your team, they are more likely to be under stress and their time stretched. When this occurs, productivity drops. The team is less likely to react quickly to projects with short timelines or to a number of concurrent projects, while most faculty increasingly expect quick response times and rapid development, and some faculty-support centers have created special rapid-response development teams to handle the problem. Severely restricting the number of members of the team will also compromise the final product's quality along with creativity and innovation. Without a full complement of skills, the kind and type of projects possible will be limited. The large number of technologies available, increasing steadily at lightning speed, requires that teams increase in size to keep up. If you must begin with a small team of web developers in support of faculty efforts, plan to add as demands expand, and they will expand after other faculty members and students see the first few successful projects. That is good thing for all involved and the education process as a whole.

23

INSTRUCTIONAL DESIGN FOR COURSES THAT USE WEB-BASED COMPONENTS

Carol DeArment
University of Pittsburgh

Faculty at the University of Pittsburgh have demonstrated a keen interest in integrating the web into their courses. The university's Center for Instructional Development & Distance Education (CIDDE) provides workshops on the Blackboard course-management system for all faculty who elect to use the software, whether to create a distance-education course or to enhance an on-campus course.

In its commitment to enhance instruction at the University of Pittsburgh, CIDDE has found that providing opportunities for faculty to consult with instructional designers is as crucial as training them to use online technologies. Although faculty recognize the importance of addressing instructional needs when incorporating technology into a course, the time and effort required to learn the new technologies can blur this focus. As a result, faculty may hesitate to apply their technological training. Those who obtain instructional design assistance at this critical juncture find they can proceed to implement online applications that address their specific course content and learners' needs.

CIDDE's instructional designers help to ensure that instructional goals are the driving force for technology-based course enhancements, both through the faculty training process and individual course-development assistance. While some initiatives are relatively simple, involving discrete units of individual courses, others are complex and involve entire courses, curricula, and the integration of multiple delivery systems.

The Instructional Design Model

Designers find that sharing the instructional design (ID) model early in the planning process helps faculty to visualize the iterative nature of integrating course components (see Figure 23.1). While faculty tend to focus more on course content and sometimes overlook how people learn, the ID model is learner-centered. The learners' academic preparedness, background, and motivation are critical to decisions about content, activities, and assessments. Instructional designers, who are more focused on learning theory than discipline-specific content, teach faculty how diverse learners acquire, organize, and retrieve information. This information often results in faculty placing more emphasis on their students and reconsidering their course objectives, activities, and assessments.

Figure 23.1

The Instructional Design Model

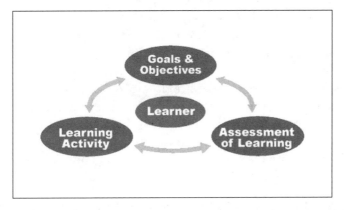

Designers initially encourage instructors to step back from their concerns with the online technologies and to articulate their instructional goals and objectives. Regardless of their teaching and subject-area expertise, many faculty find that stating instructional objectives is an essential first step, because the skills and knowledge students are expected to acquire determine other critical aspects of the course. As they guide faculty through the iterative course-design process, designers offer suggestions for instructional activities in and outside of class that will lead students toward mastery of the objectives. Assessments that provide feedback on learning to the instructor and students throughout the course are also driven by instructional objectives.

After addressing these essential course components, faculty are prepared to integrate online technologies into their course plans. Instructional designers coordinate faculty access to the specific kinds of technical support required to reach their instructional objectives. In helping faculty to develop all or parts of their courses online in the past six years, instructional designers have found four broad areas that faculty typically should address:

- the reason for using the online tools
- organizing the content to integrate activities and materials
- the technologies' effects on the instructor and students
- evaluating the effectiveness of the online components

Reason for Using the Technologies

In light of the instructional goals and objectives, designers probe faculty for the reasons why they plan to implement the technologies: "Are you doing something now that you would like to do better? Do you want to do something that you cannot do without online technology?" Often, instructors initially want to facilitate housekeeping or administrative matters, such as posting grades to an online roster. Sometimes they want a way to post handouts, lecture outlines, and course resources to allow more time for teaching and learning activities during class. These are valid uses of the technologies; however, instructional designers can help faculty to recognize and to evaluate instructional uses for the technology as well. For example, based on the instructor's objectives, the designer may point out valuable ways that synchronous and asynchronous online discussion tools can increase student engagement through active learning, feedback, or other opportunities that encourage reflective dialogue and higher-level thinking about course content.

Organizing the Content to Integrate Activities and Materials

In addition to conferring with instructors about how each course component will promote instructional objectives, instructional designers demonstrate how to organize the content so that activities and assessments are coherently integrated (see Figure 23.2). For example, faculty are encouraged to consider whether content should be arranged chronologically or hierarchically. Sharing samples from online courses, instructional designers demonstrate the importance of conceptual and visual unity between objectives, activities, and assessments. Viewing other instructors' courses helps faculty to appreciate that, for learners, lack of structural clarity is intensified in online materials. Thus, in converting content, activities, and assessments to online technologies, faculty are advised how to use a consistent, explicit structure, while organizing content in online folders.

Figure 23.2

Example of How an Online Course Integrates Activities and Materials

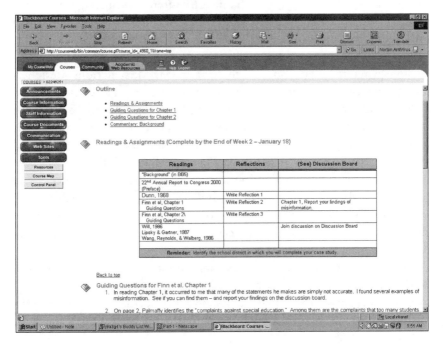

THE TECHNOLOGIES' EFFECTS ON THE INSTRUCTOR AND STUDENTS

Novices implementing online technologies are commonly unaware of the implications these technologies may have for both the instructor and students. For example, while the ease of communication that attracts faculty to online instructional technologies can lead to more time-on-task for students, the time an instructor spends replying to messages and monitoring discussions can become burdensome. Instructional designers encourage faculty to adopt online components gradually, perhaps beginning with simple, stand-alone components, such as announcements or online practice quizzes. They encourage faculty to evaluate both the effects and the effectiveness of each tool before proceeding to adopt another.

As designers share real-life experiences of other instructors with online tools, they offer advice on how to maximize instructional benefits through careful planning. For example, faculty frequently say they would like to increase student interaction and sense of community. Designers might share threaded discussion exercises that demonstrate how online group-management tools enable students in a small-group communication course to collaborate as they learn firsthand about the team approaches that they are studying. However, they would also point out that faculty interested in assigning online group projects must be aware of strategies for forming groups and assigning roles to group members.

Another priority for many faculty is the ability to promote more peer discussions when they have no time to do so in class. Instructional designers might demonstrate another instructor's virtual classroom or discussion board archives and share research about how many students who are too timid to ask questions in class feel comfortable doing so in an online session. At the same time, designers point out, if instructional objectives are not integrated with online sessions, the discussions can become chaotic; if the exchanges are not monitored, misunderstandings can cause confusion. Designers share strategies developed by other faculty who have used these online discussion tools, such as setting up procedures for synchronous and asynchronous exchanges, and encourage instructors to integrate them into their courses at the planning stage.

Faculty also often wish to increase opportunities for students to practice and get feedback on how they are learning the content. Among the alternatives, designers may suggest that studies indicate students value the reinforcement of online practice quizzes to help them to attain instructional objectives.

EVALUATING THE EFFECTIVENESS OF THE ONLINE COMPONENTS

Instructional designers encourage two types of evaluation for technology-enhanced courses. First, faculty are encouraged to assess their students' abilities to use the required technological tools, including their access to the equipment, their skills in its use, and their reactions to it. Second, designers help faculty to evaluate whether the technologies are helping students to achieve the instructional objectives. They suggest procedures to conduct and to analyze these evaluations so that immediate modifications or clarifications can be made. Sample surveys are available to elicit students' perceptions and experiences. Formative evaluations can be conducted at any time during a course through an informal class email query or a more structured questionnaire. These provide students with opportunities to express concerns that the instructor might otherwise overlook but can easily alleviate. For example, even when instructors have provided a demonstration of the online tools, students are likely to encounter difficulties using them. Formative evaluations have revealed student confusion about online navigation or course organization that the instructor can clarify by revising formatting or changing settings on the control panel. Likewise, informal formative evaluations may reveal that students are having difficulties submitting documents via a digital drop-box or accessing discussion archives; a brief review of technological procedures by the instructor often solves the problem.

SUMMARY

Effective implementation of online computer technologies, whether to create a distance-education course or to enhance an on-campus course, requires thoughtful instructional design. Faculty from diverse disciplines have found that working with an instructional designer is invaluable when they are ready to apply what they have learned from technology training to their courses. The learner-centered design process is driven by carefully crafted instructional goals and the assurance that all course components are unified and coherent. In addition to helping faculty place all or parts of their courses online, the instructional design consultation process prompts reflections on teaching that often improve the entire course.

24

SUPPORT FROM STUDENTS

Nancy Crouch
Wake Forest University

Wake Forest University values the personal interaction between students and faculty. We also value our traditions and the new standards that will move us into the future. As the university introduced technology into the teaching and learning environment, a troubling concern grew. What if we built this infrastructure, rolled out the technology, and the pace of faculty adoption was too slow to develop momentum? Our solution? STARS: Student Technology Advisors.

Now in its sixth year of operation, the program is managed by a professional in the Information Systems Department, who recruits the STARS; supervises their efforts; pairs them with faculty; coordinates training; solicits internships, presentations, and other teaching opportunities; and evaluates both the effectiveness of individual STARS and the program generally.

The first goal of the STARS program is to enhance the quality of the student/faculty relationship through sustained one-on-one contact. Recruiting STARS and faculty partners is a critical step in this process. The STARS are hired based upon their vision for using technology in the liberal arts classroom; a strong academic background; and their desire to work one-on-one with faculty, defining problems and creating solutions. Past experience at Wake Forest has shown that good academic performance (with adequate technical skills) is a better predictor of performance than strong technical skills alone.

Several factors are considered in pairing STARS with faculty. These include academic areas of personal interest and the capacity of the STAR to help the faculty member complete the proposed project. The heart of the STARS program is a two-way mentorship. While the STARS serve as mentors in the use of technology, they too benefit from the mentorship of their faculty partners. Throughout the partnership, STARS faculty are required to evaluate its success. This feedback provides the STARS and their managers with the opportunity to reassign partners if needed and to constantly improve the program.

Accelerating the adoption of technology in the curriculum is a comprehensive and lofty goal of the STARS program. The STARS program focuses on the individual nature of projects and partnerships, while promoting the accomplishments of each and every STAR and faculty partner.

To be paired with a STAR, faculty members submit proposals for joint projects designed to improve instruction in their classes. The requests are submitted online and reviewed by STARS management. Faculty outline the scope of the project, the skills they anticipate a STAR will need to assist them, and any personal information they wish to provide to ensure the best possible pairing. The proposed projects last one or two semesters.

Upon reviewing the request, STARS management begins the pairing process. No project is deemed too great or too small for the STARS. STARS and STARS management are aware that many faculty members requesting STARS may not yet know the entire scope of the project. These faculty members set forth a goal, and it is up to the STAR to set the course. Careful consideration is given to scheduling, personal interest in the subject, and the skills that each STAR brings to the partnership. To truly accelerate the adoption of technology, this student/faculty pair must be able to focus on transferring the skills to the faculty member. This transfer accelerates the adoption for the faculty, one person at a time.

Time is critical in any learning process. A primary goal of the STARS program is to leverage faculty time through the use of skilled assistants. We could ask faculty to attend training sessions. However, they would still need to find the time in their schedules to apply their new skills in a way relevant to their teaching. Instead, STARS provide the support for learning these technical skills and help the faculty identify ways in which the technologies are applicable to their teaching. STARS are able to interpret the goals of each faculty partner and spend time learning and researching the most relevant applications. Then, during the time scheduled between the two partners, they can focus specific applications.

The projects completed by the STARS and their faculty partners vary widely. As the faculty improves their base of knowledge, the STARS raise the bar again and again. At one time, STARS were teaching their faculty partners to use a three-button mouse, surf the web, and even retrieve email attachments. STARS now teach their partners to use courseware, create web sites, develop multimedia presentations, provide online quizzes, and use databases. Recently, one STAR and his partner used Visual Basic to adapt an older psychological experiment to include new technologies. Where pigeons (yes, pigeons!) formerly pecked on switches and boards when they wanted food, they now use a fully computerized model to retrieve their food. With these "peck" screen monitors and a pigeon feeder adapted to a computer, all the data collection is now done by computer for faster, more accurate results. Each project is as unique as the classes the faculty teaches. Each project provides a wealth of learning for the faculty and their STARS. Current and past STARS projects are described on the STARS web page.

The students receive an hourly wage for their work. On average, each STAR spends ten hours per week for 36 weeks per year working in the STARS partnership, including one-on-one sessions with their faculty partners, hours spent planning and preparing for these sessions, and STARS staff meetings. Time sheets and logs are monitored by STARS management.

The STARS program also works to provide students with enhanced skills for future career opportunities. STARS receive extensive training in the software tools used by the university. Training is scheduled in two ways. First, all STARS, except first-semester freshmen, return to campus up to five days prior to the beginning of each semester to attend a technical training class. The STARS can adequately pursue the course without it competing for study time during the semester. Second, shorter, less technical classes are offered throughout the semester. These classes are typically scheduled in two-hour blocks during the evening. Some of these classes are specific to software applications; some are specific to hardware, and some are focused only on soft skills relevant to the STARS.

Another goal of the program relates closely to the previous goal of skills development. STARS are frequently exposed to highly trained colleagues. Fellow STARS as well as Information Systems staff are considered colleagues. STARS and staff share their proficiencies through STARS staff meetings. Meetings are held biweekly. STARS and STARS management enforce a strict attendance policy.

The sixth and final goal of Wake Forest's STARS program is to pioneer a technology internship program for both companies and nonprofits. The program allows all interested STARS to receive summer internships in a variety of corporate and nonprofit organizations, which provide a solid background for career experiences. Funding of the internships includes summer salaries, housing costs, and transportation costs. The corporate partners fund their internships, while contributions and sponsorships fund nonprofit internships. The internships allow STARS to enhance their skills and bring valuable information back to the campus community. The internships also strengthen university ties to corporate and nonprofit partners.

STARS has become part of Wake Forest University tradition and will continue to help shape our future.

25

SUPPORTING FACULTY ADOPTION OF TECHNOLOGY WITH AN ACADEMICALLY FOCUSED TECHNOLOGY RESOURCE

Robert Vidrine
Wake Forest University

With the Instructional Technologist Group (ITG), Wake Forest has armed its faculty with a unique resource to tackle new technological solutions. This group of 16 individuals is ranked by accomplishment and experience from Specialist to Consultant to Analyst. ITSs, ITCs, and ITAs are not only trained in computers and technology but also hold a degree in the academic discipline of the department(s) they serve.

The departments select their technologist in the same way they might select a new faculty member. The similarities between our positions are many, except that my colleagues and I don't teach classes for credit but stick to enrichment workshops and tutorial sessions that augment specific undergraduate or graduate classes. We also share the knowledge we have gathered from our departmental research with other interested parties in the university community. My colleagues and I represent some of the best learning resources for technology solutions to pedagogical problems.

While most of my work involves manipulating computers to ease the teaching and learning process, the Instructional Technologist position requires experience with the subject matter of the department(s) we serve. I hold a bachelor of arts degree in anthropology, which has helped me to focus the solutions I suggest for that department to match their teaching mission. When the chair said that she needed a field recorder for her trips to Mexico this summer and fall, for example, I was able to anticipate that she would want something capable of recording everything from clear and distinct voices in a quiet interview setting to culturally significant public performances. I quickly located online discussions among several anthropologists from various universities and colleges to gather real-world recommendations for the type of recorder that would provide reliable service.

Like most of the ITG, I serve more than one department. My mother was an elementary school teacher in several public school systems, and my father was a philosophy professor at a bilingual university in Mexico. Thus, I have an acute and intimate knowledge of teaching and education that helps me to lend my talents and expertise to the education department, the other department I call home. I know, for instance, that the education department's web site serves its students best if it exemplifies the design standards that ensure its compliance with the Americans with Disabilities Act.

Of course, a position like mine requires diligence to stay current with the most effective and promising solutions. The university has shown an exceptional willingness to support the ITG's professional development. Had I not flown to a conference on video streaming in California last summer, I would not have learned about digital video production from the leaders in the video compression and delivery industry. The same follows for the working conference on technology portfolios for student teachers that I have attended in Boone, North Carolina, for the past three years. Not only did I represent Wake Forest faculty, helping to shape the North Carolina teacher licensure policies regarding technology portfolios, I was able to collaborate with faculty from a variety of other institutions, sharing ideas for improving the portfolios' creation and evaluation stages. Without such university support, my knowledge of technology solutions would rapidly become outdated. In fact, Wake Forest's teacher preparation programs are among six winners of the first National Educational Technology Standards (NETS) Distinguished Achievement Awards. Sponsored by the International Society for Technology in Education and funded through the US Education Department's Preparing Tomorrow's Teachers to Use Technology initiative, the NETS Project works to develop national standards for educational uses of technology that facilitate school improvement (see http:// cnets.iste.org/). Ann Cunningham, assistant professor of instructional design, said, "WFU does an outstanding job supporting our technology needs: It's the accomplishments of the department and the university's technology initiatives that have earned this award."

Although my position is budgeted through the dean of the college, I rarely have meetings with the dean in any formal capacity. I have an office in each of my departments and discuss matters with members on a regular basis. Sharing my time between the anthropology and education departments, I help them learn to shape and to direct technology into educational solutions, ranging from showing someone how to easily email a syllabus to several students at once to researching the capabilities of various satellite phones for a professor who directs a research center off the coast of Honduras. The variability of this position is both its biggest strength and its greatest challenge.

Faculty members have a lot of pressures and demands on their time. ITs who are worth their ergonomic keyboards know this and do not shy away from jumping in to address a technology-related problem or question. They don't mind explaining, in detail, what a POP server is or what SCSI stands for. However, when the professor's immediate interest is automatically adding a signature to every email, the conscientious IT explains only the details that don't make the learner's eyes glaze over. The people I work with need me to bridge the gap between technology and their own area of expertise and to show them how to make it work for them, not the other way around.

Technology designers have started to use some familiar terms that seem to suggest that it's reliable and easy to use: *tool, assistant, wizard.* Unfortunately, as Henry Petroski shows in *To Engineer Is Human* (1985), no solution can exist without a point of failure. Even the simplest tools have to be in good condition to produce results reliably, and sometimes I must take on one of the least exciting of my roles: repair. In an attempt to maintain my users' faith that new technologies can be seamlessly incorporated into what they already do to make themselves more efficient and productive, I must be able to deal quickly and efficiently with the inevitable failures. When the screen starts flickering violently, colors changing randomly, it can be very hard to embrace the computer as a needed tool. Not everyone *wants* to know what a video card is, but faculty require a usable computer as soon as possible if they are to learn to use it with their classes.

My position has only been in existence for about six years, but in that time, we've learned a lot about how to make it valuable. While some of the original members of the ITG are still here, supplying their constituents and colleagues with superlative technological research and assistance, several have gone. It has become clear that this position requires someone who not only has a broad knowledge of computers and technology but also knows how to relate to people diplomatically and generously. Since the academic environment offers each person the freedom to find individual solutions, requests can amount to a scheduling nightmare unless carefully managed.

Many universities have instituted programs similar to Wake Forest's ITG. However, Wake Forest has designed this group as a resource that can give the faculty not only very focused, personal attention but also a deep knowledge of the needs and challenges posed by their specific subject areas.

REFERENCE

Petroski, H. (1985). *To engineer is human: The role of failure in successful design.* New York, NY: St. Martin's Press.

26

SUPPORTING FACULTY IN THE USE OF TECHNOLOGY

Ed Schwartz and Shannon C. Phillips
Virginia Polytechnic Institute and State University

Supporting faculty in the use of technology for instruction and research at Virginia Tech is a daunting task at best. Diverse needs range from basic computing skills to the development of complex, highly interactive instructional materials. With the inception of the Faculty Development Institute (FDI), it was clear that faculty needed a well-defined avenue of support to help them embrace technology. The Virginia Tech New Media Center (http://www.nmc.vt.edu) was set up as the focal point for faculty support on campus. The center was immediately faced with a number of challenges. How do you keep current with fast-changing technologies? How do you provide a high-quality support staff on a limited budget? How do you provide support for a wide range of platforms and applications? The list goes on. One of our greatest challenges was the lack of existing models for a comprehensive faculty technology support program at a large institution.

Many of the larger support concerns were incorporated into the Instructional Development Initiative, including upgrading classroom facilities, creating and maintaining student computer labs, and funding faculty efforts to develop materials using the new technologies. Many of these larger issues were fairly well defined, but supporting over 1,600 individual faculty with their unique needs was an unknown. The goal was to create an environment that was flexible, friendly, responsive, and nonthreatening. As budget resources were inadequate to create a production facility, this resource had to assist faculty in creating materials on their own.

Another concern in the development of this support center was the identification of software. Looking at the needs of the campus beyond the faculty, a list of functional areas were identified along with one or more applications that were currently in use. These functional application areas included database, desktop publishing, e-paper, graphics, multimedia program development, presentation software, project management, spreadsheet, video editing, audio editing, word processing, web development tools, 3-D tools, and various utilities.

FACULTY SUPPORT CENTER

What was needed to support faculty needs? Quite frankly, at the outset, a great deal of guesswork accompanied constant assessments of faculty needs. Classroom space for teaching FDI classes and places to support special needs and projects were certainly needed. In its first year, the New Media Center consisted of a 21-station classroom/open lab with scanning and a host of high-end multimedia software, staffed by two half-time directors, a full-time operations manager, a graduate student, and three undergraduate lab assistants, and available during regular hours. A small back room had a few high-end computers with specialized hardware and software (video/audio digitizing, and burning). As the FDI program introduced faculty to the new technologies and digital possibilities, the New Media Center became more and more popular. As the site for most faculty training, it provided a wonderful opportunity for faculty to obtain access to scarce resources and assistance.

Today, the New Media Center is far different. We have worked to evolve the support along with the FDI program and the needs of the campus. Because of budget constraints, the center was not able to hire a large staff of full-time employees. We chose to create a team of undergraduates who would be trained to provide faculty support. Training was critical, and a bimonthly mandatory training program was established for all student employees. The student employee training soon evolved into an online program with monthly, instructor-led sessions. Student employees were trained in the same environment that they would eventually assist faculty in creating and maintaining. As for the physical resources, it was felt that we had to stay ahead of the hardware and software curve, meaning that we had to have hardware and software that is not normally accessible. Currently, the popularity of our scanning hardware is giving way to video digitizing and more creation of Director, Flash, and 3-D objects.

In many ways, the FDI and the New Media Center are inextricably linked. The people and facilities are obviously connected, but the content of the FDI workshops ultimately provides direction for the hardware and software that are supported in the center. The center has to be aware of what is taught as well as how it is taught. The student employees have to understand such matters, so they can quickly pick up what faculty need. Often student training will slightly precede faculty training on the same topic. A good example is the introduction of OS X to Macintosh users. It was critical to train the students before the faculty so they knew something about the questions that they would be asked in a few days.

NEW MEDIA CONSORTIUM

Membership in the New Media Consortium (http://www.newmediacenters.org) has played an important role in the development of support services. This nonprofit organization is composed of over 100 academic and corporate members who explore new ways of teaching and learning through new media. As a member, we were able to get a limited number of licenses to very expensive software at a very affordable rate from the corporate members. We also received valuable advice and shared knowledge with many colleagues who were doing similar things. It was encouraging to interact with others facing the same challenges and enlightening to look at similar problems in different ways.

CURRENT NEW MEDIA CENTER SUPPORT

The New Media Center at Virginia Tech today provides the hardware, software, and individual support for faculty to create media-rich learning environments. Center facilities, services, and personnel are utilized year-round to ensure a consistent level of support to those using technology in curriculum developed at Virginia Tech. Although the center has grown into a broader support mission for the larger university community, it maintains a very close relationship with the FDI and considers its participants a top support priority. However, faculty's dramatically increased use of technology has similarly increased student use. Today, the center's main users are students creating multimedia for their courses.

The center maintains an inventory of multimedia equipment for loan. Digital still cameras are regularly checked out to students, while digital still cameras, digital video cameras, tripods, lighting kits, QTVR rigs, and other creation/capture devices are available for faculty loan, ensuring that all faculty have access to the most current technologies to create materials. The equipment can be borrowed with or without assistance from the staff. The fastest growing area in the center is video digitizing and digital video editing. The current resources consist of two computers with Media 100 configurations and nine other computers with a host of other video editing tools and CD/DVD burners. These computers are connected to a two-terabyte server with a one-gigabyte network hub. All of this provides a very powerful, friendly, and accessible environment for campus digital video development.

Center staff maintain the three FDI training classrooms, including their computer maintenance, software updates, AV equipment upkeep, and the development of instructor station operation materials. By maintaining these classrooms, the center is able to ensure a certain level of consistency among what the faculty will see on the computer in the FDI classrooms, at the New Media Center lab, and on the computers that they will receive from their FDI experience. This consistency goes a long way toward establishing a level of comfort for faculty members working outside of their offices.

Full-time staff members frequently teach for the FDI. This tie is crucial. Using New Media Center staff as instructors ensures an early introduction to the New Media Center's multimedia support. The sessions will end with the news not only that faculty should contact the New Media Center for help but that they will find their instructors there should they have specific questions.

Faculty members are given the center's service desk number and location as a first point of support. The center's student employees operate this desk on a daily basis and provide many services through it. They field questions, build sample projects for instructors, digitize material for use in classroom presentations and on course web pages, and provide one-on-one help sessions by appointment.

PERSONALIZING FACULTY SUPPORT

The FDI program at Virginia Tech has provided a unique training experience for faculty and, in its tenth year, is striving to personalize the experience as much as possible. This year, the center is providing limited production support for the 400+ faculty attending the summer sessions. The undergraduate staff will scan images, digitize video and audio, create streaming files, and provide other production support services. Faculty can always call, email or come to the center for assistance with their specific materials.

ASYNCHRONOUS SUPPORT

One of the FDI's goals is to put all of its workshop content online. If faculty have questions outside of the workshop, chances are they can get answers through the web site. Virginia Tech has recently contracted with an online training company to provide over 500 online training modules for many of the most-used computer applications on campus, a 24/7 solution to this type of training need for faculty, staff, and students. Again, the student employees are required to take selected modules as part of their training. They become familiar with the product and get up to speed on many of the critical software products without engaging the full-time staff.

ONGOING SUPPORT

Whether they are in a multiple-session workshop or a single training session, faculty are welcome at the New Media Center year round. Support does not end with the workshop. Faculty will often attend a training session to explore new ideas in teaching technology. The next step occurs when they are ready to create media objects for use in their presentations and web materials. They are encouraged to come to the center when they are ready to get the services that they need. The center provides the facilities, support, and guidance to successfully integrate the knowledge they gained during the faculty-training program into their course materials.

Using well-trained undergraduates can provide a reasonably high-quality support staff when working with a limited budget. Providing support for a wide range of platforms and applications is difficult, but having such tools as online training modules is very helpful. Virginia Tech is creating its own model for support within a comprehensive faculty development program.

27

RESPONDING TO THE INDIVIDUAL, REACHING THE MAINSTREAM: A HYBRID APPROACH TO FACULTY SUPPORT

Janet R. de Vry
University of Delaware

Although it may sound like an oxymoron, the University of Delaware (UD) has found a way to offer faculty support that is individualized and flexible while also being standardized. Faculty are unique individuals with their own teaching and learning styles, learning goals for their classes, and understanding of technology. Clearly, one size does not fit all. Yet staff time is too limited to create individualized approaches for each faculty member, and standardization offers certain efficiencies. The challenge at UD has been to see how we could extend individual solutions to similar support situations and how we could make any standard solution flexible.

The five critical elements that make up our faculty technology support structure include the following:

- appropriate staffing
- a faculty technology development consulting site
- a faculty technology development web site
- faculty technology projects
- outreach to departments and other units interested in faculty technology development

In addition, classes and seminars play a significant role. A new initiative, in collaboration with faculty, is to adapt a problem-based learning approach to some classes (see Chapter 55).

APPROPRIATE STAFFING

The faculty technology professional support staff are part of the User Services unit in Information Technologies (IT). However, half of the support staff have master's degrees in education or educational technology and considerable classroom teaching experience. The other half are skilled technologists with strong people skills and significant experience in applying technology to learning. Faculty opinion is always solicited in their hiring. Every staff member knows and is committed to the premise that learning goals come before technology, and each has a strong commitment to service.

Staff will do whatever it takes to help faculty members, including going to their offices or classrooms to provide individualized support. This commitment to service has won the faculty's trust and respect. On the other hand, whenever staff find themselves doing something repeatedly, they are encouraged to document it and make it available on the faculty technology development web site. Increasingly, the support staff are using multimedia to document their own processes.

Each staff member has a primary area of responsibility and expertise, such as handling instructional design, evaluating emerging technologies, managing faculty projects, administering UD's course management system, programming, or running the site and servers. Wherever possible, the staff are cross-trained and partnered with other staff members who can provide backup assistance. Each staff member has an assigned time to be the primary consultant. Thus, the staff have specialized skills and responsibilities and yet are flexible enough to provide wide coverage.

FACULTY TECHNOLOGY DEVELOPMENT CONSULTING SITE

UD's teaching, learning, and technology center is known on campus as PRESENT (Practical Resources for Educators Seeking Effective New Technologies). It epitomizes the concept of flexible standardization. The one central location on campus where all faculty can come for assistance, the site itself is flexible and largely reconfigurable. All the chairs are on wheels, and the round consulting table that greets visitors is really two hexagonal tables. The sidewall is movable and opens onto a conference room, allowing more space when needed. Behind the consulting table, we have six multimedia workstations where up to three people can work, and the tables include enough space to add a laptop computer (de Vry & Watson, 2003).

For some, standardization of equipment means that each system is identical, while flexibility means a variety of unique, high-end workstations. Supporting a number of unique systems translates into a nightmare of documenting how to use those systems and teaching staff and faculty how each unique system works. "We achieve standardization of capability by having high-end interchangeable peripherals," said John Hall, the site manager. "We can quickly reconfigure any workstation to become whatever the faculty member needs." Since UD's campus supports both Macintosh and PCs, the site has two Macs and four PCs. It offers software that works with both Macintosh computers and PCs wherever possible. An AV cart for recording high-quality audio and customized high-end digitizing can be hooked up to any workstation. Providing additional flexibility, we have one check-in station that can take digital information from approximately 15 different types of media, such as Zip drive, Smart Media, and DVD. The staff can transfer our server over to any other station in the site. Again, we do not need to replicate every drive on every workstation.

FACULTY DEVELOPMENT WEB SITE

The PRESENT web site provides assistance through tools and templates. It showcases exemplary faculty work and connects learning goals and technology. It also notifies faculty of upcoming events and classes, informs the campus about PRESENT services, and provides easy access to resources both on and off campus.

The Tools and Templates section best exemplifies our commitment to individualized standardization. Several tools available from the web site began as requests from individual faculty members. Before tackling any major support request from a faculty member, the staff scrutinize the request to see if anything from the proposed finished project could be extended to other faculty. If so, we consider the final step in completing the project to be the creation of a template or program and self-serve instructions available from our Tools and Templates web section. At the simplest level, the web site contains a standardized syllabus template done in a variety of graphic styles that can be customized to any discipline. The staff programmed Surveyor for a faculty member who wanted to survey his class for political attitudes and display them graphically. At that time, no commercially available surveying tool met his needs. The staff and student programmers worked to make the tool simple to use, and a technical writer added do-it-yourself documentation to the web. We stopped additional programming when more powerful commercial products came on the market. Nevertheless, this free tool is in wide use at the university by both faculty and classes. I have presented a number of preconference sessions at the EDUCAUSE national conference on enhancing curriculum through faculty technology development. In these sessions I have used the Surveyor tool before delivering a session to solicit information about participant background and expectations. Another PRESENT tool offers the possibility of adding questions and answers to PowerPoint slides or any web image to reinforce what was taught in class or for pretesting. The beauty of this tool is that it adds interactivity and flexibility to standard software (see http://www.udel.edu/present/tools/).

FACULTY TECHNOLOGY PROJECTS

All our flexibility in meeting expressed faculty needs did not necessarily lead to major curriculum redesign. It helped the faculty member who already wanted to use technology or was struggling with a piece of equipment that would not work. In 1999, we began soliciting competitive grant proposals from faculty and awarding staff and student time. We began to participate in redesigning portions of courses to increase interactivity or to make more efficient and effective use of space and time. The standard use of WebCT in 2000 as the university's course management system enabled us to change our approach from programming individual solutions for faculty to seeking how faculty could take advantage of standard features to add more flexibility to their courses.

Our approach to managing projects has changed from matching one student with one faculty member to assigning a team composed of staff and students to faculty needs. This approach has been so successful that the university has announced a new program to redesign courses through grants that now include staff and student time. The larger goal is to engage chairs and deans in the process and ensure that the courses most in need of redesign with the best overall strategy for improvement are the ones selected (see Chapter 42).

OUTREACH

Partnerships continue to be a mainstay of UD's faculty technology development efforts. These partnerships usually begin with individual contact that leads to trusting relationships between whole units offering vital pieces in the faculty support process. Beginning in 1995, UD began offering collaborative faculty institutes with IT, the library, the Center for Teaching Effectiveness, and the Office of Instructional Technology all contributing. The institute's format is flexible, with each unit offering its own courses, but advertising and registration are centralized. More recently, we have done considerable department-based training.

Over the years, these initial relationships have deepened, and new ones have taken hold. In 1997, the Institute for Transforming Undergraduate Education (ITUE), a faculty-led movement to transform the curriculum through active learning, began (de Vry & Watson, 2003). The leaders of this faculty group understood the promise of technology and solicited the IT support staff to assist in the technology training during their weeklong institutes for faculty. Some of these faculty have become enthusiastic adopters of technology. The ITUE leaders routinely post faculty development technology classes and special events on their web site and publicize them to all faculty fellows. In June 2002, it is sponsoring an International Problem-Based Learning Conference in Baltimore, and IT staff will join the ITUE faculty in offering a workshop on adapting course management systems for problem-based learning.

"Relinquish control and aim for influence" (Suter, 2001) is the principle at the heart of our various partnerships and outreach efforts. To do this, we approach each potential partner, looking for the individual strengths of each unit and offering whatever we can to move the process forward. For example, IT does not control a number of departmental computing sites on campus, but we contribute expertise whenever possible. The faculty lab designer in chemical engineering designed her own configuration for a collaborative computer learning classroom, but came to IT for help in choosing appropriate collaborative software and training the faculty to use the site. The director of IT/User Services participates on a Center for Teaching Effectiveness committee that funds faculty high-technology projects. She solicits advice from the IT faculty technology development staff before supporting a proposal. Likewise, the user services director and I participate in the Teaching Learning Technology Roundtable, a group of faculty and administrators interested in promoting teaching with technology. The vice provost chairs this group.

CONCLUSION

Remaining flexible and attuned to the needs of individual faculty members while providing standards wherever possible is the hallmark of our faculty technology support efforts. The seemingly opposite goals of individualized yet standardized support are achieved as we seek the best of both approaches and refrain from easy fixes and prescriptions. This hybrid approach guides us as we seek new ways of offering services and support, as we explore new opportunities provided by new hardware and software, and as we form new partnerships.

REFERENCES

de Vry, J. R., & Watson, G. H. (2002). *University of Delaware's faculty-IT partnership: Educational transformation through teamwork.* Retrieved from http://ts.mivu.org

Suter, V. N. (2001). Managing complexity in a transforming environment. In C. A. Barone & P. R. Hagner (Eds.), *Technology-enhanced teaching and learning* (pp. 25–34). San Francisco, CA: Jossey-Bass.

SUGGESTED READINGS

de Vry, J. R., Greene, J., Millard, S., & Sine, P. (1996, Fall). Teaming up to develop a faculty institute on teaching, learning and technology. *CAUSE/EFFECT, 19* (3), 22–33. Retrieved from http://www.educause.edu/ir/library/html/cem9635.html

de Vry, J. R., & Hyde, P. (1997, Fall). Supporting faculty exploration of teaching with technology. *CAUSE/EFFECT, 20* (3), 45–48. Retrieved from http://www.educause.edu/ir/library/html/cem9730.html

RESOURCE

University of Delaware PRESENT web site: http://www.udel.edu/present

28

SUCCESSFUL STRATEGIES FOR FACULTY SESSIONS

Cordah Robinson Pearce
Indiana University–Bloomington

In a year, the Teaching & Learning Technologies Lab (TLTL) hosts workshops, presentations, panel discussions, and development sessions for faculty interested in integrating multimedia instructional technologies into their teaching. Indiana University-Bloomington faculty and instructors attend these events enthusiastically, providing feedback that helps organizers continually improve presentations. Because faculty support these sessions and because of the support of TLTL's sponsoring units, University Information Technology Services and the office of the Dean of the Faculties, TLTL has been able to dedicate time and resources to the ongoing organization of these events, developing a strategy for the successful presentation of instructional technologies.

During the 2000–2001 school year, TLTL hosted 44 faculty development sessions for 1,106 faculty from nearly every school, department, and academic program in the university. Most events occurred in the summer. TLTL collaborates with service units across campus, including the main libraries, IU counsel, Instructional Support Services, and Information Technology Services in providing sessions for this series. To put the technology in its instructional context, we always try to begin with an IU–Bloomington faculty member or instructor presenting his or her use of the technology to be discussed in teaching.

TLTL faculty development sessions include workshops, panel or roundtable discussions, faculty project showcase presentations, and presentations by university or national experts. Hands-on workshop topics include using office software for gradebooks and conferencing software to form communication groups among students; scanning images; editing scanned images for the screen in six steps; creating a course web site without using HTML; and paperless editing. IU–Bloomington and outside experts have presented topics as varied as educational intellectual property and fair use in a digital environment, interface design for multimedia and web-based instructional projects, capturing and editing sound files, the anatomy of a multimedia project, and "found" software for short classroom demonstrations and interactive projects. Roundtable and panel discussions have explored topics such as finding funding for instructional technologies projects, using an online course management system, and using digital video in instruction.

Over the last seven years, TLTL has maintained the same philosophy of presentation, reinforced by our faculty audiences: Focusing on their pedagogical objectives, faculty and instructors present their instructional technology projects to an audience of peers. In addition to this crucial approach, the TLTL consultant/developer is available during the presentation to provide background and technical support information. Experts emphasize the instructional potential of their material. Rarely do we deviate from this plan, which has succeeded for nearly all our presentations and programs.

Breaking TLTL programs into strategies that work yields six core points:

- Faculty and instructors present their instructional project experiences to an audience of peers.

- Presenters focus on instructional issues.

- Technical consultants and developers provide background and support information for instructional technology projects at the faculty presentations.

- Local and outside experts showcase projects from an instructional point of view.

- TLTL collaborates with other service units on campus to offer a broad range of topics of interest and to pool resources.

- TLTL provides information resources for follow-up (web-based, email communications, hand-outs, informed staff, etc.).

By preserving these strategies in planning faculty development events, TLTL creates and maintains a collegial atmosphere in which faculty and instructors feel free to discuss their teaching, investigate technological solutions to instructional objectives, examine support and development issues with consultants, explore applications across disciplines, and initiate the planning process for their own projects.

TLTL instructional technologies consultants and developers Madeleine Gonin, Kathryn Propst, and Amy Lawson contribute their experiences with three specific examples of TLTL faculty programs that have proved successful over the years.

Example #1 by Madeleine Gonin, Instructional Technologies Consultant and Developer

In the summer of 2000, Charles Pearce, instructor in the School of Health, Physical Education, and Recreation (HPER) elective program, came to TLTL to discuss his one-credit-hour course, Introduction to T'ai Chi Ch'uan (enrollment: 80+ students each semester). In this course, students have two performance exams and one written exam covering the history, philosophy, and characteristics of T'ai Chi Ch'uan. The exam prepares students to describe why and how this art is performed, but in elective courses, students are often unwilling to spend much time preparing for exams.

After talking with TLTL consultants, the instructor decided that an online quiz would help reduce grading time, reinforce students' study of the history and culture of the subject, and provide immediate feedback. He used a model similar to written first-aid tests, taken for mastery. To accomplish this, students were allowed to take a practice exam unlimited times. All took the final exam at the same time in the same room.

The ability to assess the effect of online quizzes on students' grades was helpful in showing that the time spent implementing this new tool was justified and helped students to prepare better. As the use of instructional technology increases, faculty see a greater need for assessing the value of time spent in development and implementation. Since this course had also been taught by the same instructor without using the online quiz, we could compare the results using student grades and found a dramatic increase in the class average and that most students practiced for the final exam. The average for students who had practiced for the exam was 10% higher than for those who had not had an opportunity to practice.

After the first semester, the instructor and the TLTL project consultant gave two presentations, one for HPER faculty and one for TLTL Summerfare. The instructor spoke about the reasoning behind testing for mastery and the general results. The TLTL consultant spoke about quiz construction, implementation, and specific results and drawbacks of this type of testing. Both HPER and TLTL Summerfare faculty were interested in this new method of testing. They felt that students retained material better, especially for a year-long course with a break between semesters. Audio and video features available in these online quizzes helped students to understand and to evaluate movement patterns better. Faculty saw potential for such methods in foreign language instruction, geology, nursing, history, and fine arts.

Example #2 by Kathryn Propst, Instructional Technologies Consultant and Developer

In the early spring of 2001, TLTL, in conjunction with the IU–Bloomington Medical Sciences Program, sponsored a lecture and seminar series with Patrick J. Lynch. Lynch, co-author of *Web Style Guide* and director of web design and development at the Center for Advanced Instructional Media at the Yale University School of Medicine, has experience as a photographer, illustrator, graphic designer, programmer, and multimedia producer. His work has garnered many awards, in part due to his elegant solutions to complex issues in information and user-interface design.

While other web design experts had spoken on campus, we believed Lynch's expertise in developing educational materials would be of special interest to faculty and instructors. Faculty and instructors had expressed an interest in better understanding the principles of design and information organization for the web. We believed an outside expert would strengthen our internal efforts to provide training and guidance on these issues. Partnering with another department on campus helped us to finance transportation, lodging, and the honorarium.

During Lynch's two-day visit, we offered four venues for faculty and others (students, staff, and web developers and designers from other units): one large open presentation and three smaller seminars limited to approximately 25 attendees. To track interest and to control attendance in the seminars, we asked everyone to register. We also asked attendees to provide feedback after the presentations to help us plan for future speakers. Attendance was excellent, and feedback extremely positive. Some sample comments include:

> I enjoyed the relatively non-technical approach to design—didn't get bogged down in coding details.

> The presentation was very useful as I have already emailed several of my friends links to his... site. His resource links and suggestions are excellent—and... his presentation—very credible.

> He helped me think of better ways to design my own web page.

> The application of technology in teaching is always an interesting topic as well as... the impact of technology and information on student learning.

As a follow-up, we posted links to some of the projects Lynch discussed in his presentations on our web site.

Example #3 by Amy Lawson, Instructional Technologies Consultant and Developer

TLTL Summerfare offered a roundtable for faculty about ways to fund technology projects. Organizers gathered a panel of internal and state sponsors of projects that, in part or whole, fall under the umbrella of instructional technology. Because teaching goals are diverse and these projects take many forms, we worked hard to have the panel cover a wide range of funding sources. Grant amounts and durations differed significantly, from a one-time award of $500 or $1000 to approximately $150,000 over three years.

The panelists explained their organizations and funding resources and described examples of successful projects. The faculty audience, seated at the same table as the panelists, asked questions about the grants, sponsoring organizations, application processes, and the relevance of their own projects within the scope of the awards represented.

We strive to stimulate faculty enthusiasm for the possibilities in integrating technology and teaching. Providing information about funding sources, gathering sponsor representatives, and discussing the topic together was an effective way to show support for faculty projects. Putting faces with funding sources helped diffuse the tension that discussions of money and competitive funding can elicit and helped these faculty realize that they do not have to undertake their projects in isolation. Most of the panelists were involved in reviewing proposals and allocating awards. Their willingness to discuss candidly the intricacies of writing successful proposals made the session collegial and encouraging.

Several faculty attendees later made contact with TLTL staff, and we were able to advise them on their proposal writing as well as offer letters of support for inclusion in their grants. A measure of this session's success is that most of these faculty received the funding they requested.

TLTL staff also assembled a funding resource page for the TLTL web site. The "Funding for Teaching and Learning" page charts 11 funding sources, links to the sponsoring organizations, and summarizes each program's focus, the amount of the award, and the approximate deadlines. This site has been accessed 545 times in the ten months since it was published, July 2001 through April 2002, with peak access during the month before the majority of the grant proposals listed on the page were due. The page is updated regularly with new, relevant awards as they are discovered.

RESOURCES

TLTL web site: http://www.indiana.edu/~tltl/

TLTL Summerfare Faculty Development Series: http://www.indiana.edu/~tltl/summer/

TLTL Faculty Project Gallery: http://www.indiana.edu/~tltl/projects/

TLTL Funding Resources: http://www.indiana.edu/~tltl/projects/funding.html

ISS BEST Quizsite: http://www.indiana.edu/~best/web-based_services.shtml

Patrick Lynch's Web Style Guide: http://info.med.yale.edu/caim/manual/

Information about Patrick Lynch: http://patricklynch.net/

29

UNTANGLING THE WEB OF SERVICES: THE RESOURCES WEB SITE

Chris Clark
University of Notre Dame

The modern university provides a wide range of online services to students and faculty. Students register for classes, check grades, and read campus news. Faculty view course evaluations, print class lists with photos, and set up electronic mail distribution. All of these functions are only the tip of the virtual iceberg, so it is not surprising that faculty have difficulty keeping track of all the resources available to them—and if seasoned veterans can't locate resources, imagine the predicament of a freshly hooded assistant professor who has just arrived on campus.

In the summer of 2001, the Teaching, Learning, and Technology Roundtable (TLTR) at Notre Dame issued a report on the state of faculty development in technology at our campus. The TLTR declared that before we can improve technology use in the classroom, our faculty members must first be able to identify the tools, resources, strategies, and support available to them. Specifically, the report recommended that the university "Create a clearinghouse to inform faculty of available resources and direct faculty inquiries to the appropriate support area" (2001).

At the Kaneb Center for Teaching and Learning, we decided that one relatively easy way to tackle the problem and address the TLTR's recommendation would be to create a web site that would list resources and help identify the right resource for a particular need. I was originally intrigued by UNC–Chapel Hill's Compass site but decided to try a different approach.

The site we created provides easy access to resources that support teaching and learning as well as general online resources. A total of more than 50 services are described under eight categories, and visitors have three choices for locating a resource:

- Proceed through a series of hierarchical menus.

- Use a search engine tuned to the site.

- Browse a comprehensive index.

In each case, only two clicks are required to reach information on a resource.

To employ the first strategy, the user begins by clicking a category, such as Campus Reference, on the site's home page. A secondary menu then displays a list of specific services. For example, under Registrar Services, one sees *Class information lookup* and other choices. After the user clicks the name of a specific service, a short description is presented, and users can follow a link to the service's web site, which should prevent visiting multiple sites before finding the desired information. Long explanations of the resources are found only on the web site of the actual service. If users have to keep looking, they haven't wasted time loading large, full-blown home pages.

In the second strategy, users enter a term of interest in the search box on the site's main page. After the user clicks *find*, the search engine looks through the resource pages—not the university web site—and presents a list of matches. At this point, the user can click a link to view a resource description page.

The third path, the comprehensive site index, is comparable to the index of a printed book. A short name for each service is listed, and the user simply clicks the name to view the service description. Some items are listed under multiple names. For example, Notre Dame calls computer labs *clusters*. A new faculty member might not be aware of that term, so the term *computer lab* is also listed.

The web site will require constant updating, and we are counting on the different offices on campus to help us keep our descriptions and links up to date. We are also actively seeking faculty feedback on the site by means of a brief, online survey accessed from the main page. We hope users will let us know when a description is unclear, when we should add an item to the index, or when a site should be added.

Our site debuted in March 2002, and the initial response has been very positive. The pages were designed to be visually soothing and easy to follow. They also incorporate elements of the university home page for the sake of consistency. There are very few graphics, so faculty who view the site via modem will not have to wait long for pages to load. These wonderful resources can make life easier and contribute a great deal to teaching and learning. The Kaneb Center hopes that our site will play a small part in counteracting the frustration cast by the tangled web of information presented every day to faculty.

REFERENCE

Teaching Learning and Technology Roundtable. (2001, Summer). *Teaching, learning, and technology at the University of Notre Dame in the 21st century.* Available: http://www.nd.edu/~tltr/2000-2001_TLTR_Report.pdf

RESOURCES

Online Resources for Faculty: http://www.nd.edu/~learning/resources/

Compass (UNC–Chapel Hill): http://compass.unc.edu/

30

THE WHO, WHAT, WHEN, WHERE, WHY, AND HOW OF PROVIDING QUALITY COLLEGE-LEVEL SUPPORT FOR FACULTY

Rick Peterson
University of North Carolina at Chapel Hill

INTRODUCTION

Doctorate-granting and research institutions, composed of multiple colleges and schools, provide a complex setting for determining how best to deliver information technology support to faculty. Who should provide this support: central university technology services; individual department support personnel; college- or school-level support organizations? In this article, I will describe the support model used by the University of North Carolina at Chapel Hill's College of Arts and Sciences information technology (IT) support organization. Using a journalist's questions—who, what, when, where, why, and how—as a framework, I will document our strategies for delivering support, generalize on that limited basis, and offer some subjective advice. Readers involved in providing technology support for faculty at a large university will benefit most from reading this paper.

As background, Carolina's College of Arts and Sciences is home to 72 departments and units located in almost 40 buildings with approximately 850 full-time and fixed-term faculty, teaching approximately 12,000 undergraduates and 2,000 graduate students. The college's IT support group, OASIS (Office of Arts and Sciences Information Services), employs 22 full-time staff plus associated full- and part-time temporary and student workers. OASIS's organizational structure and mission may be viewed in detail at http://oasis.unc.edu. Since 1999, its staff has grown from 3 to 22 full-time employees with funding from the Carolina Computing Initiative (CCI). In North Carolina, the CCI supports life-cycle computers for full-time faculty, staff, and graduate teaching assistants and requires that all incoming students possess a laptop. OASIS's main goal is to integrate technology into the life of the college in support of the CCI.

WHO

Who should provide support to faculty at the college or school level? For brevity, I use the term *college level* to denote services performed at the level of a college or school as opposed to across colleges or schools (*university level*) or for one particular department (*department level*). We firmly believe that a strong, customer-focused, college-level support group, aggressively collaborating with central information technology services, can provide the best service to faculty under most circumstances. Resource-challenged departments that cannot afford their own IT support personnel obviously benefit from college- and university-level IT services. Conversely, large departments with significant technology missions (for example, a computer science department) will benefit most from providing their own support. Perhaps only the largest departments—those able to afford three or more full-time professional IT staff members—should manage their own IT support personnel. Chairs of departments currently managing less than three full-time IT personnel will consistently advocate for maintaining their small staffs, citing the customized services they receive. Many also fear losing control of these positions.

In our experience, a college-level organization can match and exceed services currently provided by most departments, because it can:

- share and allocate multiple resources (Pooling resources, especially staff, enables us to provide more individualized services to meet faculty and departmental needs.)

- better understand central IT services already available

- effectively manage IT personnel

- maintain more significant institutional memory during times of staff turnover

- provide an active environment for learning and cross-training among our technology generalists (techs)

Also, local departmental personnel often must answer to multiple bosses, especially in departments with a fractious faculty. They have a hard time being all things to all people technologically and may have no real power to effect positive change. Hiring customer-focused techs at the college level who can communicate clearly and confidently with faculty and who are backed by collaboration-focused college and university IT specialists, such as network engineers, research support personnel, and help-desk problem solvers, will provide the best service to faculty. We can better explain and help faculty make better use of central services, which may be underutilized without us.

WHAT

What technology services should be supported at the college level? If central IT provides excellent service in given areas, then there is no need to duplicate it at the college level. Then the challenge is to effectively identify and express your trust in those services to your faculty. For example, is a college running its own email server, even though central IT provides that service? Why? Don't they trust central IT to deliver email reliably? If you do not trust central IT's services, address that fact in a straightforward fashion with central IT management.

What if central IT advertises a service that is not well received or well supported? Should that service be provided at the college level? No. First, find out if central IT's senior management wants to provide that service. If they do, then spend time advocating that they raise the profile and quality of the service as opposed to spending time recreating the service at the college level. Work together with central IT for your faculty's benefit. Finally, if your faculty want services that are not being or will not be provided quickly by central IT, research the costs, both human and technological, of providing it at the college level. Make sure that the service will meet the needs of multiple departments, and avoid providing individual solutions that benefit only a single department. Aim for high-impact, low-complexity solutions.

WHEN

When should these services be provided at the college level? It depends on the college's or school's mission. Medical schools are different from business schools, which are different from engineering or liberal arts colleges. We provide services from 8 a.m. to 5 p.m., Monday through Friday. We clearly communicate to our faculty when they can expect services to be available and let them know in advance when services will be down. In our case, after our business hours, faculty can call a central IT help-desk number or submit an online service request to our group (which we monitor after hours in case of emergency).

WHERE

Where should faculty services be provided? In the best of all circumstances, they should be provided anytime, anywhere. If at all possible, deliver applications that do not require client-side loading of special software. Provide faculty access to their files from their offices, labs, homes, and from the road. For example, we have had success providing terminal services (via Citrix) to our faculty. These types of services don't necessarily scale well from central IT's perspective, and we are able to tailor the provision of software resources to meet our faculty's needs. Most licensed application software that faculty use is available for execution from any net-connected computer running a current web browser.

Our services mainly differ from central ITs in providing faculty support *on site* in their offices and labs. We send a tech to visit them and address their question and/or fix their problem. If the tech cannot solve the problem right there, it rises through our organization until resolved. Our on-site visits to faculty establish good working and often personal relationships that enhance our service. The personal touch of our professional service is our main asset.

Finally, do we house our support personnel in the departments themselves? Currently, most of our techs are dispatched from a central location. We feel that this policy enhances group cohesiveness, training and information-sharing opportunities, and oversight. In special cases (for example, foreign language labs or in the mathematical sciences), we assign staff with particular content-area skills to specific departments or buildings to meet demonstrated needs that are shared by more than one department.

WHY

Why should there be a college-level support organization? Wouldn't it be better to just have a central IT organization, communicating directly with department-level support personnel or individual faculty? OASIS plays a crucial liaison role in delivering support to, and advocating support for, our faculty. We protect our school from looking stupid in the eyes of central IT; for example, without our help a stand-alone department may not *know* that support for *that particular* email client was dropped two years ago. Sometimes, we prevent central IT from looking stupid in the eyes of faculty. We can explain why things are the way they are; for example, we can explain why central IT really should *not* support multiple word processing applications. We are in a unique position to pass information up, down, and across the various levels of the university. Information about central IT services can be passed down to faculty, who may pay more attention to a group email from their college IT group than one from central IT. We can aggregate information about our faculty's needs and advocate for solutions to central IT. Aggregated requests to meet broad needs always are better received (and appreciated) by central IT. Information about how other college-level, faculty-support organizations work can be shared, disseminated, and debated.

Playing this liaison role is crucial to success. We believe that partnership and collaboration and discourse are good things. Sometimes we have to let go of services to central IT. That is no easy task, especially if you are a proud IT service provider. It also involves advocating to departments and department chairs that they should surrender control of their IT services to the larger organization, which is difficult, especially if you have not built up the trust necessary even to begin the conversation. There is always enough work to go around; it is important to manage the available resources effectively and not duplicate services or provide poor service.

College-level support organizations can also reduce inefficiencies and save money by pooling individual departmental requests for software and hardware. For example, we solicit software and hardware requests from all departments, aggregate them, and gauge whether our college or central IT can provide these resources across multiple departments. We are reluctant to have many departments managing small, expensive technological equipment for checkout to a few faculty a few times a semester, when fewer resources and a well-managed, central checkout procedure can meet the same needs for less cost with better utilization of the equipment.

Finally, college-level organizations yield qualitatively better service. We are more closely bound with our faculty, as they know that we exist just to serve them. We are better able to advocate with college administrators, because we have the best interests of the college or school at heart. Our presence at department and department chair meetings and faculty gatherings is accepted and, we think, valued.

How

How should college-level support be provided to faculty? We aim to provide it professionally, with feeling. We look to establish professional and even personal relationships with faculty that will last. We all start out not knowing each other well but build on successful experiences to reach a point where our group is trusted to deliver great service in support of a faculty member's or department's needs.

To a great extent, we have relied on the technology of our help-request system to ensure the delivery of great service. Faculty in our college submit all help requests via the web; we do provide a phone number, but it is seldom used. We place an icon on their computer's desktop that, when clicked, will take them directly to a simple form requesting service. Problems then queue up in the help-request system. Most requests are acknowledged within two hours and resolved within the same day. Our techs may schedule appointments or show up as soon as possible with the faculty member's permission. Once they feel that they have successfully resolved the problem, we email the faculty member for corroboration. Often, we follow up by phone as well. Their responses go to the manager's email. Once the faculty member responds favorably—and faculty know that by not responding within 30 days they signify that all is fine—the problem ticket remains open until our technical manager reviews the problem and its resolution. Once the technical manager reviews the problem and is satisfied, the ticket is closed.

All of our techs know that their work will be evaluated by the technical manager based on how many faculty they help and how successfully they resolve problems. Feedback from faculty largely determines a tech's performance rating. It is in everyone's best interest for problems to be solved effectively, and there are many opportunities for review and for bad solutions to be rectified. Faculty have been trained to submit requests via the web, because they know our pool of techs will respond quickly, solve problems, and be held accountable if they do not. Faculty can also monitor the progress of their service requests.

We are also successful because of our aggressive partnering with central IT. We know what services central IT provides and how they provide them, and we communicate that to faculty. More often than not, faculty do not know the range of services available to them.

CONCLUSION

To successfully deliver exceptional IT services to faculty at the college or school level in large institutions, develop a strong college- or school-level technology organization that delivers professional and personalized service. Deliver this service in aggressive collaboration with the central IT organization. Proactively seek out ways to improve central IT's services and to improve your own in collaboration with them. Make sure that you build a strong customer-support–oriented management team. Make sure you have a bulletproof help-request system in place to keep service requests from slipping through the cracks. Make sure that all techs are properly trained. Nothing will upset someone more than watching a service request go unheeded or remain unresolved. Following these steps will help build trust with faculty, central IT, and administration and result in better service provision to your faculty colleagues.

31

BUILDING ONLINE
SUPPORT FOR BLACKBOARD

Suzanne Cadwell and Lori A. Mathis
University of North Carolina at Chapel Hill

In the past few years, Blackboard's easy-to-use courseware program has become a core instructional technology at many universities and colleges. At the University of North Carolina at Chapel Hill (UNC–Chapel Hill), we began using Blackboard's CourseInfo 3.0 in fall 1999 and have experienced exponential growth in its use since that time. During the fall and spring semesters of the 2001–2002 academic year, UNC–Chapel Hill's installation of the Blackboard 5.5 course management system was used for an average of 600 courses each semester and had an average of 7,000 students and instructors logging in weekly.

Meeting these demands has required collaboration among several groups within UNC–CH's Academic Technologies and Networking (ATN) and Academic Information Systems. Our group, ATN's Center for Instructional Technology (CIT), assists instructors and instructional support staff who use Blackboard. CIT offers Blackboard training classes and small-group consultations, and we provide on-call and email support during regular business hours.

CIT has also created a sizable body of Blackboard documentation (see http://www.unc.edu/cit/bb). Although some might argue against creating in-house documentation when the product includes online user's manuals, CIT has found that placing this custom documentation in the Blackboard portal is critical in providing just-in-time, all-the-time support to faculty and students. The manuals, linked within course sites, answer "*What* does this do?" questions but not the more frequent "*How* do I do a particular task?" or "What do I do when this feature isn't working as expected?" or "*Can* I do this task at all?" While Blackboard's documentation describes the software's features, it does not outline its shortcomings, nor does it provide troubleshooting or task-oriented information. To fill these needs, CIT began expanding its own task-oriented documentation, customized to reflect our particular installation, and we used the Blackboard portal to place the documents within users' lines of sight.

The need for extensive documentation emerged in summer 2001, when the campus upgraded from Blackboard's CourseInfo software to Blackboard 5.5, Level 3. Based on faculty and IT support professionals' input, ATN decided that our Blackboard installation would use data from Student Information Systems to create Blackboard courses (sites) for each course listed with the registrar. Instructors of record would be granted access to these sites automatically and, in turn, make the sites visible to students officially enrolled in the courses by changing one simple setting.

To use CourseInfo before the upgrade, individual faculty members (or, in some cases, school or department IT coordinators) completed an online form requesting a course site. Upon creating a site for individual instructors, CIT sent them an email message with basic information about using the software and URLs for links to more detailed documentation published on our support site. Because the system made it necessary for instructors to place course requests, CIT had an unambiguous record of who was using the software and, therefore, a clear idea whom to notify when system maintenance was scheduled, training classes were offered, and new documentation was posted. With the move to Blackboard 5.5, CIT relinquished its former role as gatekeeper and initially lost its ability to direct information to identifiable individuals. Instead, we had to broadcast information to a much larger and less specific audience, relying on the options offered by the new Blackboard portal product for placing information in instructors' and students' view upon log in.

We availed ourselves of every portal option we could customize: We edited the log-in page to link to our help site, targeted instructors and students with important information in the small spaces that Blackboard's portal modules afford, and also set one of the tabbed portal frames to link to our help site, giving it more prominence than the default help icon at the top of the portal frame.

In response to requests and questions from faculty, we continue to expand this documentation. Some instructors have generously allowed us to copy their Blackboard courses as demonstration sites to share with their colleagues across the university. We are working with these volunteers to write materials that contextualize the sites, including course descriptions, decisions the instructor made when customizing the site, and how students used these materials and tools.

In our consultations with faculty and support staff, we have also found that they were concerned about training and support for their students. CIT's traditional client base consists of instructors, teaching assistants, and support staff across the university. With only one full-time position at CIT devoted to

Figure 31.1

Blackboard.unc.edu's Help Site for Instructors

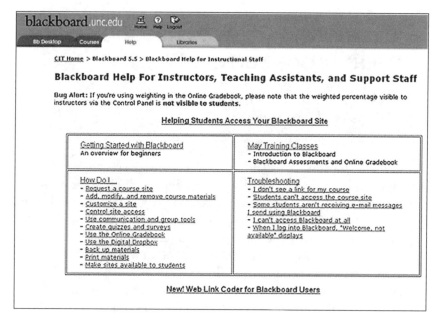

Blackboard and the part-time help of a graduate assistant, the support our office can offer students is limited. However, we did have the resources to write documentation to which instructors could refer students, including a basic orientation to Blackboard.unc.edu, information for troubleshooting common problems, and directions for using Blackboard's communication tools. Again, these documents were published so that they could be easily found via the help tab.

During the spring 2002 semester, over 1,100 users at UNC–Chapel Hill, including students, faculty, and staff, have consulted these help documents through the help tab. Though we do not yet have survey results regarding how faculty rank these help documents in relation to other support mechanisms, we know they are being used extensively. Because our documentation allows users to receive just-in-time, all-the-time support, the documentation also helps us to maintain our on-call and training services with only one full-time Blackboard consultant. Looking forward to future versions of Blackboard, we will have to invest a great deal of time to revise our customized documentation, but we have little doubt about the return on our investment.

32

CREATING A FACULTY INSTRUCTIONAL TECHNOLOGY SUPPORT FACILITY

Nick Laudato and Restiani Andriati
University of Pittsburgh

In 1995, the provost of the University of Pittsburgh created a centralized, comprehensive unit dedicated to supporting faculty in their pursuit of instructional excellence. The new unit, called the Center for Instructional Development & Distance Education (CIDDE), provides a rich variety of faculty development, instructional design, and technology support services. While CIDDE is composed of a diverse array of professionals and technical specialists, its services are purposefully integrated.

This chapter explains the development and operation of the newest component of CIDDE, the Faculty Instructional Development Lab (FIDL), a New Media Center. It focuses on practical working strategies for providing resources, staffing, and facilities in support of faculty using the web and other technologies to improve instruction. It addresses the challenges of keeping up to date with tools and technologies that are available to enhance teaching and learning.

INTRODUCTION

CIDDE is a centralized academic support unit dedicated to the pursuit of instructional excellence. It assists schools and departments in designing and developing curricula and course materials, expanding access to academic programs, facilitating distance education, and supporting noninstructional and community activities in areas where its specialized expertise is required. Its staff includes 55 professionals in the roles of instructional designers, instructional technologists, graphics artists, document designers, photographers, video producers, systems analysts and programmers, classroom engineers, media specialists, and administrative and support staff. About 50 graduate and undergraduate students supplement the staff.

In 1998, the provost allocated CIDDE additional funding and space to create the FIDL as another front door to its faculty services. The FIDL is a physical and virtual gateway to CIDDE's many human and technical resources. Its purpose is to provide faculty with the opportunity to investigate and apply instructional theory, learning theory, information technology, and multimedia technologies to instructional development projects. The FIDL is staffed by a core team of five instructional technologists, supplemented by CIDDE instructional designers and technology specialists.

FIDL MISSION

The FIDL is primarily a training and self-help facility. It provides faculty with the specialized hardware, software, and consulting expertise to allow them to accomplish their instructional goals. FIDL staff can also provide the full range of production or application-development services. The lab addresses the following goals:

- to support a centralized multimedia facility to provide faculty with training, access, and assistance in using specialized instructional technologies, including authoring languages for computer- and web-based applications and graphic, photographic, video, audio, and group work technologies

- to develop active-learning courseware in collaborative teams of faculty, instructional designers, instructional technologists, programmer/analysts, artists, photographers, and video producers

- to support the university's transition to an active-learning environment, which includes the design and development of various instructional activities that teach the principles and practice of active learning and illustrate active-learning courseware

- to evaluate and to introduce new and emerging technologies for direct application to instruction, and to provide technology transfer to the academic and support units

DESIGN OF THE FIDL

The FIDL provides office space for the five full-time core staff of instructional technologists and is organized into six areas:

- Training room: The FIDL training room is equipped with 14 networked PCs, an instructor PC, a touch-sensitive LCD panel, video/data projector, Insight PC control system, and Polycom 4000 Codec (IP and ISDN). The training room was designed to enable the presentation of computer-related content, while facilitating open discussion and hands-on experiences.

- Consulting areas: Three small-group consulting areas are each equipped with a rear-projector SMART Board, networked PC, and data/video projector. They are intended for collaborative group work between faculty and instructional designers and/or instructional technologists.

- Audio booth: A sound-conditioned booth is equipped with a microcomputer, audio mixer, audio-capture equipment, and editing software for creating audio clips for use in web-based instructional materials.

- Video booth: A multi-purpose video-recording room is equipped with two microcomputers, a touch-sensitive LCD panel, Polycom 4000 Codec (IP and ISDN), audio and video mixers, a Tegrity system, and audio/video-capture equipment. Although not nearly as sophisticated as the university's video studio (a professional production-quality facility run by CIDDE in another location), the video booth is designed for interactive video conferencing (ITV), ITV training, creating audio and/or video clips for use in web-based instructional materials.

- Video editing area: A specialized technology area dedicated to video editing is equipped with four high-end microcomputers along with software and peripherals for video conversion and editing.

- Technology areas: Four technology areas are equipped with high-end microcomputers and high-end flatbed scanners with negative and slide attachments and document feeders.

The FIDL does more than simply provide technologies. It gives faculty a work environment with specialized staff assistance close at hand. If the resident instructional technologists cannot provide assistance, the FIDL extends to include CIDDE's instructional design, faculty development, systems analysis, programming, graphics arts, photographic, video production, media and engineering expertise.

Visit http://www.pitt.edu/~ciddeweb/FIDL/ for detailed information about the technologies available in the FIDL.

FIDL ACTIVITIES

The FIDL exists primarily to support teaching and learning. It offers a wide variety of activities, including training, consulting, small-group conferencing, video conferencing, audio and video recording and editing, scanning and imaging, and instructional applications development.

The FIDL has evolved in three distinct stages. The first, its training room, came online in February 2000 in response to the heavy training demands associated with CourseInfo/Blackboard implementation. The sec-

Figure 32.1

FIDL Floor Plan

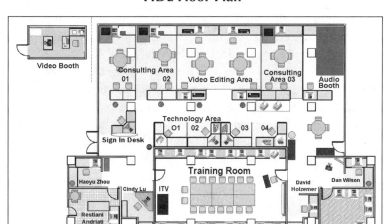

ond phase, in March 2001, opened a portion of the consulting and technology areas, providing some new and specialized technologies to support faculty instructional needs. The final phase completed the facility in April 2002 by opening an audio recording booth and a video recording facility, and providing additional consulting and technology areas.

During the nine months preceding its formal opening, the FIDL had approximately 900 faculty visits. Because of its open-door policy, tracking every use of the facility has been impossible, but 632 of the visits were logged on a paper sign-in survey.

Figure 32.2

Recorded FIDL Visits for From May 2002 Through April 2002

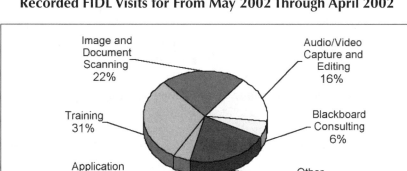

TRAINING

Training activities constitute about 31% of the total visits. These statistics were taken during a nine-month period when the technology areas were limited and the video editing areas and recording booths did not exist. The most popular scheduled training seminars address the use of Blackboard, classroom annotation hardware, and using web-based anti-plagiarism software. A total of 1,680 faculty have received training in using Blackboard/CourseInfo since the project began in 1998. The Blackboard course management system is a key instructional technology at the University of Pittsburgh. Its implementation, called CourseWeb, serves about 60% of the university's 32,000 students. Most of the nearly 2,000 courses that have been developed use Blackboard as supplemental material, with about 5% supporting distance education. The Blackboard implementation is a cooperative effort between CIDDE and the centralized computer group, CSSD.

The FIDL training room is optimized for computer-based presentations and group discussions around a conference table. It also allows training participants to break out to work on microcomputers located around the periphery. The microcomputers are networked via an Insight system to allow the instructor to call up and control any computer's display and show it on the projection system or on everyone's computer.

This design has been extremely effective for faculty training. It allows faculty to focus on the concepts and content that make up the presentation, to comfortably engage in open discussion, and then to spin around in their chairs to apply what they have learned. Placing the PCs away from the conference table prevents a common problem with the use of computer classrooms: PC access is often distracting and interferes with the classroom presentation and discussion.

CONSULTING AND SMALL-GROUP CONFERENCING

In addition to providing formal training seminars, the FIDL staff also provides one-on-one consulting sessions with faculty on demand. These individual sessions address a wide variety of topics, including scanning images, capturing audio/video, and recording a presentation and uploading it to the web. FIDL staff also help faculty via video conferencing or phone calls, and also make "house calls" to individual schools, departments, or faculty. The principle governing FIDL activities is to make every reasonable effort to accommodate faculty needs in terms of topics, level, content, and availability.

The three FIDL consulting areas are designed to support collaborative work between and among faculty and CIDDE instructional and technology staff. Each area can comfortably accommodate at least six people, with the intent of hosting instructional development meetings, which typically involve one or more faculty content specialists, an instructional designer, an instructional technologist, and other relevant technical staff, such as programmer/analysts, graphics artists, or video producers. These efforts are usually coordinated by a CIDDE instructional designer, a professional with a background in the application of learning and instructional theory as well as in the instructional design process and procedures.

VIDEO CONFERENCING

The University of Pittsburgh has supported interactive television (ITV) using compressed video technologies for nearly 20 years. The university's mainstream ITV facilities are managed by CIDDE's Instructional Media Services unit and supported by its Classroom Engineering team. The University maintains T-1 connections dedicated to ITV to its four regional campuses and to the AT&T global ITV network, and ISDN connections to other locations throughout the world. The university's six high-end ITV facilities are designed as hybrid classroom/studios to optimize the quality of the ITV sessions and to make the experience as simple and transparent as possible to its participants.

The FIDL supports a range of mid- to low-end interactive audio and video conferencing capabilities. Its training room and video booth provide multi-point conferencing over IP and/or ISDN lines (up to 512 kbps) in a multi-camera conference-room format. In the consulting areas, the FIDL also supports small-group and desktop videoconferencing over IP.

AUDIO AND VIDEO RECORDING AND EDITING

Faculty members can receive a demonstration, instruction, and ongoing technical support for capturing, digitizing, and editing video clips for inclusion in their web-based course materials. Audio and video capture can be performed in the audio booth and video booth. Some of the popular options include:

- PowerPoint voice annotations: Instructors can use the FIDL audio booth to record voice with their PowerPoint presentation and bundle it for use over the web or in Blackboard.

- PowerPoint video and voice: Instructors can use the FIDL video booth to record video and voice with their PowerPoint presentation and bundle it for use over the web or in Blackboard using either Real Presenter or Microsoft Producer.

- Tegrity: Instructors can use the FIDL video booth to record video and voice over their PowerPoint presentation, along with pen-based annotations on an LCD graphics panel. They can also incorporate ad hoc additions, input from a document camera, or screen dumps. A Tegrity session's output can be played within a web page using Windows Media Player and a plug-in from Tegrity that can be downloaded for free. The output includes the PowerPoint slide, a synchronized audio/video of the instructor, and animated drawings and annotations on the surface of the PowerPoint slide. The recording can be made available in real-time (multicast) and archived for distribution via CD or streamed at either high or low bandwidth over a Microsoft media server.

- Audio/video editing: Four high-end computers are dedicated solely to audio and video digitizing and editing, with software including Adobe Premiere 6, Cleaner 5, Pinnacle Studio 7, and SoundForge 5.

- Streaming video: The FIDL staff is currently developing streaming video services on two platforms, RealServer and Microsoft Media Server.

SCANNING AND IMAGING

The FIDL is equipped with a variety of scanning equipment and graphics panels as well as software to allow faculty to capture and manipulate electronic images. The scanning equipment can accommodate flat art, slides, negatives, and APS film, and also has document handling and optical character recognition (OCR) capabilities. Technology and consulting areas are equipped with software, such as CompuPic and Adobe Photoshop, to manage and manipulate the scanned images, and Adobe Acrobat to create PDF files. One of the most popular technologies is the HP Digital Sender, a device that can scan a stack of papers and email the scan as a PDF file.

INSTRUCTIONAL APPLICATION DEVELOPMENT

The FIDL staff provide a wide range of multimedia and application development services. For example, they can collaborate with faculty to enable them to translate their course-development ideas into reality using software such as Authorware, Director, Flash, Photoshop, QuickTime, and Premiere.

As a central component of CIDDE's mission, the FIDL supports instructional-development projects as part of the annual Innovation in Education grants program as approved by the Provost's Advisory Council on Instructional Excellence. For funded projects such as these, FIDL staff, in consultation with faculty members, instructional designers, and other CIDDE technical staff, can design and implement production-quality multimedia and application-development efforts. To date, these have taken the form of mediated, computer-based learning materials using tools such as Macromedia Director and Flash. Examples include a video CD on anger and argument for the School of Social Work and a series of Japanese language exercises for the Japanese language program.

CONCLUSION

The design of the FIDL training room has been a resounding success. It provides a comfortable environment for learning and information exchange with easy access to supporting technologies. The small-group consulting and technology areas, in place for one year, have also been well received by faculty. The majority of training and consulting services have focused on the use of Blackboard and related technologies. The most popular services have been the digital sender (creating PDFs by scanning documents), slide and print scanning, and OCR. At the time of this writing, the audio and video recording and editing facilities have been available for only one month, but already are attracting faculty use.

The most important ingredient in the FIDL's success to date has been the quality and service orientation of the staff. Core staff all have backgrounds in teaching and learning as well as computer technology and the arts. Their strongest feature, however, is their ability to collaborate with their faculty customers and CIDDE instructional designers and technology specialists.

The challenge for the FIDL is to continue to provide the basic core instructional technology training and consulting services in support of popular applications such as Blackboard and to collaborate on the development of technology-enhanced course materials, while at the same time evaluating and introducing new and emerging technologies with direct application to instruction. The FIDL staff must meet the significant day-to-day demands of its faculty constituents and serve in a technology transfer capacity to the academic units.

33

PRESERVING AND PROMOTING THE SCHOLARSHIP OF TEACHING: THE TEACHING ACADEMY WEB SITE PROJECT

Shannon O. Wilder
University of Georgia

DESCRIPTION

The University of Georgia (UGA) is fortunate to be one of the institutions involved in a national network of Teaching Academy Campus Programs initiated by the Carnegie Foundation for the Advancement of Teaching and the American Association for Higher Education. Established in the fall of 1999 by a core group of faculty, the Teaching Academy is a forum to discuss, to celebrate, and to promote teaching excellence. This distinguished group consists of faculty members who have been recognized by peers and students as excellent teachers as well as campus leaders who advocate a university culture that endorses all aspects of academic professionalism, including the scholarship of teaching. The vision of the Teaching Academy is to foster a community of scholars who are actively engaged in thinking, talking, modeling, mentoring, and promoting all aspects of teaching excellence.

The central mission of the Office of Instructional Support and Development (OISD) is to provide campus-wide leadership on matters relating to instruction, so naturally it has been actively involved in the formation and continuing support of the Teaching Academy. OISD is responsible for the design, implementation, and management of the Teaching Academy's web site. This evolving project seeks to promote the goals of the Teaching Academy and the experience of its members among campus colleagues, current and potential students, and other institutions.

CRAFTING A MESSAGE AND PRESENCE

Instructional efforts, such as WebCT, along with a highly visible web site and news center have contributed to an active online community at UGA. Most offices, departments, organizations, and student groups have web sites that are regularly maintained and used for campus communication. Whether the goal is information dissemination, distance education, or program promotion, this vibrant online campus culture encourages new groups to establish a web presence.

The academy's initial goal for its web site was merely to provide information about its mission, history, and membership. Each arm of the UGA mission—teaching, research, and public service—has a web site linked to every initiative and program that supports that mission. As an initiative of the Office of the Vice President for Instruction (OVPI), the Teaching Academy is a primary link on that web site.

OISD took on the task of designing this site and worked in conjunction with the Teaching Academy's Executive Committee to craft a cohesive and clear message. It became apparent during this process that the web site should not only provide information about the academy but actively promote its goals for fostering teaching excellence. Several components in the design process were necessary to accomplish this function:

- Create a flexible and attractive visual design.

- Clearly articulate the academy's mission and goals.

- Actively update the web site regarding special events.

- Archive academy documents and reports.

- Establish a database to collect member profiles and document teaching philosophies and methods.

While each of these components is important, the database distinguishes the Teaching Academy web site and provides a great service in documenting and modeling effective and innovative teaching on campus.

THE MEMBER PROFILE DATABASE

From its inception, the Teaching Academy has been driven by faculty who not only have distinguished themselves as outstanding teachers but also have worked as advocates for the scholarship of teaching and learning. Each member brings a unique perspective on teaching and the desire to share his or her experiences with the university community. The Teaching Academy believes this collective scholarship on teaching is worth preserving and developed the member database.

Each profile provides a range of current information about academy members, including:

- contact information

- educational background

- biographical information

- courses taught, along with links to any course web sites

- teaching philosophy statements

- teaching methods

- teaching awards and honors

The database is searchable by keyword, academic department, professor's name, and course name and number. Users can also browse through a complete alphabetical listing of member profiles. Future plans include linking to streamed video segments of members demonstrating teaching methods in their courses.

The information is intended to increase the visibility of the academy on the UGA campus and within the larger academic community. Other faculty and teaching assistants can use this resource as a model for reflection on their own teaching careers.

When it comes to scheduling their courses, students are highly interested in teaching styles. The Student Government Association publishes a web site each semester with grade distributions for each instructor on campus; however, this web site does not provide any information about the instructor's teaching methods or the quality of teaching and learning that goes on in the classroom. Current students can benefit from the Teaching Academy database by planning their schedules around challenging courses with creative instructors.

These profiles are potentially useful for recruiting prospective students who are attracted by the university's research-oriented reputation but unaware of the UGA's concern for excellence in teaching.

LESSONS LEARNED: MARKETING THE TEACHING ACADEMY WEB SITE

It is sometimes difficult to alert an active online community to a new web resource. OISD and the academy have worked together to make the academy more visible by linking from other web resources, targeting new faculty, and keeping members involved in the web site's development.

OISD's biggest challenge has been to alert other faculty to the presence of the Teaching Academy's web site so that they may get involved by attending special events sponsored by the academy each semester or by becoming members. Links from other instruction-oriented web sites, such as those of the OVPI and the OISD, have helped increase the academy's presence on campus. OISD has also created an online resource for new faculty who are just learning about the university community. This web site is an excellent way of introducing the members of the Teaching Academy to new faculty who are looking for mentors.

Another challenge has been promoting the web site to the academy's own members. OISD is working to design an interface so that faculty can immediately update their profiles as information changes instead of filling out a form that must be processed.

The Teaching Academy serves as a focal point for thoughtful and informed conversation related to UGA's teaching mission, and the academy web site is an important and ongoing thread in this dialogue. This project provides a way to document and preserve the legacy of teaching and learning at the University of Georgia.

RESOURCES

University of Georgia: http://www.uga.edu

University of Georgia Teaching Academy: http://teachingacademy.uga.edu

UGA Office of Instructional Support & Development (OISD): http://www.isd.uga.edu

UGA Office of Vice President for Instruction (OVPI): http://www.uga.edu/ovpi/

Carnegie Foundation for the Advancement of Teaching: http://www.carnegiefoundation.org/

American Association for Higher Education (AAHE): http://www.aahe.org/

National Teaching Initiative (CASTL): http://www.carnegiefoundation.org/CASTL

34

FACULTY DEVELOPMENT INCENTIVE AT THE UNIVERSITY OF FLORIDA

Terry Morrow
University of Florida

The Center for Instructional Technology and Training (CITT) is a division of the Office of Academic Technology at the University of Florida. As part of the services offered to faculty, CITT provides training, technical support, and access to equipment for the development of multimedia for instruction.

The CITT staff present workshops on the use of technology and software, assist in the evaluation of software for media-based instructional development, consult with faculty on the pedagogical issues related to web-based instruction, and provide access to equipment for media production.

Since 1999 there has been an increasing emphasis on the development and delivery of training relating to the effective use of technology for teaching and learning. The CITT hands-on classes no longer emphasize skill development in the use of software, but instead emphasize the pedagogical basis for using increased technology in the classroom and for online delivery of materials. Major effort is devoted to supporting the use of course management tools such as WebCT. Training is also offered in such diverse areas as videoconferencing, video streaming, accessible web design, using PDAs for teaching, and digital media. Details are available at http://www.citt.ufl.edu/training.

In 1999, the College of Education approached the CITT concerning the development of a faculty initiative that would provide a notebook computer to faculty who completed a series of training classes and consultations. The program resulted in more than 50 faculty in the College of Education being awarded a computer.

The success of the College of Education program prompted the College of Health and Human Performance to fund a similar program for about 30 faculty. Following that experience, central administration decided to offer a similar development program to faculty throughout the University of Florida. In fall semester 2000, proposals were solicited and 200 faculty were selected to participate in a training program. The program required 16 hours of hands-on training. Most of the training was conducted in a portable class-room environment using 30 notebook computers identical to the ones to be awarded to the participants. Faculty were allowed to choose training segments from a diverse slate of offerings. An introduction to "Using Technology in the Classroom" and a final segment dealing with "Effective Use of Laptop Com-puters" were the only required classes. The program was offered four times during FY 2000–2001 allowing the faculty to pick class times convenient to their schedule.

During 2001–2002, the program was repeated for another 100 faculty, but "Using Technology in the Classroom" was no longer required, and offer-ings were repeated two rather than four times. Most of the classes were again taught using the mobile notebook computer bank. Details concerning this initiative are available at http://www.oir.ufl.edu/laptop.

For FY 2002–2003, several changes are being considered. Participants will still be required to take the "Effective Use of Laptop Computers," but the remainder of the required classes will be selected from hands-on classes offered in the conventional CITT classroom. Participants will be given a machine including an MS-Windows operating system but no other software. They will be allowed to choose software from a short list including the soft-ware provided in the training classes. They may also choose to eliminate some of the software and substitute a mid-range PDA, probably using the PALM operating system.

Consideration is also being given to the development of a parallel pro-gram dealing with the use of PocketPC based devices. Participants in that track would be awarded a PocketPC device and required to take fewer hours of training than participants in the notebook program. The PocketPC devices would include wireless capability, attachable keyboards, and display devices allowing them to be used for projection in a classroom.

The Faculty Development Program has been very successful, but a num-ber of changes are being made because of experience gained during the early years of the program. These include such concerns as:

- Excessive time is required for setting up and dismantling the mobile notebook laboratory. Since most of the classes are identical to those taught in the CITT classroom using desktop computers, most classes will no longer be taught using the mobile facility.

- The notebook computers are awarded to faculty for their use but remain property of the University of Florida. This necessitates getting college and departmental authorities to accept the transfer of the computers from the Office of Academic Technology. Much effort is required in maintaining a proper tracking record.

- Software distribution has been a continuing problem. During the first year of the program, the University of Florida purchased licenses for all installed software and provided an image to the manufacturer who then pre-installed all of the software and provided a restore CD-ROM. That method did not work well at all because faculty did not have access to the media for the individual software components. Changing to a different operating system, for example, caused great difficulty in reinstalling the software. During the second year of the program, the CITT pre-installed all of the software and gave a copy of the media to each department having participants in the program. That method required a lot of extra effort in tracking and distributing the licenses and software. For FY 2002–2003, plans are to provide each participant with a license and uninstalled media for each piece of software they have selected. This method will be a bit more expensive because of the extra media needed but will save considerable administrative overhead and be much more convenient for the participants.

- Surveys have been taken during each of the classes offered to participants but no overall pre and post evaluations have been conducted. An effort will be made to collect more comprehensive evaluations during the next phase of the program.

In summary, the Faculty Development Program has been very rewarding for the CITT, and participants have been most appreciative. Please contact the author of this essay if you wish more detail about the program.

RESOURCES

Office of Academic Technology: http://www.at.ufl.edu

Office of Instructional Resources: http://plaza.ufl.edu/ctm

CITT Training: http://www.citt.ufl.edu/training

Center for Instructional Technology and Training http://www.citt.ufl.edu

Faculty Development Program: http://www.oir.ufl.edu/laptop/

PART IV
TEACHING ENVIRONMENTS

35

CLASSROOM TECHNOLOGY: BECOMING A "COMMON UTILITY" FOR TEACHING

Dennis Williams
University of Delaware

In 1994, the University of Delaware began a systematic, campus-wide upgrade of classroom technology. This initiative involved 165 general-purpose classrooms, ranging from small seminar rooms to large auditoriums, and was based on the following five planning and design principles:

• Establish room technology levels, from simple to sophisticated, to meet faculty need and facilitate scheduling.

• Provide user-friendly technologies to diminish faculty resistance.

• Standardize technology to promote faculty self-sufficiency, minimize on-site maintenance, and secure favorable procurement outcomes.

• Link classroom technology improvements to classroom renovations.

• Implement a technology skill development program.

The first principle recognized the need to provide facilities that serve different teaching/learning styles and situations. To do so, the classroom technology initiative established the following four levels of technology:

• Level I was limited to the display of videotape materials on a 32-inch monitor in small classrooms.

• Level II provided the capability to project both video and computer signals on a screen size appropriate for the room.

• Level III added an integrated touch-screen system to control the equipment and room lights.

• Level IV added a wide range of equipment, including a video/data projector, electric screen, VCR, CD player, audio cassette recorder/player, laser disc player, 35 mm slide projectors, 16 mm film projector, full sound system, and a custom-built lectern with a connection panel for laptop computers and auxiliary audio and video inputs.

In assigning classroom space, the registrar's office considered the type and frequency of technology use requested by the faculty. As more and more faculty use laptop computer screens in their teaching, there is less demand for the Level I and Level IV rooms. The Level I rooms cannot project computer displays, and the Level IV rooms have rarely needed capabilities that complicate their use.

The need emerged for a uniform minimum standard that accommodated the high-quality projection of video and computer screens and their accompanying sound tracks with minimal effort for control and connection and minimal orientation and training. Faculty need a variety of technologies, packaged in a transparent and intuitive way that will not detract from, or compete with, the pedagogy.

In January 2002, the university equipped 12 new classrooms, using the experience gained in supporting nearly 100 previously established rooms. The goal was to display computer and video presentations, with audio, appropriate to the room size in an intuitive and reliable package.

Rather than using touch screens or hand-held remote controls, a basic modular control/connection panel provides easy access to all functions. One button turns the video/data projector on and off. One button selects computer display. Another selects video display. One knob adjusts the volume, regardless of its source. In this case, the time-honored admonition to "keep it simple" has proven itself. Faculty response has been overwhelmingly positive, and problems have been nil. The money saved on the simpler systems will accelerate the goal of equipping every classroom for using and displaying technology.

RESOURCE

University of Delaware Classroom Technology: http://www.udel.edu/UMS/classroomtech/

36

LEARNING SPACES AT THE
UNIVERSITY OF NOTRE DAME

Thomas C. Laughner
University of Notre Dame

The University of Notre Dame prides itself on providing quality under-graduate education. DeBartolo Hall, a state-of-the-art classroom build-ing when it opened in fall 1992, demonstrated the university's commitment to providing world-class facilities for its students. Over 700 groups and organizations have visited the building to learn about its capabilities.

As wonderful as the facility is, we have since learned many lessons about classroom design. Through the experiences of Notre Dame's faculty and stu-dents as well as faculty and students elsewhere, we have learned the impor-tance of flexible classrooms to allow both technological and nontechnological activities in the same space. We have learned of the importance of faculty/stu-dent interaction and the effect a classroom-only building has on that interac-tion. We have also learned about the level of support required for a building with a significant amount of technology.

Notre Dame's Teaching, Learning, and Technology Roundtable (TLTR) report of spring 2000 drew attention to the importance of well-designed learning spaces and some general recommendations. During the 2000–2001 academic year, a group of faculty and administrators began a discussion of specific recommendations and how they might be implemented at Notre Dame. While there is still tremendous work to be done, the committee is heartened to see many activities taking shape.

A learning space is defined as any location where learning occurs. It is not necessarily limited to a classroom. It can also be a lab, a quad, a faculty office, or a student snack shop. *Well-designed learning spaces should reflect the same quality standards as other Notre Dame traditions, characteristics, functions, research, and teachings.*

Below are excerpts from the text of that group's report. The report lists several issues pertaining to the design of learning spaces and some recommen-dations to address those issues.

2001–2002 TLTR REPORT:
DESIGNING MORE EFFECTIVE LEARNING SPACES

Use Learning Spaces to Increase Faculty-Student Interaction

The configuration of DeBartolo Hall, where there are very few faculty offices, provides minimal opportunities for faculty and students to easily interact before or after class. Likewise, many faculty office buildings can be uninviting to students and provide little opportunity for students to easily interact with their professors.

Recommendation 1: Improve opportunities for interaction between faculty and students in academic space.

• New construction and renovation should intermingle faculty and graduate offices and classrooms.

• Create social spaces in office and classroom areas.

Recommendation 2: Provide seating outside faculty offices so that students can sit comfortably while waiting to speak to their professors.

Design Classrooms to Provide Maximum Classroom Flexibility

Many classrooms on campus do not provide sufficient flexibility to allow multiple teaching strategies to be used in the same space. A room should not inhibit movement by students or instructors. Students should be able to freely move into any space where public discourse is produced or projected. Instructors should be able to move throughout a room to consult individually or with groups of students. The room should allow, as much as possible, direct exchange of physical materials between student and instructor. Not only is time during class important, but the design of a facility should allow interaction before or after scheduled class time.

Recommendation: Identify a campus advocate who can suggest alternate ways to design flexible and technology-enhanced learning spaces. The advocate's work should be brought to bear prior to the completion of final architectural rendering. A group of people, possibly a subgroup of the TLTR, could fill this role. So that exemplary learning spaces can be studied, the advocate should have a modest annual budget to visit other campuses.

Develop Guidelines to Assure Consistent Classroom Design

While the registrar oversees classrooms, the department closest to a room normally has the greatest influence on how much technology is added during construction or remodeling. This becomes problematic for faculty who are assigned different technology classrooms from one semester to the next.

Recommendation: Develop a consistent model for technological implementation in learning spaces across campus. A minimum set of standards should be developed, and any new or remodeled classroom must meet them. They should be incorporated into the plans during the architect's initial design.

Develop A Support Structure for Learning Spaces

Once outside of DeBartolo Hall, support for technology is problematic. It is difficult, under the current model, for support staff to get to remote classrooms in a timely manner. Often, class sessions are lost because of technological difficulties.

Recommendation 1: Develop a support model so that technology can be brought to any learning space, regardless of its location. Learning spaces should not be limited to those locations that already have technology and wires.

Recommendation 2: Develop a support model so that when technology does fail, every effort is made to assure that class sessions are not lost.

RESOURCES

Learning Technology Consortium's Classroom Design and Support Site: http://www.nd.edu/~ltc

Notre Dame's TLTR: http://www.nd.edu/~tltr

37

ENVIRONMENT: EVOLVING TOWARD SIMPLICITY

Mark McCallister
University of Florida

Like most schools and universities, the University of Florida continues to pursue strategies to provide greater access to technology in the classroom. Successful implementation of technology-enhanced learning in the university classroom snowballs as increasing numbers of faculty experience positive feedback from their peers on the use of technology in their particular disciplines. Central service organizations are pressured to provide technology support in more and more classrooms, often without the benefit of increased resources.

The University of Florida provides classroom technology on a wider scale with a strategy of simplifying the technology in each classroom and standardizing technology across all classrooms. During the mid-1990s, significant resources went into making technology available in the classroom by installing multimedia consoles in most of the large lecture halls on campus and by making mobile technology carts available for use in other classrooms. Many different types of media equipment and interface/switching devices were utilized in this technology, creating a very complicated system to use and maintain. Great effort and expense went into making devices available that were used only once or twice a year.

More recent efforts have been focused on reducing system complexity, making the technology easier for faculty to use and easier and less expensive for support staff to maintain. The first simplification was to remove the Macintosh desktop computers from the consoles, replacing Macintosh users with on-demand laptops that can be plugged in like other instructor-provided laptops. An entire platform was eliminated, taking advantage of equipment that had to be there anyway—the laptop connections. The second effort eliminated the laserdisc players, which were used only by a small group of faculty. Temporary specialized equipment installations could be made for such faculty on demand, without imposing the side effect of complexity on everyone else.

After eliminating the redundant equipment, attention was turned to furniture. The 6-foot-long console was replaced with a 24x24 inch podium with just enough room to accommodate a stalk-mounted document camera, laptop computer, VCR, and, if necessary, a sound system and related gear. One of the most important things eliminated in this change was the control system. Expensive, difficult-to-maintain, active control systems are no longer needed, when the projector itself can be used as an audio/video switch along with simple, bulletproof automatic and manual switches where needed. Complicated and failure-prone matrix switches are eliminated, along with the programmable interface controllers that users often find more confusing than simple buttons labeled, for example, *on* and *off.*

While keeping the amount of equipment installed in each classroom to a minimum is important, maintaining a flexible technology environment is key, so that unusual requests can be accommodated with minimal advance notice. A large variety of equipment can easily be delivered to classrooms and plugged in to auxiliary input ports, which keeps things simple for the average technology user, and at the same time provides the flexibility to keep the power users satisfied. The heaviest users are the ones most likely to understand what the A/V staff has to do to accommodate the instructor's requests and work with them accordingly!

One of the most interesting phenomena we have observed is the continued preference of some faculty to use permanently installed computers in classrooms. A significant number of faculty are much more comfortable walking into a room that already has a computer in it, expecting to load their presentation files either from removable media or a remote network location. There appear to be two reasons for this. First, instructors are often more comfortable knowing that the installed computer is designed to work with the installed projection system. Many faculty have been to conferences and similar environments where their laptop didn't work correctly with the audio/visual equipment provided in a room. Second, many instructors simply would rather not carry their equipment around. They have plenty of other things to worry about than lugging in a computer and making sure that they can connect all of the wires and boot up before class starts. While laptop computers continue to get smaller and smaller, higher-end laptops with large screens are still quite heavy to tote around on a daily basis.

The preference toward installed computers has a significant effect on classroom technology design. First, it is not possible to abandon the concept of the installed classroom computer as soon as might be preferred, at least from a budgetary standpoint. The rapid advancement of PDA technology, which might be labeled "microportable computing," will change this situation, but until all instructors have a fully functional computer in their pocket or purse, their expectation of a classroom-installed computer will remain. Second, the University of Florida is moving toward installing desktop, rather than laptop, computers in the classroom technology podium. The desktop computers are much cheaper, less attractive to steal, and almost universally favored by support staff, because they are more robust, and because broken parts can be changed out without return factory shipments for repair or replacement.

The computer space in the technology podiums was originally designed for laptop computers, which meant that finding a way to fit a desktop computer and monitor in the podium was a challenging design problem. CRT monitors are of course too large, and most LCD monitors are not designed to fold down flat for storage like laptop screens. The solution was to install interactive LCD panels, which function as LCD monitors, fold flat like laptops, and have pens and other features that allow instructors to annotate and to interact with their presentations in ways not possible with a laptop computer. As a replacement for the overhead projector and chalkboard, this technology allows faculty to make high-resolution recordings of the audio and writing surface of their entire lecture, which can be used in a variety of ways to assist learning by both local students and students at remote locations.

What are the next steps toward simplicity in classroom technology? Any remaining redundant devices and cabling must be eliminated, and wherever possible complexity must be hidden from the user, but without adding hidden complexity to compensate. Automatic, self-contained equipment must be used wherever possible, modeled on the appliance that works as simply and reliably as a toaster or a refrigerator.

38

WIRELESS LAPTOP COMPUTERS IN A PROBLEM-BASED LEARNING CLASSROOM

Araya Debessay and Paul Hyde
University of Delaware

When Araya Debessay earned his doctorate in accounting in 1979, Visi-Calc had just been introduced as the first electronic spreadsheet program. When he received his CPA in 1985, Microsoft launched a program called Excel, which ran only on Macintosh computers. Today, the American Institute of Certified Public Accountants (AICPA) web site reports that "keeping abreast of new technologies is critical to the accounting professional's success." Debessay, professor in the Department of Accounting and Management Information Systems at the University of Delaware, recognized that a fundamental change from the way he had been taught was required to prepare his accounting students for the challenges of the twenty-first century. At a Center for Teaching Effectiveness presentation, Debessay remarked, "The information technology revolution has dramatically impacted the manner in which accounting information is being prepared, processed, and communicated. Realizing this fact has influenced me to design my courses with the view of helping my students to be able to integrate computer applications in the courses that I teach."

In recent years, Debessay, who is also an advanced fellow of the Institute to Transform Undergraduate Education, has been using the "Group-based Active, Interactive and Collaborative Teaching Approach" in the classroom. He has explored problem-based learning, adopted electronic distribution of his PowerPoint presentations, and incorporated an online course management system. For fall 2001, Debessay was one of four faculty members who proposed and was granted the installation of wireless laptop computer carts in two problem-based learning classrooms.

On the first day of each course, Debessay uses the wireless laptop computers to provide a hands-on experience of his WebCT course. His extensive WebCT resources range from an assignment schedule, time-released solutions for homework problems, additional problem sets and solutions, chapter notes, PowerPoint slides, answers to textbook questions (released after the questions are discussed in class), and discussion and chat areas for group exercises. This first-day, hands-on introduction encourages students to start using the WebCT resources immediately. In the past, some students were easily discouraged by minor problems they encountered when first accessing WebCT. The online materials have been designed to maximize in-class discussion of the underlying conceptual issues, and the laptops function as a bridge between in- and out-of-class group activities and individual study habits.

ADDING TECHNOLOGY TO THE PROBLEM-BASED LEARNING STRATEGY

On a sunny Thursday afternoon, 49 students amble into 208 Gore Hall. What once might have been just another lecture has been transformed into an active, group-work session: Roles are assigned, students gather corporate data, real-world problems are tackled, a collaborative effort is applied to analyze options, and solutions are synthesized. Experience and understanding are gained, as results are shared with the entire class. No one is slouching in the back.

The most exciting learning opportunity for students is the use of the wireless laptop computers to access companies' financial statements. After discussing their nature and content theoretically, Debessay asks students to search for, and to review, the financial statements of their favorite companies. They then compare and contrast their nature and content with the ones discussed in class or presented in the textbook. The real-life demonstration makes the class lively and interesting and helps students grasp the application of generally accepted accounting principles. The interactive, real-life approach has been a noteworthy benefit of using the wireless laptops in the classroom.

Despite the extra demands, student response has been favorable. Students are engaged and seem likely to remain so. Comments like, "I want to have this professor for all my accounting classes," and "I wish there were more professors like Professor Debessay teaching at the University of Delaware," have been expressed. A student's comment that "cooperative learning and groups is an effective instructional method" indicates that students appreciate alternative classroom teaching approaches.

The wireless laptop computers have afforded this new learning opportunity with minimal disruption. The students still meet in the same problem-based learning classroom. The computers are neither the focus nor a distraction, as they might be in a traditional computer lab. They are distributed only at strategic points during particular class sessions and can be shared within a group, like a textbook. A small sacrifice of class time for the distribution, startup, shutdown, and collection of the laptop computers does occur.

How Wireless?

"Wireless" is a misnomer of sorts. While an ethernet cable is no longer necessary, electrical power is. Without sufficient electrical outlets, a cart with power adapters for each laptop is *de rigueur*, and with a battery life of two hours and a corresponding recharge cycle of two hours, usage is cut by 50%. To provide continual use, the installation of a second set of batteries and chargers is under consideration. Because the campus is fully wired, a wireless web-surfing experience is somewhat slower for faculty and students and can have an impact on class time.

The system software configuration is maintained with Faronics' Deep Freeze program. Computers are configured with floppy disk drives but without CD-ROM or DVD drives. The laptop cabinet is attached to the wall and padlocked. A surveillance camera provides additional security. Faculty members are given individual orientations regarding their responsibility to maintain the system in a secure and organized manner.

Two variations to the wireless laptop cart might prove useful in other settings. The two classrooms selected for this project were chosen because of their problem-based learning seating configuration. Alternatively, case study rooms that already have network and power outlets at each student's seat could be considered. While not the traditional problem-based learning classroom arrangement, this setup would facilitate small group activities and allow students to work together with a shared laptop.

Certain technical concessions were made to obtain the wireless laptops within budget; they have small video screens, limited processing and removable media capabilities, and no printer. Due to the nature of classroom scheduling, the use of the laptops is largely restricted to semester-long courses. Another approach would adapt a room configured for problem-based learning with network and power outlets at each seat. Although significantly more costly, this alternate model has been successfully deployed in a new engineering classroom on campus that can be visited online.

The authors wish to thank Suzanne Nanis at the University of Delaware for her editorial assistance.

RESOURCES

Wireless Technology for Collaborative Learning at UD: http://www.udel.edu/pbl/wireless/

AICPA web site: http://www.aicpa.org

University of Delaware's engineering Computer-aided Active Learning Classroom (eCALC): http://www.che.udel.edu/ecalc

39

CHANGING THE WAY WE TEACH WITH CLASSROOM ANNOTATIONS

Nick Laudato and Michael Arenth
University of Pittsburgh

This chapter discusses the development of a new capability, named *Janus*, in classrooms at the University of Pittsburgh. Janus enables faculty to control and to enrich their classroom presentations. The deployment of this technology offers faculty a powerful tool that, while innovative, is based on traditional teaching presentation methods and practices.

INTRODUCTION

For centuries, the most dominant feature in classrooms has been the blackboard. Instructors use blackboards to illustrate concepts and principles, to highlight important notes, and to work through problems and examples. In the 1950s, the overhead projector added an important capability to the classroom. Instructors could prepare a presentation in advance using the software precursors of Microsoft PowerPoint, print it on clear transparencies, and project it onto a screen. As with a blackboard, the overhead projector also allowed the instructor to be spontaneous and write notes or draw illustrations and equations with a grease pencil. This capability addressed two important deficiencies of the blackboard. First, it allowed classroom presentations to be reused both by allowing them to be created in advance and by providing a medium to record in-class annotations. Second, the overhead projector allowed the image to be displayed on a large screen so it could be seen by students in the rear of larger classrooms, where writing on a blackboard would be too small and indistinct to read.

The combined technologies of microcomputers and LCD (liquid crystal display) data/video projectors enabled instructors to display their computer screens to the entire class and reduced the need to print transparencies. Companies such as SMART Technologies wedded the blackboard to computer and projection technologies to create touch-sensitive white boards. Their product, the SMART Board, allows an instructor to draw on the displayed surface, making annotations or creating new images. The drawings or notes can be saved as files and used in subsequent classes, posted to the web, or printed. The result provides the instructor with virtually unlimited whiteboard space and an electronic recording of the class displays.

At the University of Pittsburgh, SMART Boards became popular in rooms that met their physical requirements. Two problems limited their more wide-scale application. First, faculty who use wheelchairs cannot reach all areas of the board. Second, their application is limited to rooms that are small enough for all students to view a six-feet diagonal image (the largest possible SMART Board). In response to these problems, innovators at the University of Pittsburgh combined existing technologies. The solution adds a touch-sensitive LCD panel to the microcomputer/projector model. The LCD panel doubles as graphics tablet and preview screen, allowing the instructor to stand or sit, facing the class, and make drawings and annotations that the entire class can view on the large projection screen. Pitt named the innovation Janus after the Roman god of portals who is typically depicted with two faces looking in opposite directions.

Figure 39.1

The Janus Concept

Janus

The term "Janus" refers to a combination of hardware and software technologies that define a new classroom capability. Janus is being implemented at the University of Pittsburgh in several different configurations and modes. It can be built into media-enhanced classrooms or delivered to any room as a standard service of the Instructional Media Services (IMS) group within the centralized faculty support unit, the Center for Instructional Development & Distance Education (CIDDE).

In the classroom, Pitt is deploying Janus in place of preview monitors. Pitt's classroom design standards specify that a monitor be built into the instructor's console, so instructors can view their presentations while facing the class. Without a preview monitor, they must turn away from the students to see what is being projected. Implementing Janus simply involved substituting a flat LCD panel for the traditional CRT preview monitor. Although significantly more expensive, the touch-sensitive LCD panel that is the basis of Janus can be used in four unique ways that make it ideal for classroom presentations:

- *Pen as mouse:* A pen (stylus) can be used in place of the computer mouse, providing an interface device that some presenters find more natural and allowing more precise drawings and annotations. Buttons on the pen perform the double-click and right-click functions of a normal mouse. Instructors can use the pen in any way a mouse can be used. For example, during a PowerPoint presentation, the instructor can draw on the surface of the image (via the "Pointer Options" and "Pen" selections) much more precisely than with a standard mouse. Instructors can use this feature to highlight important phrases or graphics, make spontaneous notations, work through problems, or draw illustrations related to their presentations.

- *Virtual whiteboard:* Using specialized software, Janus can also act as a virtual whiteboard. In conjunction with a data projector, it creates an effectively unlimited chalkboard space. This feature is especially attractive in larger lecture halls where viewing distances make chalkboard use impractical. Annotations on the multi-paged virtual whiteboard can be displayed, saved, and then recalled later for review. The instructor can prepare illustrations and notes in advance and then modify or supplement them in the classroom. For example, a math instructor might prepare some pages with the Cartesian coordinate system to make it easier to graph spontaneous examples in the classroom. Software with this capability is sometimes bundled with the LCD panel but may be proprietary (its license may allow use only on a computer connected to the panel), making it difficult to prepare notes in advance or share them with students. Some vendors provide whiteboard software, such as Microsoft's NetMeeting, that offers similar functionality with no significant licensing restrictions. At Pitt, Hitachi's MultiMediaNotePad and SMART Technology's SMART Notebook fulfill this function.

Figure 39.2

Sample Virtual Whiteboard

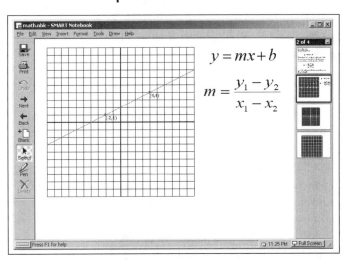

- *Screen capture and annotation:* Janus captures and saves pen annotations made on a transparency layer over whatever appears on the computer screen. For example, an instructor can annotate over the slides of a PowerPoint presentation during class with the pen and then save the transparency with the annotations embedded for inclusion on the course web site. Students can later review the annotated presentation. Annotations can be made over any application and saved as .JPG or .BMP files using such software as Hitachi's ShareWizard Pen.

- *Screen capture movie:* Special software can record the computer desktop, mouse movements, and screen annotations during a session and store them for subsequent playback as a digital movie. An example is TechSmith's Camtasia.

As a result of the long tradition of writing notes on a blackboard in class, most faculty are accustomed to turning their backs on their students and often simultaneously talking to the wall. Janus changes everything. With Janus, they can always face their students, while still using all of the capabilities they had with a blackboard—and more. This seemingly small change can have a profound effect on the dynamics of the classroom. It makes the class more intimate, allowing the instructor to maintain more eye contact with students, thereby getting a better assessment of students' understanding and improving communication.

Janus overcomes many of the traditional presentation problems faculty have faced in classrooms, especially faculty in wheelchairs and those who teach in larger classrooms. By incorporating the power of a PC with the image size of an overhead projector and the flexibility and ease of a pen and paper, Janus literally revolutionizes instructional technology opportunities in the classroom environment.

JANUS IMPLEMENTATION

The technology in the University of Pittsburgh's classrooms is planned and implemented through the work of the Classroom Management Team (CMT), a committee chaired by the university registrar and reporting to the provost. The CMT establishes standards for instructional technology installations, recommends classroom renovation priorities, and manages and monitors their implementation. The CMT is staffed by faculty and staff from the office of the registrar, CIDDE, Facilities Management, the Faculty Senate Plant Utilization and Planning Committee, the office of the provost, Health Sciences, and Computer Services and Systems Development.

With the development of Janus, the CMT has upgraded its minimum installation standards to include this technology in all future renovation plans. As of May 2003, 24 classrooms have been equipped, and another dozen are planned for the remainder of 2003. Because it will take several years to retrofit Janus into rooms that have been previously renovated, CIDDE's Instructional Media Services unit allows faculty to request daily delivery and setup in classrooms throughout the campus. Special priority is given to faculty in wheelchairs.

Technical Details

After experimenting with several generations of LCD panels and tablet PCs, CIDDE's classroom engineering staff selected the Hitachi Starboard product for the implementation of Janus. The Hitachi Starboard weighs 9.15 lbs and offers a 15-inch diagonal LCD screen, capable of native 1024 x 768 resolution and 24-bit color depth. It uses a DVI or VGA interface for video and either USB or serial mouse connections. The panels are manufactured for Hitachi by Wacom. Most of the panels installed in classrooms are electromagnetic instead of touch-sensitive, allowing users to rest their hands on the surface without affecting the drawing. These EM panels require a more expensive stylus.

The Hitachi panel is connected to the computer and to a data/video projector. For most of its classrooms, Pitt's standard implementation uses the Sharp XG-P10XU LCD projector. The standard lectern (teaching station) configuration allows the projector and the Hitachi panel, through an Extron switch, to be driven by a built-in microcomputer or by a wild laptop. For the portable version delivered to the classroom, an Altinex DA1907SX VGA Splitter allows the laptop image to be viewed on the laptop, the Hitachi panel, and the data/video projector.

The built-in computers and the CIDDE and faculty laptops must run the Wacom panel drivers and the Hitachi software to fully use the configuration's capabilities. The Hitachi software includes the virtual whiteboard (MultiMediaNotePad) and screen annotations (ShareWizard Pen) applications.

Future Directions

In experimenting with different configurations to meet the functional goals of the Janus project, CIDDE researchers have experimented with, and continue to explore, three different variants:

- *Large format:* In a special, integrated-curriculum classroom in Pitt's School of Engineering, the instructor's console contains a 40-inch diagonal plasma screen with a Matisse overlay, manufactured by SMART Technologies, to allow it to be touch sensitive. This configuration allows the instructor to use a plastic marker or even a finger to annotate over the data/video presentation. Software to enable the virtual whiteboard and captured annotations, analogous to the Hitachi software, is available from SMART Technologies. School of Engineering faculty have been using this configuration since early 2001.

Figure 39.3

Large Janus Console in the School of Engineering

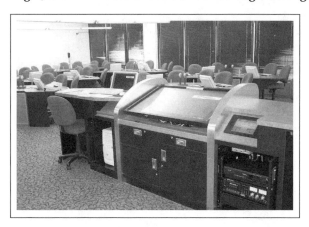

- *Tablet PC:* QBE released a tablet PC in 2000 with many of the characteristics needed for Janus. The QBE device is a portable tablet PC running Windows 98, with a touch-sensitive surface and virtual keyboard. The QBE was capable of 1024 x 768 resolution, the Pitt standard minimally acceptable display resolution, but was not deployed because of difficulties using the machine in landscape orientation. More recently, the Fujitsu B-Series Lifebook tablet PC provides a touch-sensitive surface on a traditional laptop platform, with the proper resolution. Its small size (10-inch diagonal screen) and portability allow it to be easily moved and quickly set up in the classroom but limit its application to simpler annotations.

- *Handheld:* Another exciting area of investigation centers on the use of wireless connections between a PDA and either the PC or the projector directly. The connection can be made via Ethernet 802.11b in peer-to-peer mode or via Bluetooth. Special software, such as SlideShow Commander, then allows the PDA (either Palm OS or Windows CE) to communicate with the PC and control a PowerPoint presentation. The instructor is therefore free to roam the classroom and remotely change slides, read the PowerPoint notes pages, and even make drawings and annotations on the projected image by writing on the surface of the handheld.

These technologies are evolving at a rapid pace and promise to dramatically change the way faculty can make classroom presentations and interact with their classes.

40

CREATIVE HIGH-TECH/LOW-TECH TEACHING IN AN INTEGRATED TEACHING ENVIRONMENT

Carol Burch-Brown and Ann Kilkelly
Virginia Polytechnic Institute and State University

During the spring semester of 2001, we tandem-taught two different women's studies courses at the same time in a single, large classroom in Torgersen Hall, Virginia Tech's new, high-tech research and classroom facility. We experimentally combined, traded, and recombined our students in a series of projects that centered on gender and the arts. Ann's class, Women, Culture, and the Arts, is a popular core curriculum course that meets general education requirements in the humanities; Carol's class, Women with Cameras, is a studio course in photography and gender. Both are sophomore-level courses. Each enrolled about 30 students, who were not primarily in the arts but drawn from many academic programs. About two thirds were women. Both courses employed readings, lectures, discussions, and laboratory/studio experiences to focus on women's issues, to stimulate students' analytic and imaginative capacities, and to look at the role of the creative process in understanding social inequity and potential change.

Our experience with the flexible space of Torgersen Hall and its technological capabilities not only enhanced but also qualitatively shifted the teaching and learning experience in a variety of ways. Direct access to the central library and special resources, such as the New Media Center, led students to embark on collaborative projects of greater imaginative range. Their practical academic skills improved, as did their overall level of achievement, to an extent that neither of us had experienced before.

The Classroom Space
Unlike most general assignment classrooms, the classrooms in Torgersen are designed for flexibility. The tables on rollers and comfortable chairs can be quickly rearranged or moved aside to create multiple work stations, open areas, and study environments, rather like a higher-ed application of the open

classrooms used in progressive elementary and secondary schools. The room includes a lockable closet where faculty members can store special equipment and materials as well as some of the students' works-in-progress. Within a matter of minutes, a faculty member can transform the room into a rehearsal space, workshop, movie theater, traditional lecture/demo classroom, or any arrangement needed. What tops off the flexibility of the classroom space, however, is its continuity with the other facilities and support staff located in the building.

Digital capabilities include large-scale video projection for any materials accessible through the room's central computer pod, including playback for videos, CDs, and DVDs, as well as "Elmo," a digitized cross between a camera, a traditional overhead, and an opaque projector. Other connection links in the floor and walls are accessible to both students and faculty. Students can check out laptop computers from the Electronic Reading Room and bring them to the classroom for individual and small-group use.

The macro and micro space of the building, along with special equipment and support staff, provides a continuity of access to central university resources heretofore scattered: the library, an electronic reading room located strategically between the classroom space and the library, the New Media Center, flexible furniture, and the closet. The combined laboratory modes of the class, we believe, shifts the gaze of the learner from the stable authority figure/teacher to a collective focus on the questions at hand. The visual technology allows everybody to gaze at a common image and each other rather than down at a desk or paper and, therefore, away.

The class becomes less a conduit for information, in Paolo Friere's sense of a "banking" mode, than an active "making" mode, where information and skills are generated by active participation. Students learn about, and become much more comfortable with, digital equipment and processes, which carries over to other classes. They learn to use, as a logical extension of class time, a demo classroom, well equipped and staffed, in the New Media Center. They get to know the staff, and the staff become familiar with the types of projects the students are doing.

Many students have trouble initially adjusting to a classroom that is more chaotic than most. They must focus their activities and be responsible for their choices. The class cannot be experienced in the abstract but relies on group presence and variable modes of learning, which may not work with another kind of subject matter. Having to organize and work out a timeline for their production, although reflecting real-world working conditions, requires more trial and error than a top-down structure. Students are sometimes angry that what they thought would be free and easy (it's an art class about women, after all) requires their engagement and a lot of work, which is why we believe it is a quality learning experience. We offer here a few examples of imaginative possibilities this integrated space suggested.

Music and Performance Work

Students in Ann's class looked at a variety of women artists, including well-known blues and jazz musicians and guest artist Elise Witt, who conducted singing workshops during a portion of the semester. Witt performed in the classroom space for and with students. Subsequently, the room became a rehearsal space for group projects, where students could reteach each other the material. All singing materials were connected to course themes, including civil rights, global empowerment, and women's work. In final reports and presentations, students combined music with original visual imagery.

Ann also used a variety of interactive theater and image-making games. These games included works by Augusto Boal, Michael Rohd, Anna Deavere-Smith, Celeste Miller, sociometric games, and Ann's own performance techniques. They literally repositioned class and faculty in the space and discussed topics/subjects without using words. Controversial and emotionally and intellectually challenging ideas about race and gender, for example, could be explored by shifting how we stood in relation to the group. Students' and teacher's gazes are constantly refocusing and self-assessing, a direct function of both space and technology.

Another performance unit of Ann's class was quilting, introducing the concept of women's art and labor, and employing the skills of Mary Ellen Connaughty, Ann's sister and an expert quiltmaker. One of the surprising lessons of this unit was the awareness, caught poignantly by one of the male students who had never before threaded a needle, that sewing is a technology. This vital insight allowed us to link the domestic work of functional quilt-making and its history to the photographic reproduction of quilt images using much more current technology. Scanned photos of the quilt patches made their way into the final project of every student in the class: a limited-edition, digital book.

Imagemaking and Digital Processes

Ann's interactive classroom activities and guest artist performances naturally grew into photo opportunities for the students in Carol's Women with Cameras classes. In fact, the students, teachers, and guest artists became willing subjects for photographic assignments at a number of points during the term. Students actually saw themselves at work and play through the eyes of other students in the class. Students in the photography classes learned to make digital contact sheets and then to post their photographs on the class web sites, using our online discussion groups. We projected some of these images and comments in class, thereby deepening our collective class discussion about the audience's response to works of art and to gender issues in images.

Students thus had the benefit of watching the creative process unfold in the works of their peers at the same time as both classes examined the careers of major female photographers. The benefits of their exposure to the twists and turns of the creative process became clear when we studied the relationship between photographer and subject in Dorothea Lange's work. From our class web site, we projected large-scale photographs. Arranging furniture and open space in the room, we then staged the positioning between photographer and subject to understand better the composition and emotional impact of Lange's work.

Using the classroom and the students themselves as basic photographic resources produced other benefits to the fledgling photographers. For example, two of our guests were elderly women who were quite willing to have the students photograph them. Improvising a photo studio in a corner of the room was not difficult. The floor outlets made it possible for students to move portable lights to various locations as interesting activities caught their attention. This unusual practice opportunity led to some remarkable photographs that members of both classes valued and encouraged improvisation and freedom in the culminating joint photographic project, which was on the genre of photography. Students in both classes willingly became subjects, photographers, and assistants to each other. They worked well together, because they had seen firsthand during class how the often tiny decisions at every stage of the creative process affect the outcome and impact of the work of art.

Ann's students used watercolors to produce original work in class, using techniques Carol had created in a previous class. This "deep doodling," as she called it, was designed to familiarize students with a range of visual materials in a context where they would not be inhibited by previously absorbed ideas about their own skills or the nature of the creative process. Painting sessions were keyed to readings and other course material. After reading Toni Morrison's *The Bluest Eye*, for example, classes painted and drew, while listening to a range of female jazz and blues musicians. Students then scanned and printed out original work in the New Media Center and Digital Imaging, located down the hall. The remarkable results challenged and surprised students and encouraged them to become more adventurous. In almost every case, the students emerged with a detailed knowledge of texts and of the material process of making art.

Writing-Related Skills and Technology

We read and wrote in the classroom or the comfortable atrium area just outside. Sometimes, reading accompanied performance work, often using laptop computers available from the library upstairs or electronic reading rooms we created. Students did online library research during class time, bringing resources back into the room itself.

All students revised their prose, using video and online materials that were projected during class. Students could download and typeset literary classics from online sources like Project Gutenberg; they could combine text with original illustrations and personal reflections for later hand-binding into a book.

The Book Project

All student imagery and writing culminated in a book project, where groups from each class, Carol's with expertise in photography and visual imaging and Ann's with quilting, writing, and performance experience, edited, assembled, and produced about seven printings of a book. Carol demonstrated and coached students in book-binding techniques: Japanese stab binding, sewn-signature binding with hard covers, comb and spiral binding, and original approaches with wood, Plexiglas, and handmade paper.

Part V

MODEL PROGRAMS

41

THE FACULTY DEVELOPMENT INSTITUTE

John F. Moore and J. Thomas Head
Virginia Polytechnic Institute and State University

BACKGROUND

Faculty development is a critical component of the Instructional Development Initiative, which is part of Virginia Tech's strategic plan for creating an educational environment that will meet the needs of the 21st century. Created in 1993, the initiative's goal is to offer all faculty members the opportunity to attend instructional improvement workshops every four years, while continuing to upgrade classroom and laboratory facilities.

The goals are structured into three components:

Faculty Development

- Encourage all university faculty to participate in the Faculty Development Institute (FDI), with the overarching goal of motivating them to investigate, to create, and to utilize alternative instructional strategies.

- Provide participants who complete the program with access to state-of-the-art instructional technology, the knowledge to use it, and the incentive to collaborate with their colleagues in enhancing their courses.

Student Access

- Advise all students on their investment in computer technology to maximize its usefulness during their college careers.

- Provide access to computer labs and computer-intensive classrooms that run software unique to disciplinary areas (e.g., Geographic Information Systems, Mathematica, and Daedalus).

- Provide orientation and online training software for all students to ensure that they have a solid foundation in computing and instructional technology resources.

Course Development

- Support faculty in developing and implementing network-accessible courseware and instruction. An OnLine Course Support unit provides faculty with robust course management system support, including Blackboard, WebCT, and other services. The New Media Center was developed to provide access to high-level multimedia and web development facilities. The center is open to faculty, staff, and students.

- Facilitate electronic libraries of scholarly materials supporting designated courses.

- Improve classroom and presentation facilities to support faculty efforts in introducing new technologies into core courses.

FACULTY DEVELOPMENT INSTITUTE

The FDI program is a long-term strategy to provide the time and resources for faculty to investigate alternative instructional strategies designed to improve the productivity of the teaching-learning process. Its workshops allow faculty to reexamine their curricula and the instructional methods that will help them to adapt to students' changing needs. Attendees' evaluations have been consistently positive over the past ten years. After the workshops, faculty participants receive a state-of-the-art computer and a suite of appropriate software applications. About 40% now select a wireless laptop computer.

August 2001 marked the completion of the second four-year cycle of FDI workshops, in which 1,560 faculty participated. During each four-year cycle, about 95 % of the university's faculty participate without charge. The provost's office allocates four years of participation to each college. The college deans and department heads select the faculty who will attend the workshops each year.

The third FDI cycle is now underway. The 2003 FDI has been designed to focus on specific projects for most FDI summer workshops to encourage faculty to undertake course enhancement and transformation based on their specific needs. Faculty can choose among or are appointed to one of 12 tracks: New Faculty Computing Orientation; Basic Computing Skills; Developing a Web Course using Dreamweaver and Blackboard; Developing Web Course Interaction; Creating Digital Media Content; Using AutoCad; Using MatLab; Creating Learner-Centered Instruction; Developing and Delivering Online Instruction at a Distance; Instructional Media/Web Production Studio; Research Presentation Tools; and Visualization and Virtual Environments. A series of spring workshops will serve as a suggested prerequisite, or quick start, for the summer sessions. Lab assistance is provided in all summer workshops, and the New Media Center will continue assistance to complete the projects successfully.

The FDI workshop tracks and the increased emphasis on project-orientation reflect the increased complexity of emerging technologies. Several of the 2003 FDI tracks support web content creation and multimedia integration for interaction. Others, such as MatLab, visualization, and research presentation, support research activities. A team approach is encouraged for several tracks, so that graduate students or staff are invited to participate alongside the faculty with whom they work. This team approach increases the focus on achieving desired outcomes in advanced course-transformation projects.

An alternative format was tested in spring 2002 for faculty whose schedules prevent attendance at summer workshops. The hybrid format combined occasional small-group meetings with independent study, online content, and tutoring. About 50 faculty selected this alternative approach.

Access to information outside the workshop has become increasingly important to ensure that the knowledge gained is in fact useful. A contract with ElementK.com now provides continual access to over 550 online tutorials covering desktop productivity, multimedia, web development, databases, project management, and related software. Access is provided by request to faculty, staff, and students.

Winter focus groups are also conducted for each track. Details of workshop topics, instructional pace, and hands-on activities are adjusted based on the participants' interests. FDI workshop topics will continue to reflect the stated needs, interests, and instructional objectives of the participating faculty.

The workshops' content has radically changed since the pilot workshops in 1993. At the beginning of the FDI, the core skills being taught were email, introduction to multimedia, developing classroom presentations, and principles of computer-based instruction. As the FDI's effects have spread across the campus and with increased awareness of the Internet, changes have been implemented. The core skill set has become more advanced, reflecting the more sophisticated computer skills and awareness of the participating faculty. For example, core content now includes computer security as an important topic. Principles used in designing the 2003 FDI workshops were developed from the feedback received during workshop sessions in previous years. With changing technology and the evolving needs of faculty, the content of the FDI must be constantly updated and evaluated for effectiveness.

Most workshop instructors and facilitators have been Educational Technologies' and university libraries' staff. Each track has a facilitator, who recaps each topic presentation, introduces each new presenter, and underscores the connection among workshop topics relative to the desired track outcomes. Their work is supplemented with presentations by selected faculty and staff from the departments of geography, forestry, English, entomology, mathematics, computer science, veterinary medicine, engineering, architecture, art, music, and humanities, where appropriate. A very effective feature of the FDI, which was continued during the 2002 sessions, included presentations by faculty who had previously attended its workshops. These sessions demonstrated how faculty had changed their courses and answered questions about effects on student learning, productivity, development time, and similar topics.

Beyond the core skills, many workshops have focused on discipline-specific software. For example, the mathematics department is engaged in large-scale experimentation in the Math Emporium, a student-centered, advanced-learning center that provides interactive, self-paced courseware, diagnostic quizzes, small-group work, and faculty-student tutoring for over 17,000 undergraduates. The aim is to overcome conceptual barriers and thereby broaden the range of students who succeed in making mathematics an effective tool for later course work and careers. This new approach encourages more realistic problems to be brought into even elementary courses, speeding the transition to professional-level work. The first of its scale in the nation, the Math Emporium is a bold example of the use of instructional technology to systematically improve student learning and faculty productivity.

In another workshop, the focus upon specific software involved professors from a number of different disciplines. Faculty involved with design concepts, such as architecture, art, apparel design, geographical information systems, landscape architecture, and theater arts, examined and debated the use of computer-based tools to enrich both two- and three-dimensional design instruction. Other groups chose to supplement their introductory sessions with more in-depth sessions on specific aspects of multimedia development and use.

Most workshops included general sessions that were attended by all participants. Breakout sessions permitted participants with different experience levels or interests to focus on topics that were most appropriate to them individually. In addition to gaining a basic understanding of the computer-based tools, faculty spent time discussing the possibilities for using technology to facilitate student learning.

Open lab time gives faculty the opportunity to practice what they've learned in each workshop session and to begin development of new course materials for the 2003–2004 academic year. Most faculty have left the workshops with a multimedia presentation for use in a lecture or with a framework for an Internet-accessible course. These introductions to instructional tools set the stage for more extensive workshops on specific topics, which will continue throughout the year.

RESOURCE

Faculty Development Institute home page: http://www.fdi.vt.edu/

42

Special Programs: Grants for Course Redesign

Leila Lyons and Janet R. de Vry
University of Delaware

Using Technology to Transform Learning

Demand for technology to transform learning is driven by an information-based economy, changes in student demographics, the need for an adaptive and flexible workforce, and increased accountability for educational outcomes. Technology's potential to transform education sometimes seems beyond reach—like the proverbial pot of gold at the end of the rainbow. Those seeking a technology-based solution plead for additional technical staff, more money, a feature-rich course management system, while others advocate a revised faculty reward system, better technology training for faculty, or a renewed emphasis on teaching. All these factors contribute, but none by itself will provide a sustainable transformation.

At the University of Delaware (UD), we are implementing a strategy to engage the campus in the educational redesign process. To dovetail with UD efforts to revise the general education curriculum, beginning in 2002, we are offering Technology-Enhanced Course Redesign grants. These grants, ranging from $2,000 to $20,000, must be matched by the applicant's department or college, which must also approve their impact on the curriculum. Freshman-year experience courses—L!FE, interdisciplinary Pathways courses, and senior-year Capstone courses—are specifically targeted.

This initiative builds on a previous program that offered faculty small grants of expert time and strategies adapted from the Pew Grant Program in Course Redesign. Its three years saw tangible examples of active-learning opportunities not available in the traditional classroom and innovative uses of space and time not previously possible. The new round of grant proposals promises to take these successful strategies, create new ones, and apply them to the systemic transformation of courses deemed critical by the academy.

Evolution of Grant Programs to Enhance Learning

The UD Teaching, Learning, and Technology Center (PRESENT) for faculty was established in 1997 and served almost 200 in its first year. Although faculty were very content with its service, staff realized that in the traditional consulting role, they could only provide a quick fix. We needed a mechanism to focus both faculty and staff on applying technology to critical learning issues. Our solution was for PRESENT to offer small grants to create pilot projects and modules for technology that enhances teaching and learning. We were particularly interested in receiving applications for small-scale, active-learning modules and tools that could scale to other courses and disciplines. A student technology assistance grant paired faculty with a student employee to work on small projects that could typically be completed in about ten weeks. This short timeframe enabled faculty to focus their ideas within a circumscribed period.

We solicited proposals from faculty and, in 1999, funded ten projects that were all successfully completed. We continued implementing these small projects until we exhausted the funding that supported the students: over 30 projects in three years. We also changed three aspects of our approach. First, the adoption of a course management system in 2000 led to a shift in emphasis from custom programming to helping faculty design learning activities that use the collaborative features of WebCT. Second, we have increasingly hired students from a broad range of disciplines, but especially from Education. Third, we shifted from assigning one technology-savvy student to one or two faculty members to assigning a team of staff and students to the faculty members. The importance of instructional design became apparent, and, in 2001, we hired our first instructional designer, who will play a key role in the new round of grant proposals. Some examples of projects funded by small grants can be seen at http://present.smith.udel.edu/showcase/

FIRST STEP—THE SMALL GRANT PROPOSAL PROCESS

Our small-scale grant program is better described as "boutique style" (Buckley, 2002) course redesign rather than systemic transformation. The program's simplicity makes it a suitable starting point for any campus. UD now has an enthusiastic group of faculty who have transformed portions of their courses and are keen evangelists for applying technology to teaching. Many of them are now presenting at national conferences, publishing in national journals, and obtaining funding from external sources to complete the work begun in these small grants. All of these continued efforts tie into the traditional faculty reward system.

The program philosophy was to keep the proposal process simple to encourage a broad range of faculty responses. Initially, we considered the use of leading-edge technologies but gave preference to proposals that sought to effectively integrate existing campus and technological resources into creative and effective teaching and learning strategies. To apply, faculty were asked to respond to five questions (see grant application http://www.udel.edu/present/center/grantform.html):

- Briefly describe what you plan to do with the grant.

- Please specify at least one or two learning goals or principles that will be furthered by this project.

- What will be your role in the project?

- What will be the role of the PRESENT staff in the project?

- How will you assess the effectiveness of your project?

Those faculty completing successful projects have willingly showcased them. They have expressed overwhelming satisfaction with the program. In response to the question, "What has been the most valuable aspect of the program to you?" we received such comments as the following:

Because of the program and the assistance that I have been getting from the PRESENT staff, I have been able to integrate technology into my teaching. Frankly, without the assistance of the PRESENT staff and the student technology assistance, I would have been discouraged from even trying to integrate any technology in my classes. (Araya Debessay, business and economics, accounting, and MIS)

I have benefited from PRESENT because they got me thinking about ideas and provided the seed money/people to get them going. The main project we worked on became a pilot for a much larger project and a substantial grant from an external source for further development of the pilot project. (Lesa Griffiths, director of the Center for International Studies, formerly associate dean, agriculture and natural resources)

I got a lot of creative ideas from the various people involved, things that I never would have thought of myself. (Mark Huddleston, formerly chair of political science and international relations, now dean of the College of Arts and Sciences)

The grant assistance (from ITUE) provided the freedom for me to spend the time to redesign one of my classes.... The PRESENT program offered a large dedicated block of time from the consultant. (Joshua Duke, food and resource economics)

SECOND STEP—TECHNOLOGY-ENHANCED, COURSE-REDESIGN PROJECT GRANTS

During 1999–2002, UD adopted a course management system, WebCT, that enabled many faculty to incorporate active-learning strategies into their classes. However, the combination of course-management system support and student technology assistance grants has, so far, primarily affected individual classes taught by individual faculty. Large introductory courses have been scarcely touched by these grants.

To address the need for curriculum reform on a larger scale, UD funded a program of grants for technology-enhanced, course-redesign projects in 2002. This program was announced jointly by the acting provost and the vice president for information technologies in mid-April. To encourage a university-wide impact, grant proposals will be approved by department chairs and prioritized according to their programmatic impact on the curriculum by deans. See http://www.udel.edu/present/grant/ for an online description of the application process. During the 2002 Summer Faculty Institute, an overview session targeted toward potential grant applicants will summarize resources and tips for redesigning a course. Participants can learn proven strategies for engaging students in active learning, techniques to off-load repetitive tasks to online resources, and methods for assessing student comprehension. Follow-up sessions to refine strategies and to complete the redesign application will also be offered.

Possible Variations That Might Be Useful in Other Settings
A departmental approach to transforming learning through the use of technology assists people with common disciplinary needs to become equally comfortable with technology. To achieve this goal, exposure to the technology and services provided at the university, including an overview of available tools and features that enforce active learning and an introduction to the supported course-management system, could be useful.

PRELIMINARY CONCLUSIONS

Curriculum transformation requires rethinking classroom teaching and examining what is best achieved in face-to-face settings and in the online environment. We are offering special programs on course redesign in our Summer Faculty Institute to help faculty think through the process of restructuring their classes to take advantage of the opportunities that technology affords. We firmly believe that the new grant program supported by our educational outreach and consulting through the library, Center for Teaching Effectiveness, and PRESENT will begin the systemic transformation in learning that will meet the needs of our campus. By offering a campus-wide program, we hope to capitalize on interdisciplinary efforts currently under way. Small, individual grants to gain faculty confidence and to create a faculty support base on campus are certainly beneficial. UD's course redesign grants offer the dedicated time of instructional design and technology experts to faculty on a competitive basis. Two benefits are included in the new grant process. First, faculty can apply for funds that support a development team to assist them, and, second, the advocacy of department chairs and deans will ensure that the results align with institutional goals and will be sustained. We see this program as energizing and engaging the entire campus in an effort to transform education with an appropriate use of technology.

REFERENCE

Buckley, D. P. (2002, January/February). In pursuit of the learning paradigm: Coupling faculty transformation and institutional change. *EDUCAUSE, 37* (1), 29–38. Retrieved from http://www.educause.edu/ir/library/pdf/erm0202.pdf

RESOURCES

PRESENT site Small Grant application: http://www.udel.edu/present/center/grantform.html

Technology-enhanced, course-redesign projects: http://www.udel.edu/present/grant/

L!FE (Learning: Integrated Freshman Experience): http://www.udel.edu/life

Pathways: http://www.udel.edu/pathways

Brown University: http://www.brown.edu/Facilities/CIS/itc/services.html

Wilfrid Laurier University, Canada: http://www.wlu.ca/~wwwtlt/STAprogram.shtml

The Pew Learning and Technology Program web site: http://www.center.rpi.edu/PewHome.html

43

BETTER, CHEAPER, SLOWER: EVOLUTION OF AN INSTRUCTIONAL TECHNOLOGY DEVELOPMENT PROGRAM

Bob Henshaw and Lori A. Mathis
University of North Carolina at Chapel Hill

Institutions of higher education continue to experiment with faculty development programs that emphasize the successful integration of computer-based technologies into courses and curricula. The University of North Carolina at Chapel Hill has adopted an instructional technology development model that seeks to recognize faculty across a continuum of interests and experience levels. The model is based on the following principles learned from our experience:

- Small grant awards still offer a much needed incentive for work with instructional technology.

- Most faculty members implement computer-enhanced teaching strategies incrementally over a number of semesters.

- Ongoing support for instructors at all experience levels is critical to continued innovation on campus.

BACKGROUND

During the mid-1990s, when the use of Internet-based technologies began gaining mainstream popularity, the university funded a series of annual grant competitions for instructional technology projects. Their budgets ranged from $5,000 to more than $100,000. One of the goals of the early grant programs was to generate a few projects with broad lay appeal that could be used to promote continued interest among state funding agencies. As a result of these and other factors, the majority of the funding went to projects led by faculty members whose previous experience using instructional technology made them more likely to succeed in the eyes of the reviewers. While the benefits of some of those projects are still being realized on campus today, many were not sustained beyond the life of the grant.

Support for less ambitious instructional technology implementations began in 1999. Program sponsors, under the aegis of the Faculty Information Technology Advisory Committee (FITAC), a subcommittee of the Faculty Council, structured the new grants program to accommodate a wide range of faculty experiences and skill sets. This shift occurred, in part, because of a much smaller budget. However, the shift also reflected a realization that the widespread adoption of computer-enabled teaching strategies by instructors with many responsibilities, and perhaps no inherent enthusiasm for technology, was unlikely without legitimate rewards and incentives.

PROGRAM DESCRIPTION

At research institutions like UNC–Chapel Hill, where instructional innovation is less likely to be recognized in the tenure and promotion process, faculty have few built-in incentives to experiment with new instructional techniques. As with any change in teaching, the successful implementation of a computer-supported resource, strategy, or assignment occurs through a process of trial and error. The time this trial and error requires is a real cost for many faculty members who are rewarded primarily for research and scholarly writing. To recognize this time and the potential risks, the current program uses a one-time financial award of $2,500. Faculty can use the award as salary, student wages, or to purchase equipment and software related to their projects.

The current program also accommodates a much broader range of faculty interests and experience levels than the mid-1990s program. Rather than requiring faculty with little instructional technology experience to compete directly against those with more experience, faculty members now compete within three separate grant tracks. The first, Introducing Instructional Technology in a Course or Curriculum, is designed for instructors who have not used instructional technology but are ready to begin exploring its use in a specific course or curriculum. The second track, Enhancing the Use of Instructional Technology in a Course or Curriculum, targets instructors who wish to build on previous experiences using instructional technology. The third track, Applying Advanced or Emergent Instructional Technologies, is intended to support instructors who are interested in working with technologies that are leading edge or have limited support on campus.

Participants in the introductory track are assumed to have minimal or no experience using computer-enabled teaching strategies. They are required to attend a two-day summer workshop designed to help instructors clarify their instructional objectives, to explore computer-enabled teaching strategies appropriate to their objectives, and to develop a support plan that will provide them with the skills necessary to implement an effective instructional technology project. After the workshop, individual or small-group meetings with consultants continue throughout the participants' grant project.

Of the three tracks, the enhanced track accommodates the most diverse range of faculty interests and experience levels. Some of the participants have very limited experience using computer-enabled teaching techniques but are ready to revise or extend their initial implementations. For instance, a quarter of those who participated in the introductory track of the 2001 program received grants for the enhanced track in 2002. Other participants in this track have years of experience using instructional technology and are interested in either refining current techniques or trying something completely new.

The advanced track offers instructors and university support organizations a chance to learn more about technologies that have not yet been used in an instructional context on campus. The principal investigators in this track usually, but not necessarily, have a strong background using instructional technologies. The active collaboration of campus support organizations in every step of the proposal implementation is designed to promote the sustainability of these more experimental projects. To ensure that support organizations can meet this commitment, the advanced track funds only a handful of proposals. It is the only track among the three that offers funding in addition to the stipends for each team member, since many of the proposals require hardware or software that is not yet a campus standard.

Neither the enhanced nor the advanced tracks require grant recipients to attend a workshop. The proposals in these tracks are too varied for the standard workshop format used in the introductory track. Instead, participants begin meeting soon after the grant announcements with a small group of consultants who will serve as their primary support contacts throughout the program year. The purpose of these initial meetings is to clarify project goals, to identify support needs, to establish working relationships between the grant recipients and consultants, and to develop a tentative schedule for implementing the proposals.

A crucial part of this development model is the continued support by consultants throughout the grant year. The program relies on the active participation of the libraries, the Center for Teaching and Learning, the Center for Instructional Technology, and the academic technology groups of the College of Arts and Sciences and School of Nursing. The collaboration among these organizations makes it easier for program participants to draw on a wide range of expertise, and it has also helped to limit administrative overhead costs for the program to less than 3% of the overall budget.

After the implementation of the projects, faculty participants are required to submit a written reflection on their experiences. It includes a review of the pedagogical plan for technology in the course or curriculum, the evolution of the plan and its educational results, and thoughts on future directions. In addition to helping faculty grantees reflect on their experiences, these profiles offer other faculty specific examples of teaching with technology projects on their campus. (The initial reflections are available in a searchable database called TLT Profiles located at http://oasis.unc.edu/fitac/profiles/search.asp.)

Finally, in order to balance individual project work with the invaluable exchange of ideas that can occur across disciplines, a spring colloquium, featuring presentations from each grant track, was held for the first time this year. Both new grant recipients and recipients from the previous year were invited and encouraged to compare notes during the event.

CHALLENGES

Faculty feedback on the program has been generally positive. In a survey administered at the end of the 2001 program year, 96% of grant recipients agreed with the following statement: "This grant program is an appropriate way to encourage the effective use of instructional technology at UNC–Chapel Hill."

Still, a number of challenges must be addressed as the program evolves. One current shortcoming is the limited ability to serve instructors who may have project ideas that require additional support and funding but do not employ emergent or advanced technologies. In addition, providing the $2,500 stipend is increasingly difficult in tight budget years. Finally, we continue to explore effective ways to ensure that program requirements are met. FITAC awards the grants in good faith that the proposed project will be implemented, barring unforeseen barriers to completion. Instructors who do not complete the requirements for the grant are ineligible to participate in future FITAC-sponsored programs.

CONCLUSION

Most faculty members have little time to devote to developing new teaching strategies in any given semester. Furthermore, our experience working with instructors at UNC–Chapel Hill suggests that successful implementation of higher-level computer-enhanced teaching strategies is more likely to occur iteratively over a number of semesters. This realization marks a shift in faculty development efforts in the area of instructional technology. The UNC–Chapel Hill grant programs of the 1990s that emphasized large awards for quick, leading-edge results have evolved into a program that encourages incremental adoption over several semesters and serves faculty members who have a wide range of experience in using instructional technology.

RESOURCE

Instructional Technology Development Grants: http://www.unc.edu/cit/fitac/grants/itdev2002/

44

FUNDING INSTRUCTIONAL TECHNOLOGIES PROJECTS

Kathryn B. Propst and Cordah Robinson Pearce
Indiana University–Bloomington

The Teaching & Learning Technologies Lab (TLTL) at Indiana University–Bloomington is a service partnership provided by Instructional Support Services and University Information Technology Services. TLTL assists faculty in developing multimedia web sites, CD-ROMs, and class presentations and in using class communications and online course management systems.

Our faculty clients, staff members, and university administrators had all identified the need for funding small purchases of equipment, software, or training as well as support for assistants with content-area expertise to help instructors complete instructional technology projects more efficiently. When the Office of the Dean of the Faculties provided TLTL with $7,500 for faculty clients, we created the TLTL grant program. We quickly drafted a plan and sought feedback from faculty, librarians, and former TLTL clients. We asked: Are these the right kinds of programs to offer? Is the amount of the awards about right? What other kinds of things should we consider?

Based on the feedback we received, we finalized the program. It supports technology projects with well-designed instructional objectives that focus on learning activities. The program was divided into two parts: TLTL Media Assistants and TLTL Grants-in-Aid.

TLTL Media Assistants: This program funded an assistant who specializes in multimedia to work with a faculty member and TLTL staff to help to develop or to implement an instructional project. It was designed for projects that needed discipline-specific or other specialized knowledge or talents and/or for projects that required intensive efforts. Faculty members helped to select the media assistant for their projects. Each media assistant award was initially set at $1,500. Four grants of varying amounts were awarded for 2001–2002.

TLTL Grants-in-Aid: This program funded small grants up to $1,000 each to enable faculty to purchase equipment, software, or other materials or for other purposes, such as to defray workshop or other expenses necessary to complete a project or to make project development or implementation proceed more efficiently. The total program amount for the 2001–2002 year was $3,000. The number of grants was determined by the amounts requested.

Application procedures: Instructors applied for the grants online. The application asked them to briefly describe the proposed project, especially as it related to course objectives and instructional goals. Applicants described how they would evaluate the project's success in meeting teaching and learning goals they had identified in the project description. For media assistant applications, instructors described what role a media assistant would play in the project. For Grants-in-Aid applications, applicants listed the equipment, software, or materials they wished to purchase and provided a brief justification for each item, including a price estimate. They listed any workshops or training they wished to attend and provided a brief justification and the price for each.

Frequently asked questions (FAQ): On the grant application web site, we noted FAQ to provide additional information about the program. All TLTL staff were informed of the details of the program and could answer phone questions about the program as well.

Q: Do I need one of these grants to work with TLTL?

A: No. TLTL's mission is to work with faculty to integrate technology into IUB classes. TLTL will make every effort to help you with your project, whether or not you receive a grant. These grant programs are designed to provide assistance for projects that need specialized knowledge or talents, for projects that require intensive efforts, or for materials or training that will make project development or implementation proceed more efficiently.

Q: Can graduate students apply for these grants?

A: Technically, no. However, if you are an AI developing course materials and/or if you are interested in being a media assistant, talk with the faculty member in charge of the course and urge him/her to apply.

Q: Can I apply for both grant programs?

A: Yes. Note, however, that you must provide justifications for all requests, and you must have an explicit plan for using the assistance.

Q: Are media assistants supervised by TLTL or the faculty member?

A: This depends on the project and how the media assistant will contribute to it; the details will be determined by the faculty member and TLTL staff after the grant is awarded.

AWARD CRITERIA AND REVIEW PROCESS

Applications were reviewed electronically by a committee of TLTL staff and IUB faculty members according to the following criteria:

- clearly defined instructional goals

- plan for evaluating how well goals are met

- feasibility

- applicability to other disciplines

- explicit plan for using assistance

The committee reviewed applications and entered comments in an online form. Following the selection of projects to be funded, a committee of TLTL staff met to review costs, and through good purchasing strategies, we were able to provide sufficient funds for all the hardware and software products the successful applicants requested.

The committee reviewed 24 applications, a very enthusiastic response to this first-time offering. It funded four requests for media assistants and five requests for grants-in-aid. Of the remaining 15 applicants, TLTL was able to assist with 12 as part of our normal services and three were referred to other service units on campus.

SAMPLE PROJECTS

Some examples of projects for which media assistants were awarded are:

School/Department: Medical Sciences Program

Course: Gross Human Anatomy

Award: $1,500 to hire animator/graphic artist with biomedical background to develop and to implement a series of animations of the embryonic cardiovascular system to teach difficult concepts

School/Department: School of Public and Environmental Affairs

Course: Statistical Techniques and Statistical Analysis for Public Management

Award: $1,500 to hire former student from one or both classes to assist in identifying and adapting web-based applets or workstation tools illustrating critical concepts; obtaining real-world data for group projects and providing web links that document the policy context; and integrating active learning techniques into the course web pages

School/Department: Folklore and Ethnomusicology

Course: Black Music in America

Award: $750 to hire an assistant with knowledge of the subject matter and course materials to digitize music and image files and create web pages that are used as resources both in and out of class

Some projects for which Grants-in-Aid were awarded include:

School/Department: Music in General Studies

Course: Rock Music in the 1970s and 1980s

Award: $210 for supplies to convert class VHS videos to DVD

School/Department: Religious Studies

Course: East Asian Buddhism

Award: $340 to purchase Adobe Acrobat and FrameMaker+SGML upgrade for redesign and presentation of class materials according to the Collaborative Learning Archive Initiative (CLAI; www.indiana.edu/~clai/) teaching philosophy

School/Department: Classical Studies

Course: The Ancient City of Athens

Award: $875 for video camera to record student reports from Athens, Greece and to videotape Greek monuments for use in the class and in other classes on return to the USA

School/Department: School of Optometry

Course: Systemic Pharmacology and Ocular Pharmacology; fall and spring semesters, respectively

Award: $875 toward equipment for producing virtual grand rounds (case studies)

Modifications

As with any new program, some modifications were identified for the next offering:

- Strictly limit the amount of text the applicants can type in the online form's text boxes to 500 words or less.

- Provide more structure to the form to require applicants to address the application questions directly and specifically.

- Require a more detailed budget on the online form and provide links to educational price lists used for university purchasing.

- Ask if applicants have had any previous contact with TLTL, including those with whom they have worked, so we might have more background on their projects.

- Change media assistant awards to dispense sums up to $1,500.

- Enable the review forms to be edited and to track which have been completed.

EVALUATION

This grant offering was successful because it fit directly within the mission of TLTL while meeting needs not directly covered by our services. Further success was ensured by the program's organization, which included an efficient online application process, good supplemental information in the form of an online FAQ, and a well-informed staff to answer questions over the phone. The online review process was efficient, provided a way for each reviewer to examine all other reviewers' comments, and made it easy to compile committee recommendations. Careful purchase reviews by the TLTL staff made it possible to stretch available funds to cover several projects.

Faculty and instructors who were awarded grants are currently working with TLTL to develop their teaching projects. The grants further enhance IUB's supportive environment for faculty wishing to integrate instructional technologies into their teaching.

RESOURCES

TLTL web site: http://www.indiana.edu/~tltl/

TLTL funding information: http://www.indiana.edu/~tltl/projects/funding.html

45

THE LEARNING TECHNOLOGIES
GRANTS PROGRAM

William K. Jackson
University of Georgia

In 1989, the University of Georgia (UGA) established the Instructional Technology Grants (ITG) program to provide funding, on a competitive basis, for innovative projects using instructional technologies. Administered by the Instructional Advisory Committee, the program provided $1,011,239 to support 74 projects involving 147 faculty members in 36 academic departments over a period of nine years. During the same period, similar funds were available to faculty through two additional UGA grant programs: a curriculum development program administered by the office of the vice president for academic affairs and a facilities development program administered by Computing and Network Services. Beginning in the mid-1990s, most proposals submitted to all three programs involved innovative uses of instructional technologies, and the three groups responsible for reviewing proposals and issuing awards found themselves substantially duplicating effort. In many cases, the same project was submitted to all three programs, modified only to comply with varying program guidelines.

In 1998, the ITG program was combined with the curriculum and facilities development grant programs to form the Learning Technologies Grants (LTG) program, administered by the newly formed Instructional Technology Advisory Committee. In the past four years, LTG awards totaling $2.5 million have supported 66 separate projects involving 93 faculty members in 53 academic departments. Funding from the ITG and LTG programs has stimulated innovative uses of technology to enhance teaching and learning throughout the campus, and the LTG program was recently identified as a best practice nationally (Hagner, 2000).

The LTG program is now administered by the Committee for Applied Instructional Technologies (CAIT). This committee, formerly the Instructional Technology Advisory Committee, includes six senior administrators who are permanent members and nine faculty who serve three-year terms.

The permanent committee members include the chief information officer, the vice president for instruction, and representatives from university libraries, the Center for Continuing Education, and student affairs. The director of the office of instructional support and development serves as chair. In addition to administering the LTG program, CAIT's other major responsibility is the development of the annual allocation plan for approximately $5 million generated by the institution's student technology fee.

Proposals for the LTG program are due at the beginning of the academic year, and recipients are normally notified by the end of October. Although two-year awards are possible, most projects are supported for one year. Complete LTG guidelines are posted each year at www.isd.uga.edu.

The following are a few examples of the initiatives funded by the LTG program:

- Computerized testing center in chemistry eliminates the need for in-class testing.

- The Music Technology Education Center (MuTEC) provides students access to the latest digital audio, musical instrument digital interface (MIDI), and digital display technology.

- Enhancing the large-classroom experience in psychology resulted in the installation of a student response system and interactive video connectivity with animal labs.

- The Interactive Performance Studio allows students to explore the interaction between live performance and digital media.

- Interactive computer-based instructional modules develop the critical thinking skills of veterinary students.

- A multifunctional computer/technology classroom in education trains students in advanced applications of instructional technology.

- A multimedia digital imaging laboratory in environmental design provides students the opportunity to develop and to publish web-based portfolios of their work.

- Computer-based medical diagnosis/patient disease state evaluation is a new training program for pharmacy students.

- Web-based interdisciplinary math modules were developed by the Division of Academic Assistance for use by students in several disciplines.

- Haptic interface for sculptors provides students the opportunity to use a physical feedback computer interface to work with a virtual block of clay.

- The microcontroller as an engineering design tool: A hands-on laboratory formed the basis for a $100,000 NSF training grant.

- Digital hands-on practice in administering, analyzing, and applying K-5 reading diagnostic instruments; interactive DVD case studies allow students in reading education to use state-of-the-art technology to develop assessment skills.

The annual level of funding for the LTG program is $650,000. Of this amount, $400,000 is provided by UGA's student technology fee. The university's use of student technology fee revenues to support innovative projects is permissible when the projects directly benefit students.

REFERENCE

Hagner, P. R. (2000, September/October). Faculty engagement and support in the new learning environment. *Educause Review, 35* (5), 27–37.

46

DEVELOPMENT GRANT PROGRAM: ADVANCED AND EMERGING TECHNOLOGIES IN INSTRUCTIONAL CONTEXTS

William Frawley
University of Delaware

Over the past two years at the University of Delaware, all instructional development grants from the Center for Teaching Effectiveness (CTE; see www.udel.edu/cte) have had a single goal: to encourage research faculty to use the research environment to develop or adopt *very new technologies* for instructional purposes. Admittedly, *very new* is a difficult phrase when it comes to technology, where the interval for innovation can be the nanosecond. How many of us have found that in the span of a year or less, some hardware or software in which we invested thousands of dollars to be ahead of the curve is now a low-cost package bought only by Luddites? By *very new*, I mean *technologies that are beyond what one would expect to be a part of normal faculty use in instruction*—beyond course web sites and WebCT and into developments that might be quite individual, experimental, and unusually labor- and technology-intensive. Still, even this way of talking evokes the slope of relativism. What is normal? Whose expectations? Who are the faculty? Whose use? While answers to these questions can be heavily institution-specific, the questions generating them, I would argue, need less to be answered than simply to be asked in order to fix the background of discussion to make technology efforts intelligible.

Delaware's development-grant program, Advanced and Emerging Technologies in Instructional Contexts, was conceived of and administered by the CTE as a way to tie to instructional practice the high-technology environment of the research university and the teaching interests of a research faculty. By most measures—faculty response, administrative commitment, student benefit—this program has been a success. What worked in CTE?

Groundwork

As in advertising, so in the academy—you never get a second chance to make a first impression: The harder you work before you announce a Request for Proposals (RFP), the more success you will have after it is announced. At CTE, we spent months and months prior to the competition's announcement cultivating an environment that we hoped would promote maximal response. Advanced and Emerging Technologies in Instructional Contexts was a new program, so naturally it required foundational thinking, but we devoted inordinate time to planning, discussion, and brainstorming before we made anyone else aware of the program, and these efforts had a double effect. They not only got the program off on the proper initial footing, but also established the competition in institutional consciousness and so made it easier to sustain it. In essence, we applied an established faculty development lesson to ourselves—when you teach a new course, prepare it the most thoroughly you can the very first time you offer it because you will incidentally develop all kinds of spin-offs as a consequence of the initial effort.

We learned two more specific lessons. The first was the value of brainstorming from the research environment. We formed "idea groups" of faculty and professionals to rethink CTE grants. These groups were organized around research and technical expertise and consisted of individuals from across the sciences, humanities, professional units, and levels who may have had passing knowledge of one another's work, but did not speak with one other often, if at all. Importantly, these groups had no agenda other than to be as imaginative as they could. The conversations were wide open and promoted *content-driven instructional improvement:* They were explicitly organized so as *not to encourage* discussions of instructional technique. The groups, however, did have one (silent) condition: They had to come up with a small number of specific projects—just one would be enough!

Many interesting possibilities emerged from these idea groups. What about a program that addresses how we teach the hard ideas, like what structure is? One very promising suggestion was that we focus our instructional-development efforts on the latest (*very new?*) technology—Internet 2, virtual reality—tools principally associated with the research environment. As one idea-group member said, "Don't you think art historians could use virtual reality as well as those in biotechnology?" This suggestion turned out to be the winner of the idea-group conversations, mostly because of its fit with the institution's larger priorities, but it delivered many other benefits along the way. Brainstorming in the research environment gave us many concrete possibilities for proposals and programs in the future. The idea groups became ready-made review panels and fostered concern for teaching as a purely intellectual activity, very much as research itself has traditionally been seen.

The second lesson was to fan out. Once we settled on a possible grant program, we engaged in a campaign to target individuals for involvement. The idea group on technology had identified a small number of faculty working with new technologies in their research and teaching who might be good candidates for initial recipients of high-technology instructional grants. Many of these individuals had never been involved in instructional projects of this sort, or instructional projects at all, for that matter. We saw their inexperience as an advantage because their participation would send a signal that there was widespread interest from key concerns. We approached them in their own research environments, and on their grounds, and had them articulate the germ of their instructional projects on site. The overall purpose was to foster, in a personal way, proposal development that is knowledge-driven, recognizes epistemological diversity, acknowledges the variety of teachable moments in laboratories, studios, and other non-classroom locales, and reverses the typical flow of institutional interest. This last point is worth unpacking. Faculty perception is sometimes guided by the incorrect, but no less powerful, myth that the administration is hostile to and uninterested in their most imaginative ideas. Our special-operations-like fanning out into the research environment showed the faculty that the administration was taking a proactive interest in their research as it linked to teaching, created substantial goodwill.

In the end we recruited grant submissions, in the same way that NSF or NEH encourages and filters proposals. For us, the RFP became the RFYP— request for *your* proposal. Faculty saw that we wanted them to be involved and that we would work with them to produce a fundable proposal. Still, it must be stressed that, up to this point, we had not yet even announced the program! But by our groundwork, the program was becoming a fixture in the minds of key people. We then announced the program and got substantial response, not only from those whose proposals we recruited, but also from many others who had either heard about what we were promoting or saw the program as a way to do new things.

Results

Over the past two years, Advanced and Emerging Technologies in Instructional Contexts has supported the following instructional projects:

- Remote-control delivery to the classroom of electron microscope images: faculty in chemical and mechanical engineering

- Alternative sequencing of historical images for use in history and art classes: faculty in art and the Center for Material Culture
- Wireless technology in problem-based learning environments: faculty in physics, communication, accounting, and consumer studies
- Virtual meetings and business decisions in synchronous and asynchronous electronic environments: faculty in business administration
- Internet 2 for teaching the arts: faculty in music
- Three-dimensional models of organs and body structures for teaching anatomy: faculty in health and exercise sciences
- Delivery of real-time brain images and neural activation data for the classroom: faculty in psychology and cognitive science
- Interactive, web-based, problem-solving and data-analysis modules for natural science classes: faculty in bioresources engineering
- Writing on and for the web: faculty in English
- Dynamic, electronic portfolios for K-12 teachers: faculty in education
- Personal digital assistants (PDAs) for field experience in health sciences: faculty in nursing and nutrition and dietetics
- Digital images of historical costumes for instructional databases: faculty in consumer studies
- Three-dimensional images of proteins for instruction in marine sciences and biochemistry: faculty in marine studies and chemistry

Advanced and Emerging Technologies in Instructional Contexts has elicited interest from the humanities and sciences alike. One critical feature of the wide response is traceable to how we phrased the grant program—technology *in instructional contexts.* We promoted thinking about the instructional experience generally in order to be sensitive to the range of activities that count as teaching and learning, especially as they vary by disciplinary focus research program.

LESSONS

Two rounds of these grants have taught us some important lessons. First, less is more. It is better to award larger amounts to fewer projects than to have a more evenly distributed grant program (see also Chapter 9: Motivating Faculty). Indeed, if I were at an institution that had only $15,000 to award in instructional improvement grants, I would give it all to a single deserving project, because that would focus attention and afford maximal support to the project.

Second, research can drive teaching improvement. Research is indeed a source of ideas for the classroom, but also a source of ideas about technique. Faculty development efforts should capitalize on the fact that researchers not only know what they need to convey, but also have innovative ideas about how to do it.

Third, teams are the best PIs, even in the humanities. Large-scale grant programs foster teamwork, if only because a grant of $20,000 requires the PI to think of others to work with in order to spend that much money! Showing the humanists what the scientists have known for a long time—problem-solving that pools and coordinates expertise—is an important stimulus to collaboration across the academy.

Fourth, technology is not the same as computation. We tend to equate the two in instructional design and development, but technology is only one form of mediated delivery, and computers are only one kind of technology. Granted, most of our projects involved computation, but one of them— three-dimensional models of organs and body structures for teaching anatomy—centered on the development of plastinated organs harvested from autopsies. I still recall the discussion of this proposal in the review panel: "Is this technology?" The answer, overwhelmingly, was "yes," when we realized that the right question was, "Is this *a* technology?"

Fifth, few fully appreciate how to assess the effectiveness of instructional technology. We ask PIs to follow the results of their efforts to determine whether and how student learning changed, but this standard is very hard to implement. Not that we should all become Larry Cuban (2001) and throw up our hands in perplexity. But I think we need to take a hard look at how we decide, on empirical grounds, whether and how technologically mediated delivery works. In this task, we need to recognize that technologies will have as many backward steps as forward ones, and that a circuitous path is a helpful one.

Sixth, expect some unexpected effects. Advanced and Emerging Technologies in Instructional Contexts, although motivated by the very new, actually came to define the *very new* as a consequence. By focusing on cutting-edge technologies, the program helped establish a new class of instructional-technology activities at the university: those beyond courseware packages and requiring substantial individual and team effort. These activities have stimulated reconsideration of normal faculty development and even intellectual property owned by the faculty. The very new has become a set of activities that, I am afraid, will no longer be so in a very short time.

REFERENCE

Cuban, L. (2001). *Oversold and underused: Computers in the classroom.* Cambridge, MA: Harvard University Press.

RESOURCE

www.udel.edu/billf/~frawley.html has downloadable materials accompanying conference presentations on this subject.

47

SUPPORTING FACULTY DEVELOPMENT WITH WEBCT WORKSHOPS, SEMINARS, CONSULTATION, AND ONLINE MATERIALS

Margaret S. Anderson
University of Georgia

THE UGA WEBCT INITIATIVE

In 1997, a campus-wide group of teaching faculty evaluated and selected WebCT (Web Course Tools) as the course management system to provide web-based instructional resources for the University of Georgia. During the last five years, the Office of Instructional Support and Development (OISD) and University Computing and Networking Services, now known as Enterprise Information Technology Services (EITS), two distinct campus units reporting to the senior vice president for academic affairs, have jointly supported WebCT.

WebCT Support and Training

A WebCT support team, consisting of members from both OISD and EITS, provides campus-wide workshops, custom workshops for groups, seminars, consultation, online resources, and a listserv for questions. In addition, EITS provides applications support, and OISD focuses on instructional design support. This unique collaboration between EITS and OISD has been central to the success of WebCT at the University of Georgia.

Workshops

The OISD-EITS WebCT support team offers hands-on workshops to all faculty and teaching assistants at the University of Georgia. The following topics are included in the series of two-hour workshops:

- An Overview of WebCT
- Fundamentals for Course Designers
- Student Management

- Content Management

- Quiz Management

- Advanced Tools

- Creating and Editing Web Pages Using Netscape Composer

Participants in the overview workshop are faculty members who log in as students to a WebCT demonstration course designed by members of the joint support staff. This demonstration course contains many of the WebCT tools so that faculty can try out the tools as students, discuss how they might be used in teaching and learning, and then decide which additional workshops would be most useful for further instruction.

In the other hands-on workshops, participants start from a basic "model WebCT course," one created by support team members for use during the workshops so that the participants do not have to change their own courses. Using WebCT features and files created by support team members, faculty practice by adding elements that they are likely to want to use in their own courses. A description of these workshops can be found at https://webct.uga.edu/www/training/coursedesc.html.

Lessons Learned About Workshops

- The WebCT overview workshop is helpful.

- Workshops are more effective if all participants use the same files and perform the same operations than if they use their own materials and try to develop their own courses.

- Faculty members often cannot interrupt their daily schedules to attend all-day workshops. Therefore, several series of two-hour workshops are offered. Two-hour workshops fit attention spans and time demands better than three-hour sessions.

- Participants like hands-on workshops where they can actually try things out for themselves, and they like step-by-step instructions.

- Participants like having a floater, a member of the support staff available to answer individual questions, while the workshop instructor is presenting materials.

- Faculty members like to have handouts with workshop information to take back to their offices with them. Online materials also provide useful information.

- Workshop participants want to know whom to call for questions after the workshop, so providing contact phone numbers and email addresses is important.

Custom Workshops

Custom workshops are designed to fit the needs of a specific department or group of faculty or teaching assistants. OISD staff offer many custom workshops for participants of faculty development programs that are sponsored by OISD or for groups of teaching assistants. Since teaching assistants are future faculty members, they are an important component of faculty development activities.

Lessons Learned About Custom Workshops

When colleagues attend a workshop together, they continue to assist each other after the workshop is over.

Seminars

OISD and EITS have also sponsored brown-bag seminars as a way for faculty to demonstrate their courses and to show how they have used WebCT. Faculty like to see how their colleagues are using WebCT, and campus seminars are one way to offset the password protection that prevents them from doing so online.

Consultation

In addition to workshops and seminars, consultation is a very important part of the WebCT support structure. At UGA, it means one-on-one sessions between a faculty member and a support-team member or sessions among support-team members and groups of faculty or teaching assistants to work through design issues or technical problems. Consultation also refers to the availability of support-team members to answer individual questions by phone, email, or office visits. Faculty members often give support-team members designer access to their courses so that the team members can assist while the faculty members remain in their offices or homes. When faculty have questions, a support-team member responds as quickly as possible. Very often, several faculty have the same questions, which involve detailed explanations. In response, the WebCT support team developed an online resource of Frequently Asked Questions, Helplets, and additional information. Support-team members can refer faculty to these resources, which are available on the UGA WebCT homepage at https://webct.uga.edu. The online resources are grouped into several categories: Faculty Resources, Student Resources, About

WebCT, and Guest Resources. From the WebCT Demo Course Log-in, under Guest Resources, anyone can log in as a student to a demonstration course and explore the different features of WebCT. The Faculty Resources category contains the Frequently Asked Questions, Helplets, WebCT workshop schedule, and an item called *New to WebCT?* for faculty and teaching assistants who need information on how to begin using WebCT.

Listserv

Another component of WebCT support at UGA is the WebCT-UGA listserv, where faculty and teaching assistants can post questions, answers, or comments about WebCT. When someone posts a question to the list, either another user or someone from the support group will answer it for all members.

OUTCOMES AND RESULTS

WebCT was beta tested at UGA during the spring and summer of 1997 with around 70 volunteers. By July 1999, there were approximately 1,000 WebCT courses and 32,000 student seats, which refers to the number of students in all of the WebCT courses. One student taking three courses that used WebCT counted as three student seats. In October 2001, there were 2,618 courses, 53,521 student seats, and 28,569 unique users. In April 2002, there were 2,993 courses, 59,253 student seats, and 29,358 unique users. Some of these numbers include training courses and accounts for WebCT support staff, but they clearly indicate the popularity, growth, and acceptance of WebCT by faculty and students.

Between July 2001 and the end of March 2002, 660 faculty members, teaching assistants, and departmental support staff registered for WebCT workshops. Teaching assistants have been extremely enthusiastic about opportunities to learn WebCT. They use it in the courses they teach and provide WebCT support for the faculty they assist.

During the 1999 and 2001 spring semesters, OISD and EITS administered campus-wide WebCT surveys to faculty and students. Some of the survey results are located at https://webct.uga.edu/www/about/survey/. One of the questions not included on the web site is, "Has WebCT changed the way you teach?" Faculty responded that using WebCT improved their ability to disseminate information, to spend more class time on discussions when the information is available on the web, to communicate with students and respond to their questions, to make students more responsible for their own learning, to make students active learners, to give students opportunities to see each others' work, to give students access to grades, to make class management easier, and, last but not least, to improve their own course organization.

SUMMARY AND CONCLUSION

WebCT has been widely accepted at the University of Georgia by both faculty and students, as is evident by the large numbers of courses and accounts. Most of the faculty use WebCT to enhance their more traditional courses, although with the increased interest in distance learning, some courses are now completely online. With over 2,000 faculty members and 30,000 students, we do not have the staff to develop courses, but we do try to empower faculty and teaching assistants as they develop their own WebCT courses.

Our approach is to provide multiple forms of support: workshops, seminars, consultation, online resources, and a listserv. Some faculty are early adopters who need very little assistance, while others feel less secure and require more support. Having support-team members available to answer questions and to work with faculty has been crucial to our successful implementation of WebCT. The unique collaboration between OISD and EITS has made this support possible.

RESOURCES

Office of Instructional Support and Development (OISD): http://www.isd.uga.edu

Enterprise Information Technology Services (EITS), formerly University Computing and Networking Services (UCNS): http://www.eits.uga.edu

UGA WebCT home page: https://webct.uga.edu

UGA WebCT Faculty Resources: https://webct.uga.edu/www/faculty.html

UGA WebCT Designer Frequently Asked Questions: https://webct.uga.edu/www/faq/faqs.html

UGA WebCT Designer Helplets: https://webct.uga.edu/www/helplets/

Description of UGA WebCT Workshops: https://webct.uga.edu/www/training/coursedesc.html

UGA Faculty and Student Survey Results: https://webct.uga.edu/www/about/survey/

UGA WebCT Course Listing: https://webct.uga.edu/webct/public/show_courses.pl

UGA WebCT Support Staff: https://webct.uga.edu/www/contact/

OISD location and JRL 275 where workshops are given: http://www.eits.uga.edu/dms/oisd/

History of WebCT at UGA: https://webct.uga.edu/www/about/history.html

48

THE WEBCT SEMINAR

Chris Clark
University of Notre Dame

We began using WebCT at Notre Dame in 1998. Over a few months, a group of faculty met with representatives of the Office of Information Technologies to compare and to test various products. In the end, the faculty chose WebCT over competing products. At this writing, nearly four years later, one sixth of our faculty have an active WebCT course, and three quarters of Notre Dame students use WebCT in one or more courses.

We have provided hands-on instruction for faculty ever since adopting WebCT. Our training strategies have evolved continually over the years, and we are pleased with the results. Our teaching philosophy has always emphasized pedagogy and strategies for effective use.

One of the early questions we asked in planning WebCT classes for faculty was, "Which tools will they want to use?" Based on their perceived educational benefits, we focused on tools that enabled grading, content pages, web links, discussion, chat, and quizzes. Experience has shown these were good guesses. The only formal training we eliminated was on chat; we felt it was very easy to learn quickly, and relatively few people were using it.

Another choice we debated was whether to ask all participants to work on the same dummy course during training or to allow them to work on their own classes. We started with a standard course and then tried the custom approach. In the end, we returned to having everyone work on a copy of a set course.

Our training documents have also gone through a series of changes. The original materials were designed only for use in the workshops and were not much use afterward. We also made WebCT's corporate tutorial available, but our faculty did not seem to find it very useful. With the advent of WebCT version 3 on our campus in June 2001, the earlier documents were abandoned for a less formal approach, using an outline. That tactic has not proven satisfactory, and at this writing, we are developing our own tutorial documents. Our goal is to design the new materials for use either in a workshop or as self-teaching tools, should faculty prefer to learn on their own. We will also incorporate materials on teaching principles and effective strategies. Our training philosophy is to integrate pedagogy into how-to classes; faculty learn not only how to use WebCT but also how to use it effectively.

We have gradually built a series of single-page "cheat sheets" to help faculty through common processes, such as uploading grades from an Excel spreadsheet. These learning aids have proven very helpful. During the classes, we also hand out a number of reference sheets on topics such as copyright, use of Adobe Acrobat, and principles of graphic design, and we plan to incorporate them into the new documents. To encourage the faculty to be self-sufficient, we stress the use of WebCT's comprehensive help system.

From the start, we have not required faculty to attend training on all of the tools. However, we do list our introductory class as a prerequisite for each of the five succeeding sessions. The sessions were set up in small, efficient blocks, allowing faculty to learn only the tools in which they were interested.

The popularity of the sessions varies. The introduction is always the most well subscribed, usually followed by the grade-book and information-sharing sessions. Our current six-class sequence spans 12 hours and includes:

- Course Setup and Maintenance—interface, student database, course appearance, and backups (2 hours)
- Sharing Information—add HTML documents, a syllabus, and web links (1.5 hours)
- Organizing Content—create a content module integrating WebCT tools with HTML documents (2 hours)
- Conducting Online Discussions (1.5 hours)
- Creating a Quiz or Survey (3 hours)
- Posting Grades (2 hours)

Our most popular training series, without a doubt, was the WebCT Seminar held over fall break in the year 2000. Nearly 30 faculty registered, and 10 of them took all six classes. Normally, we have one presenter in our classes, but when class groups are larger than ten or 12, we always enlist help. Half of the classes that week required such helpers.

In order to create a greater sense of continuity, the seminar followed a more unified approach than earlier class series had taken. Over the three days of the seminar, there was a class each morning and afternoon; between sessions, everyone had plenty of time for work on his or her own class. Faculty were encouraged to think of the week as a single event, although they were not expected to attend all sessions. On the first day, everyone was treated to a box lunch. This amenity may not seem important, but sharing a meal early in the week seemed to put everyone at ease, and the free lunch served as a small incentive that encouraged people to register for the seminar.

Each participant received a notebook with the handouts for all of the sessions, not just the ones for which they had registered. The notebooks also contained articles on good pedagogy and teaching strategies. One strategy faculty were encouraged to explore was the WebQuest, a technique developed at San Diego State University by Bernie Dodge and Tom March (http://webquest.sdsu.edu/). In their words, "A WebQuest is an inquiry-oriented activity in which some or all of the information that learners interact with comes from resources on the Internet."

Each session highlighted one or two of Chickering and Gamson's (1987) "seven principles for good practice in undergraduate education." Faculty were frequently encouraged to share their plans and ideas for WebCT courses with the rest of the group.

The WebCT Seminar was a tremendous success, as evidenced both by formal evaluations and word of mouth. A large number of people learned a great deal about how to use WebCT well. Materials developed for the seminar notebook have been used repeatedly since that time, and the schedule formulated for that week set the pattern for all future series of classes. The hours spent planning and organizing the seminar were very well spent.

REFERENCE

Chickering, A. W., & Gamson, Z. (1987). Seven principles for good practice in undergraduate education. *AAHE Bulletin, 39* (7) 3–7.

RESOURCES

Notre Dame WebCT page: http://www.nd.edu/~webct

WebCT seminar page (dated): http://www.nd.edu/~edtech/seminar/

49

AGENDA FOR A SUCCESSFUL FACULTY WORKSHOP

David G. Brown
Wake Forest University

Our International Center for Computer-Enhanced Learning has conducted six-hour workshops for faculty wishing to use technology in their courses at more than a dozen universities. Agenda is always a problem. Participants arrive with different experiences and expectations.

All want to strengthen their courses by incorporating technology. Where to start is the challenge. Logically, one should start by asking, "What is it you want to do?" and "On what pedagogy is your strategy based?" We have, however, encountered two problems with this approach. First, few workshop participants arrive knowing what they want to do or what to say when asked. Second, faculty are most comfortable starting with the distinctive theories of their own disciplines, and most workshops include many disciplines. Economists, for example, redesign their courses using concepts such as marginal analysis, cost-benefit, and comparative advantage. For them, Bloom's taxonomy, Chickering and Gamson's seven practices of good teaching, and Gardner's way of knowing are interesting but not central. They become impatient and disinterested if too much time is spent explaining theories from other disciplines.

Another place to start is with the technology. Most participants have come expecting to learn what technology they will need to redesign their course. They want to learn what technology can do for them. They want to learn PowerPoint, spreadsheet construction, techniques for conducting virtual discussions—the specifics. Again, however, we have encountered two problems with this approach. First, participants arrive with different proficiencies, different levels of experience, and the need to learn different programs. Second, many university professors resist and should resist learning technologies before they have decided whether they will be useful.

The format that works best in most circumstances starts with strategy. We have asked 150 technology-using professors from diverse disciplines at over 40 universities to describe what they have done to improve their courses with technology. What have they been able to improve? What objectives have they sought to achieve with technology?

Our workshop now starts with answers to these questions from the "early adopters." We start from the premise that most participants will adopt many of these same strategies after they contemplate their own theories and learn how to use relevant software. Participants are asked to accept this working premise, even as they are promised that, at the end of the day, they will have an opportunity to rethink whether the premise works for them.

Five strategies emerge from the early adopters' reports. They turned to technology as a means to increase the quality and quantity of communication and interaction with and among their students. They sought out technological means to enable more teamwork and collaboration among students. Before using technology, they had found that students become more engaged when controversy is highlighted, so they looked for ways that technology could facilitate controversy and debate. They were turning to technology in order to customize their guidance of individual students according to their abilities, interests, and learning styles. Finally, they use technology in order to increase student contact with practitioners and/or other academics. In summary, early adopters sought additional means to enhance communication, teamwork, controversy, customization, and consultants through technology.

Mini-lectures filled with examples are given on each topic. For example, the lecture on communication and interaction will include a discussion of the use of email and "muddiest point" emails to the instructor prior to lecture, of student profiles and pictures posted on a course web page, and of the one-minute quiz during class. After the mini-lecture on communication and interaction, break-out groups share specific ways, both with and without computer technology, that they increase communication and interaction in their own classes.

After all five strategies are covered and the related break-out groups have met, participants are shown how easy it is to use popular software products: for example, to post course materials on the web via a Course Management System, to set up email groups for each class, to use the comment function within Microsoft Word, and to incorporate URL citations and links in a syllabus.

Toward the end of the workshop, participants are paired, and each indicates how he or she plans to augment a course. During this personal planning session, participants are urged to reconsider the workshop's premises in relation to their own objectives and theories. Usually, most participants are then willing to share their plans and ideas with others.

The feedback we've received from these workshops has been tremendously positive.

SUGGESTED READINGS

Brown, D. G. (Ed.). (2001). *Interactive learning: Vignettes from America's most wired campuses.* Bolton, MA: Anker.

Brown, D. G., McCray, G., Runde, C., & Schweizer, H. (2002). *Using technology in learner-centered education: Proven strategies for teaching and learning.* Boston, MA: Allyn and Bacon.

50

INNOVATIVE FACULTY DEVELOPMENT PROGRAMS AT IUPUI'S CENTER FOR TEACHING AND LEARNING

Elizabeth Rubens
Indiana University-Purdue University Indianapolis

Indiana University-Purdue University Indianapolis's (IUPUI) Center for Teaching and Learning is continually seeking to provide innovative programming for faculty to strengthen their expertise in effective pedagogy and the application of instructional technology. The center opened its doors in 1995 as a result of a partnership between Academic Affairs, University Information Technology Services, and University Library. Since that time, it has grown from what was initially a center solely devoted to technology consultation and training to an office that provides an entire suite of services under the umbrella of the office for professional development. Led by Nancy Chism, associate vice chancellor for professional development and associate dean of the faculties, the office now also provides programs in organizational development, instructional design and development, information resources, copyright management, multicultural faculty development, associate faculty development, an office for women, and grant writing and research. Faculty are now able to access this set of holistic services in one convenient location.

Although the office sponsors many programs, three have been developed to meet the specific needs of IUPUI faculty and are highlighted here.

THE GATEWAY PROGRAM

The Gateway Program is designed to improve the quality of students' experiences in their introductory courses. Faculty, staff, and students involved in beginning courses have met over a period of two years to discuss barriers to student success. As a result, many new policies, programs, course innovations, and services were put into place. Major activities have included:

Forums. Opportunities for Gateway instructors, students, and others within the IUPUI community to talk about promising practices or policy changes that can improve student success in Gateway courses were convened by the Gateway Group. Four forums, each repeated once, have been held each academic year. Ideas generated by the forums and other exchanges have been prioritized for action and pursued by appropriate groups.

Gateway grants. This program has funded over 30 faculty teams engaged in inquiry, development of innovative practice, the integration of block scheduling, and dissemination of best practices in Gateway courses. In addition, special funds have been awarded for orientation activities, critical inquiry, structured learning, and assessment in Gateway courses.

Web forum. A web forum containing a database of best practices, research results, questions, and ideas contributed by faculty can be searched by topic.

In addition to these main activities, regular meetings are held with the departments that offer Gateway courses to assess their progress, establish community within the instructional teams for these courses, and offer support services. An annual retreat and periodic town halls on retention along with an ongoing program of instructional consultation available to Gateway instructors are also available.

This program earned the prestigious Hesburgh Award in spring 2002 and has seeded the development of many promising new initiatives.

DIALOGUES FOR FIRST-YEAR STUDENT SUCCESS

Dialogues for First-Year Student Success also targets the needs of faculty who teach introductory courses. The series is composed of eight three-hour modules designed to give both part- and full-time faculty an opportunity to discuss strategies that can be critical to the success of engaging first-year students. Modules include Learning Theory, Course and Syllabus Design, Inclusive Teaching, Classroom Management, Active Learning, Assessment Strategies, and Student Support and Technology Resources.

The modules combine presentations by center staff, active exercises designed to allow faculty to experiment with new strategies, and plenty of opportunity for discussion among participants. Faculty have reported that they value the time to talk with colleagues from other disciplines about what works with beginning students. Additionally, many faculty—whether they are teaching for the first time or have taught for many years—are encouraged to learn about university resources that support their work with students.

Center staff are now developing a modular Dialogues Series, conducted completely online, to allow faculty who are unable to schedule enough time to come to the center to participate in all eight modules.

TECH CAMPS

Another example of IUPUI's creative approach to faculty development has been the Tech Camps developed under the leadership of Rhett McDaniel, program leader for Instructional Technologies within the Center for Teaching and Learning. Center staff looked for a way to better engage faculty who are often prevented from taking part in technology training because of multiple demands on their time and some trepidation about learning new technology skills. The staff tried to design an experience that would allow faculty time to play with the technology in a focused, yet relaxed fashion.

As a result, a series of four Tech Camps were born. Each listed a series of technology skill objectives and provided an opportunity for faculty to walk away with tangible products as a result of their three or four days of camp experience. However, what might have been just another technology training session was transformed by the creativity of the instructional technologies staff. Faculty were invited to immerse themselves in featured themes carried throughout the sessions that were designed to be fun and engaging.

The first camp, set up in a conference room in the library, featured a simulated outdoor campground, complete with a tent and campfire. Outdoor sound effects, a collection of wildlife and camp food added to the ambiance. Faculty labored to learn the basics of IU's course management software, Oncourse, and to create an online syllabus, a basic PowerPoint presentation, an electronic conference, and an online quiz. As they mastered these skills, they competed for merit badges, composed camp songs, and learned the camp pledge. Staff were initially worried that these lighthearted attempts at training might not be well received, but their fears were soon put to rest. Faculty loved the experience, and the humor and laid-back attitude allowed everyone to relax and genuinely enjoy the experience of learning new skills. At the final camp gathering, faculty showcased their beginning work on their online courses. The camp alumni are now comfortable coming to the center when they have an idea they would like to explore or when they need assistance in solving a problem.

Because of the success of this experience, three additional camps were created with new themes. Faculty visited a winter ski lodge in Tech Camp II and learned basic web page layout. In Tech Camp III, they took a simulated cruise and learned to create digital audio and video clips to enhance their online courses. Tech Camp IV featured a mock Olympics. As faculty learned basic authoring skills with Macromedia's Director software, they competed for medals. Participants had their own digital pictures placed on celebratory Wheaties boxes that they took home as souvenirs of the Olympic games.

The camaraderie that these experiences have generated has proved to center staff that the injection of fun and humor into faculty development has been a key ingredient in the success of its programs.

RESOURCE

Office for Professional Development web site: http://www.opd.iupui.edu

51

TEACHING ASSISTANTS: TEACHING COMPETENCIES OF FUTURE FACULTY THROUGH TECHNOLOGY

Kathleen S. Smith
University of Georgia

Increasingly, teaching assistant (TA) program directors have been introducing technology to graduate students to facilitate the preparation and presentation of their teaching materials. This paradigm shift challenges long-held instructional traditions and may help to identify the pedagogical structures that most benefit from technology (Liberman & Reuter, 1996). This challenge to examine how we approach teaching and learning also acknowledges that future faculty will have to address an instructional environment that includes larger classes, more diverse students, and accessing and managing ever larger amounts of information at a reasonable cost (Marchionini, 1995). In addition, since "population growth is outpacing the world's capacity to give people access to universities" (Daniel, 1997), educational technology may replace the traditional concept of a campus environment for many.

Faculty development offices are in a unique position to respond to this changing instructional environment. Since significant growth in funding for education is not predicted, consolidating and coordinating available resources will be necessary (Weller, 1993). Faculty development offices can provide cost-effective access to new uses of technology in education, technical expertise, and assistance in meshing educational objectives with appropriate teaching tools (Everley & Smith, 1996). Helping graduate assistants who are preparing for academic careers to develop teaching competencies (Smith & Simpson, 1995) that reflect this environment is the 21st century challenge for faculty development specialists.

This chapter describes how instructional technology support at the University of Georgia (UGA) facilitates the professional development of graduate teaching and laboratory assistants in a rapidly changing instructional environment. Technological support at UGA interrelates pedagogy and technology and attempts to model how technology may improve teaching competencies and learning outcomes. UGA's Simpson and Smith (1993) and Smith and Simpson (1995) sought the expert opinion of leaders in teaching assistant and faculty development programs to validate teaching competencies as they apply to the instructional role (http://www.isd.uga.edu/teaching_ assistant/tahandbook/department.html). In the early 1990s, the Office of Instructional Support and Development (OISD) and TAs representing a variety of disciplines designed a new TA-support program. It includes the introduction of instructional technologies that enhance teaching competencies and provides a place to experiment with state-of-the-art equipment, a forum for discussing new technology, and the professional staff to help mesh technology with pedagogical objectives. The technology initiative offers technical and professional expertise during the development, implementation, evaluation, and adaptation of technology to meet pedagogical goals.

Development

One of the strengths of a centralized instructional technology support program for TAs is that it can provide a learning environment not available at the departmental level. The academic year begins with a required orientation for all new graduate teaching and laboratory assistants, which apprises them of UGA support services to develop teaching skills. A series of semester-long teaching seminars are required for all inexperienced TAs and LAs before they can be considered for teaching duties. These seminars model uses of technology and provide students an opportunity to develop their skills in using hardware and identifying useful technology. In addition, a group of outstanding TAs serving as mentors works with OISD for the academic year to develop their own use of technology and to share strategies with departmental TAs. These mentors explore the use of technology as they create teaching materials, portfolios, job talks, and online professional portfolios. OISD staff also meet with individuals or groups in the Instructional Development Laboratory (IDL) or the Instructional Development Classroom (IDC) to design programs or to practice using equipment. The IDL is equipped with state-of-the-art computers. An extensive resource file of articles and texts on the educational use of technology is also available. The IDC has the most recent presentation equipment in a classroom setting. Such resources are rarely available at the departmental level for graduate teaching and laboratory assistants.

The OISD also provides media design at a reduced rate for TAs who do not have the time or inclination to develop materials. It delivers equipment to classrooms and provides technical backup for the equipment. This kind of centrally supported computer environment can provide a cost-effective means to experiment with strategies and equipment and to develop projects using technology in teaching.

OISD staff provide technical expertise, an environment for sharing and critiquing uses of technology, and a mechanism to build on the next instructional technology development to improve teaching and learning. Teaching and laboratory assistants work with OISD staff on new applications as technology changes and have conducted workshops in cooperation with OISD to model their responses to these changes.

Initial efforts by graduate assistants often lead the way for more seasoned department members to consider classroom technology. For example, an English TA, who learned HTML through an OISD workshop, designed and taught a completely web-based English 101 course that was a model for later web-based courses. Many TAs are now developing WebCT courses for faculty use. This kind of technical experience has become increasingly important in graduate preparation and has helped graduates as they move into the faculty job market and academic positions.

Challenges

One difficulty in preparing TAs involves introducing new technology in the classroom. Even technically experienced teaching and laboratory assistants find it daunting to try to get equipment up and running in front of students. In an attempt to reduce technical failures, TAs may reserve the IDC to practice the use of new equipment or to test the feasibility of a particular software package. Individual classes also may be scheduled in the IDC for a specific presentation using the equipment. OISD provides technical expertise for all classes equipped with technology.

Another challenge in developing instructional technology has been the lack of time or departmental staff to develop materials or to maintain data banks. OISD provides ongoing support by maintaining databases and video libraries. In addition, TAs may request that OISD staff design media for them at a reduced cost.

Evaluation

OISD provides a series of credit classes, workshops, and seminars sponsored by TAs as a forum for discussing technology. TAs have also led workshops on graphic design, distance learning, and web-based teaching tools. These seminars attract TAs interested in the latest applications of technology to teaching as well as those who are just beginning to use technology.

The ultimate goal in evaluating the use of technology in teaching is to determine whether more learning occurred. Considering the application of technology within the framework of the teaching competencies identified by national experts in TA support and development has been essential in ensuring that the choice of method is driven by pedagogical need and learning outcomes.

Adaptation

As new technologies establish a record of improving teaching and student learning, OISD informs others on campus through workshops, interest groups, a listserv discussion, and such publications as the *TA Newsletter* and *Teaching at UGA*. Although many TAs can use existing technical resources, strategies for a particular course must often be adapted. OISD staff consult on augmenting course design with technology.

SUMMARY

The rapidly changing instructional frontier requires that those involved in TA-support programs constantly assess where they have been, what they are presently doing, and where they are going. The OISD encourages teaching assistants to consider the use of technology early in their graduate teaching experience. They have the opportunity to develop more sophisticated uses of technology as they develop their teaching strategies. Many TAs are now working on web educational tools and beginning to explore projects in distance education. Central faculty development offices will become increasingly important in funding and supporting the development, application, evaluation, and adaptation of these efforts because of the cost of maintaining state-of-the-art equipment and the time involved in staying abreast of new technological applications.

REFERENCES

Daniel, J. S. (1997, July/August). Why universities need technology strategies. *Change*, 11–17.

Everley, M. L., & Smith, J. (1996). Making the transition from soft to hard funding: The politics of institutionalizing instructional development programs. In L. Richlin (Ed.), *To improve the academy: Vol. 15. Resources for faculty, instructional, and organizational development* (pp. 209–230). Stillwater, OK: New Forums Press.

Liberman, D. A., & Reuter, J. (1996). Designing, implementing and assessing a university technology-pedagogy institute. In L. Richlin (Ed.), *To improve the academy: Vol. 15. Resources for faculty, instructional, and organizational development* (pp. 231–250). Stillwater, OK: New Forums Press.

Marchionini, G. (1995). The costs of educational technology: A framework for assessing change. In H. Maurer (Ed.), *Educational multimedia and hypermedia, 1995, Proceedings of Ed-Media 95-World Conference on Educational Multimedia and Hypermedia* (pp. 33–38). Charlottesville, VA: Association for the Advancement of Computing in Education.

Simpson, R. D., & Smith, K. S. (1993). Validating teaching competencies for graduate teaching assistants: A national study using the Delphi method. *Innovative Higher Education, 18* (2), 133–146.

Smith, K. S., & Simpson, R. D. (1995). Validating teaching competencies for faculty members in higher education: A national study using the Delphi method. *Innovative Higher Education, 19* (3), 223–133.

Weller, L. D. (1993). Putting instructional technology to use: A cost-effective approach to satellite-center teaching. *Eighteenth International Conference on Improving University Teaching* (pp. 223–131).

52

THE GOVERNOR'S TEACHING FELLOWS PROGRAM SERVING FACULTY IN THE STATE OF GEORGIA

Patricia Kalivoda and William K. Jackson
University of Georgia

The Governor's Teaching Fellows (GTF) program is a statewide faculty-development program administered by the Office of Instructional Support and Development (OISD) and the Institute of Higher Education (IHE) at the University of Georgia (UGA).

HOW THE PROGRAM STARTED

The GTF program was established in 1995 by the Honorable Zell Miller, currently a U.S. senator and formerly governor of Georgia (1990–1998), to provide the state's higher education faculty "with expanded opportunities for developing important teaching skills. Governor Miller envisioned that this program would address faculty members' pressing need to use emerging technologies, instructional tools that are becoming increasingly important for learning in today's society" (IHE, 1995).

GTF "came about as a result of discussions during the early 1990s about the need for faculty development at all institutions of higher learning—both public and independent—in Georgia. In 1979, a large and comprehensive model for faculty development had been initiated at UGA's OISD. As new and potentially powerful instructional technologies emerged, OISD developed programs designed to facilitate the investigation and use of these technologies by UGA faculty members. The experience and the success of this initiative served as the impetus for the design of the GTF program to extend many of the faculty development opportunities available at UGA to faculty members throughout the state" (IHE, 1995). Faculty from OISD and UGA's IHE, founded in 1964 with service to the State as part of its mission, collaborated to shape and to implement the program that Governor Miller envisioned.

THE PARTICIPANTS

The GTF program is "designed for faculty members who teach at accredited public or private colleges or universities in the state of Georgia. Participants are selected on the basis of their teaching experience, on their interest in continuing instructional and professional development, on their ability to have an impact on their own campus, and on a strong commitment by their home institution for release time and other forms of support for the duration of their participation in the program" (IHE, 1995). To date, over 175 faculty members representing over 60 disciplines and close to 50 different institutions have participated in the program.

PROGRAM FORMAT

There are three options for participation in the GTF program: the Academic-Year Symposia program, the Summer Symposium program, and the Academic Year in Residence program. Most faculty members participate in either the Academic-Year Symposia or the Summer Symposium, which is a ten-day, condensed version of the Academic-Year Symposia program.

The Academic-Year Symposia program "allows participants to attend three-day symposia held six or seven times over the academic year, while also engaging in instructional improvement projects on their home campuses. The symposia include a combination of structured instructional and faculty development activities as well as self-directed activities designed to meet individual needs. Participants receive a stipend for each day of full participation on campus. Meals, lodging, and travel expenses are provided by the GTF program" (IHE, 1995).

PROGRAM CONTENT

From the beginning, the GTF program has striven for a balance between purely instructional technology-related topics and more general pedagogical topics. Feedback from participants indicates that this balance is one of the program's strengths. General pedagogical topics addressed include developing student listening skills; student learning styles; understanding and using wait-time in questioning; dealing with difficult classroom problems; test construction; measuring teaching effectiveness; and classroom assessment techniques.

The instructional technology topics have evolved with the technology. In the first year (1995–1996), technology topics included equipping a state-of-the-art classroom; a demonstration of Adam software; applying instructional technology to science and humanities classrooms; HTML; and GSAMS

(Georgia's Statewide Academic and Medical System), Georgia's network of distance-learning classrooms using a two-way, interactive, compressed video system that transmits signals over existing telephone lines. (To learn more about GSAMS, see http://gsams.gagta.com/v3/master.html.)

By 1997, instructional technology sessions had changed. No longer were sessions provided on learning HTML code. Now, they focused on using a web editor to prepare instructional materials. In addition, the first sessions on web-based course-management software were offered. WebCT was the course-management tool demonstrated, because the Georgia university system supported it state-wide. (Learn more about WebCT at http://www.webct.com/.)

In the early years, numerous sessions were held on how to develop Power-Point presentations. Today, sessions focus less on creating a basic presentation and more on how to incorporate PowerPoint in WebCT or how to incorporate images, sound, and web links. Streaming media, use of digital whiteboard technologies, such as Mimio (see http://www.mimio.com), and instructional applications for PDA are other popular topics for today's fellows.

INSTRUCTIONAL TECHNOLOGY HARDWARE SUPPORT FOR PARTICIPANTS

In addition to exposure and training on various software applications, the GTF program also provides hardware support. In the first year, the program could offer computer-lab space only when the participants were on the UGA campus. In subsequent years, the price of laptops dropped, and the GTF program was able to purchase enough laptops to lend to participants. In 2001, the GTF program purchased iPAQ pocket-PCs for each of the participants, which they can keep permanently. (Learn more about iPAQ technology at http://www.compaq.com/products/iPAQ/.) In 2002, a comprehensive equipment loan program similar to that available to UGA faculty members was developed for both current and past participants in the GTF program.

INSTRUCTIONAL CONSULTATION SUPPORT FOR PARTICIPANTS

The GTF program aims to provide participants access to many of the faculty-development opportunities routinely available to members of the UGA faculty. Instructional design and technology specialists are available in OISD to assist UGA faculty in the use of technologies for instructional purposes. These specialists are available to the GTF participants for both group presentations and individual consultations. Each time the fellows come to campus, these specialists give presentations to the group on emerging technologies, and open lab periods are included in each program to allow one-on-one interactions with the specialists and other OISD technical staff members.

SELECTED OUTCOMES OF THE GOVERNOR'S TEACHING FELLOWS PROGRAM

In the seven years that the GTF program has been serving the instructional needs of the faculty of Georgia's colleges and universities, a number of positive outcomes have accrued, including:

- a statewide community of scholars who engage in a collegial dialogue about teaching

- increased use of Georgia's distance-learning network, GSAMS, by GTF participants

- the opportunity to experience and experiment with new instructional tools for application in the classroom

- a place to explore and to construct new courseware in the instructional development laboratory

- instructional and faculty-development projects by participants to enhance teaching and learning on their home campuses (sample projects may be seen at http://www.uga.edu/ihe/GTF.html#6)

SUMMARY

The far-reaching impact of the GTF program is rooted in its three primary core values, which shape its activities: 1) that teaching is an ongoing process of scholarly inquiry; 2) that faculty members need opportunities to talk about teaching in a scholarly way; and 3) that faculty members need a low-stress, high-support environment in which to experiment with emerging instructional technologies.

REFERENCE

Institute of Higher Education. (1995). *Governor's teaching fellowship program.* Retrieved May 15, 2002, from http://www.uga.edu/ihe/GTF.html

53

REPORT FROM THE TRENCHES: FACULTY DEVELOPMENT THROUGH A SUCCESSFUL GRASSROOTS CAMPAIGN

George H. Watson
University of Delaware

The Institute for Transforming Undergraduate Education (ITUE) was established at the University of Delaware (UD) in 1997 by a group of faculty members who were interested in making the undergraduate learning experience more student-centered and technology-empowered. The National Science Foundation program on Institution-Wide Reform of Undergraduate Education initially funded this endeavor, following on funded projects for the development of problem-based learning (PBL) in introductory science classes. ITUE was established to expand the use of active-learning strategies and the effective use of technology in instruction through course design and faculty development. Unwavering administrative support and encouragement helped to achieve these overarching goals, but faculty members, all teaching undergraduate courses in the trenches, launched this grassroots effort to transform teaching. Some elements of our successful faculty development program and the lessons that we learned may be relevant to efforts on your campus.

Although our ITUE experience was a grassroots effort, many features could be adapted by centers for teaching excellence or learning and technology. These centers abound on campuses and play an essential role in faculty development and improving students' learning opportunities. By partnering with our center for teaching, learning, and technology, we strengthened our program. The purview of traditional faculty development frequently extends broadly from orientation and training of graduate teaching assistants to oversight of instructional improvement grants and from consulting with and counseling individual faculty members to evaluating and assessing learning across the entire campus. Seldom is the institutional enterprise afforded the opportunity to focus on one aspect of improved student learning. On the other hand, technology centers sometimes miss the link between technology and improved learning. The key to a strong faculty technology development program is a core group of energized faculty, committed to transforming learning, no matter what group on campus initially brings them together.

RELYING ON A FACULTY PERSPECTIVE

In Chapter 56, some of the factors responsible for ITUE's success are identified. As ITUE leaders were faculty members, their perspective was fully represented in program planning. I must admit that in the back of my mind I was always asking myself how my colleagues in physics and engineering would respond to our workshop announcements and invitations, our web site and promotional materials, our schedule of events and activities, and, finally, the program's design and delivery. Each member of the ITUE team had a similar constituency, which helped us to keep it real and relevant to the needs of faculty members also working in the trenches. We considered the following questions important to the program's success and had immediate access to the faculty perspective:

- How much supplemental funding should be made available?
- How could we best recognize and reward participants?
- How much investment of time could we invite?
- What outcomes could we expect in return?

An important advantage of a faculty-led effort is its credibility to other practitioners in the classroom. ITUE leaders are role models who have successfully made the transition from lectures to a student-centered format. They have also embraced and incorporated technology into their teaching. "As much as one can be convinced intellectually that moving to an approach such as problem-based learning is pedagogically sound and desirable, taking that first step away from the lectern and surrendering even some of the responsibility for learning can be unnerving" (Watson & Groh, 2001). Having available colleagues who have successfully navigated the transition and mastered the new strategies can help alleviate the anxieties of novices.

Early in the program, ITUE participants were given ample opportunity to discuss their courses and the approaches that they were already exploring. They were also asked to identify and to articulate their course objectives for student learning, content mastery, and skill development. Following this essential step, they were encouraged to reflect on how a transformation in the use of active learning and technology might satisfy those objectives. After faculty have articulated and reflected on their objectives, they are then poised and motivated to reform their teaching.

RESPONDING TO CHANGE

As a faculty-led, faculty-delivered enterprise, our program could be expediently changed and maneuvered from one opportunity to another and around barriers as they appeared. Although we always had an administrative adviser, we were generally afforded broad flexibility in designing and delivering our programs as we saw fit. By focusing on faculty development and course transformation within the existing curricular structure, we avoided the delays and frustrations associated with official curricular revisions that would have required approval from curriculum committees, faculty senates, and administrative leaders.

ITUE's initial focus was on active learning and web enhancement. When we launched a major project to expand PBL into teacher preparation and the social sciences, funded by the Pew Charitable Trusts and matching commitments from the university, we were able to respond quickly, develop a sharp focus, and provide additional support to associated faculty members. The ITUE leadership team added new members to broaden our disciplinary base. They were selected from ITUE fellows who had interacted positively with team members and successfully completed course-transformation projects. As UD shifted toward WebCT as a course-management system, we shifted our focus from developing stand-alone web sites to embracing the new platform's communication tools for enhancing collaborations among our students.

PARTNERING FOR SUCCESS

Our partnership with UD's teaching, learning, and technology center (Practical Resources for Educators Seeking Effective New Technologies, PRESENT) has created a program for educational reform that is sustainable and cost-effective. PRESENT was instituted in 1997 by Information Technologies/ User Services, which reports to the vice president for information technologies. The partnership between ITUE faculty leaders and IT staff has been critical to the effective infusion of technology into our classrooms and happened at the grassroots level, as staff and faculty joined forces in common cause (de Vry & Watson, 2003).

From the beginning, ITUE recognized technology's potential to help to transform learning and made it a key component of its training sessions. ITUE generates an informed and inspired group of faculty via its workshops and individual mentoring, and ITUE fellows are primed to embrace technology in achieving their learning objectives. However, ITUE leaders have limited time for in-depth technical assistance and follow-up support. Sustained technical support by PRESENT staff fills this gap and ensures the expedient transformation of ideas into finished course materials, empowering motivated faculty to improve learning by applying technology as appropriate.

PRESENT staff members assist in presenting the technology portion of the ITUE workshops, regularly teaching side-by-side with ITUE leaders. They also attend the PBL sessions so that they can reinforce ITUE-advocated teaching strategies during their work with ITUE fellows. Staff members are available to consult and to provide sustained support of both technology and active-learning strategies. PRESENT's year-round seminars demonstrate ways to apply technology to PBL.

MEETING FACULTY WHERE THEY ARE

The inaugural ITUE session included morning sessions exploring active-learning strategies and afternoons in computer labs exploring the use of technology. This two-pronged approach has continued over the past five years and accounts for much of its success. At the outset, faculty members of two different persuasions were drawn to participate as ITUE fellows: those interested in exploring active learning and those interested in using the web in their teaching. The convergence of interests during the week was quite noticeable. "Those coming primarily for the technology portion . . . had their eyes opened to the possibility of PBL and other active learning strategies. Those coming primarily for PBL saw how the Web can be used to facilitate student learning in their courses and were empowered both to design problems with rich online resources and to publish them on the Web for their students" (Watson & Groh, 2001).

Successful faculty development sessions draw on faculty interests. Although a cynic might call our approach "bait and switch," we feel strongly that our sessions should have something for everyone. Mixing faculty with different experiences within the two categories cited above is an excellent way to generate enthusiastic interactions and genuine peer-mentoring opportunities. We also believe that technology training devoid of active-learning strategies misses a perfect opportunity to engage faculty on what really matters— the improved learning of their students.

If you are responsible for designing and delivering technology development at your campus, take a hard look at your faculty. Is a nucleus using a common technique with great success? Is the technique something that would be of benefit regardless of academic discipline? Can it be incorporated into the technology training in a seamless way? Do the faculty members have the commitment to the technique and the enthusiasm for mentoring others? At the UD, a handful of science faculty who were developing PBL at the introductory level provided the catalyst for change. I suggest that you also identify a group on your campus who would serve well as partners in expanding your faculty development program and creating fresh and exciting opportunities.

ACKNOWLEDGMENTS

The success of ITUE hinges on its faculty leaders, particularly the founding leaders who continue to embrace its mission: Deborah Allen, Barbara Duch, Susan Groh, and Hal White. Also of critical importance are the support and contributions of Paul Hyde and Janet de Vry in User Services at the University of Delaware.

REFERENCES

de Vry, J. R., & Watson, G. H. (2003). *University of Delaware's faculty-IT partnership: Educational transformation through teamwork.* Available: http://ts.mivu.org

Watson, G. H., & Groh, S. E. (2001). Faculty mentoring faculty: The Institute for Transforming Undergraduate Education. In B. J. Duch, S. E. Groh, & D. E. Allen (Eds.), *The power of problem-based learning* (pp. 13-25). Sterling, VA: Stylus.

RESOURCES

Institute for Transforming Undergraduate Education: http://www.udel.edu/inst.

The PRESENT, a teaching, learning, and technology center at the University of Delaware: http://www.udel.edu/present.

54

TRAINING AND SUPPORT FOR WEB-ENHANCED INSTRUCTION

Nick Laudato, Restiani Andriati, and Daniel Wilson
University of Pittsburgh

For four years, CourseInfo/Blackboard has been an important tool, supporting faculty in their efforts to use the web to enhance instruction at the University of Pittsburgh. This paper reviews the centralized training, staff support, technologies, and facilities dedicated to assisting faculty to improve instruction and learning.

INTRODUCTION

The University of Pittsburgh selected and implemented the CourseInfo instructional management system in 1998. After just two years, nearly one half of the University's student population of approximately 32,000 was actively using CourseInfo. Upgrades to Blackboard 5 in 2001 and 5.5 in 2002 brought additional waves of faculty users.

Figure 54.1

CourseInfo/Blackboard Course Sections by Academic Year
(Estimate for 2003)

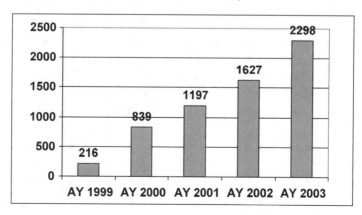

Blackboard currently serves faculty in all 20 of the university's academic centers, including its 16 schools and four regional campuses. Pitt's implementation is jointly managed by the Center for Instructional Development and Distance Education (CIDDE) and Computing Services and Systems Development (CSSD). CIDDE is responsible for training and supporting faculty and administering the Blackboard software; CSSD is the university's centralized computing group and is responsible for managing the servers, integrating with back office systems, and supporting student access.

CIDDE is a centralized academic support unit dedicated to the pursuit of instructional excellence. CIDDE assists schools and departments in designing and developing curricula and course materials, expanding access to academic programs, facilitating distance education, and supporting noninstructional and community activities in areas where its specialized expertise is required. The staff of CIDDE includes professional instructional designers, instructional technologists, graphic artists, document designers, photographers, video producers, systems analysts and programmers, classroom engineers, media specialists, and administrative and support staff.

To support the university's web-enhanced instructional efforts, CIDDE has evolved an integrated set of support services, including a rich variety of training opportunities, online communication and reference resources, instructional and technical consulting services, and a multimedia instructional development lab.

Training

CourseInfo was implemented as a pilot program in September 1998. To optimize conditions for the success of the pilot, the number of participants was limited to 20 faculty members, and a comprehensive training program was developed and implemented in the summer of 1998 under the auspices of the Summer Instructional Development Institute (SIDI). The institute focused on the application of instructional technologies to enhance learning by increasing opportunities for active and collaborative learning.

The SIDI CourseInfo training took the form of a five-day program, designed by a team of instructional designers and instructional technologists and supplemented by other CIDDE and university professionals. The training program used CourseInfo to teach CourseInfo, enrolling each faculty trainee into a special support course. This meta-course served as an exemplar of CourseInfo structure and concepts and as a repository of training and reference material. Completion of the five-day program was a prerequisite for participation in the pilot. The program included the following modules:

- Basic Web Concepts
- CourseInfo from the Student's Perspective
- Instructional Design Model and Process
- CourseInfo Content Creation
- CourseInfo Administration and Course Management
- CourseInfo Testing and Grade Book Functions
- Using Microsoft Word to Create HTML
- Virus Prevention
- Using Microsoft PowerPoint in Web-Enhanced Courses
- Designing and Acquiring Images in Web-Enhanced Courses
- Using Audio and Video in Web-Enhanced Courses
- Copyright and Legal Issues

An important factor contributing to the success of the CourseInfo training is the concept of a course template, created by CIDDE instructional technologists and instructional designers. Instead of starting with an empty course shell, faculty were provided with a course shell containing components that reflected the instructional design model used as the basis of the training program. For example, the template course defined a standard structure for the "Course Information" area, including an introductory document, course goals, class meeting times, course description, and rationale. The "Course Documents" area implemented a series of folders for each course module. Each folder contained documents for an introduction, learning objectives, lecture notes, assignments, and quizzes. The template reinforced the instructional design model and helped faculty arrange and organize their material in CourseInfo, providing students with a consistent structure when they moved from one course to another.

After a successful pilot term, faculty interest in using CourseInfo increased dramatically and demand threatened to exceed the capacity to effectively support the service. The policy of requiring training as a prerequisite to using CourseInfo was extended in an effort to increase the probable success of the project, to help contain ongoing staff support requirements, and to help control the demand for service.

Clearly, it was impossible and unnecessary to require every faculty member to devote a full week to CourseInfo training, especially outside the context of the Summer Institute. To accommodate faculty support needs and schedules, the original SIDI was unbundled into smaller pieces and offered more frequently throughout the year. The core training options now include:

- *Standard:* An eight-hour course introduces faculty to the use of Blackboard at the University of Pittsburgh. It is offered as two half-day sessions or one full-day session. It focuses on the application of web-based instructional technologies to enhance learning by encouraging active and collaborative learning and is intended to help faculty learn how to use Blackboard authoring, communication, and management tools.

- *Web Novices:* An expanded, 12-hour version of the standard training is offered as three half-day sessions over three weeks. It includes all the features of the standard training plus devotes additional time to explaining how the web works and how to use desktop productivity tools, such as Microsoft Word and PowerPoint, to create content for Blackboard. More time is allocated to hands-on work and individual tutoring.

- *Web Experts:* A condensed, one- to two-hour version of the standard training introduces the web expert (someone who is facile at creating HTML-based course materials) to the features of Blackboard and focuses on its management tools and operational procedures. This training is also recommended for faculty who may have used Blackboard at another institution, because it details the idiosyncrasies of Blackboard implementation at the University of Pittsburgh.

- *Self-Instructional:* A self-instructional course in Blackboard use, supplemented with a one-hour orientation session to cover procedural and operational topics, provides pedagogical applications and links to useful web resources.

The keys to the success of this training program are that 1) it is a required prerequisite to using Blackboard; 2) it focuses on the instructional application more than the technology; and 3) it is tailored to the technical literacy of the individual faculty member. Although mandated, the program is administered in a low-key manner, with every effort made to accommodate faculty needs and schedules, even to the point of providing individual sessions in faculty offices, if necessary. Approximately 1,680 faculty have taken CourseInfo/Blackboard core training as of May 2003.

In addition to the required core training, several supplemental training modules are offered to faculty. Participation in these modules is optional, based on each faculty member's goals and interests. The supplemental modules address virus prevention; using PowerPoint; using such software as Microsoft

Figure 54.2

Faculty Taking Core Blackboard Training
(AY 2003 Estimated)

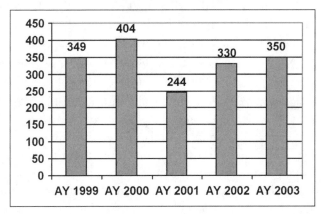

Word and FrontPage to create HTML; incorporating images, audio, and video into web pages; using anti-plagiarism software; and identifying and addressing legal and copyright issues. Consultations with instructional designers are encouraged.

Support

Providing an effective training system helps to reduce the need for ongoing support but does not eliminate it. Faculty need ongoing support if they have limited technical skills, use the software infrequently, use advanced features, have innovative ideas that stretch current capabilities, or wish to make use of newly released functions. To address these ongoing needs, the University provides a range of support services:

- *Support organization:* Upon completion of Blackboard training, every faculty member is enrolled in a special support organization implemented within Blackboard. Part of this organization contains information and links to browser plug-ins commonly used in Pitt's Blackboard courses and is available to both students and faculty. Other parts of the organization are restricted to faculty and contain notes on upgrades, technical tips, sample student surveys, a threaded discussion board, and other features.

- *Managed mailing list:* Faculty who complete training are also enrolled in a managed mailing list. This Majordomo list server is used to proactively communicate technical and operational information to faculty using Blackboard.

- *Public web site:* CIDDE staff also maintain a web site that targets faculty and students not currently using Blackboard. It contains information and documents about the Pitt implementation of Blackboard, current and archived announcements, and information and training schedules for faculty who use or wish to use Blackboard. The URL for this site is http://www.pitt.edu/~ciddeweb/COURSEWEB/.

- *Technology support facility:* The Faculty Instructional Development Lab (FIDL), a New Media Center, is a physical and virtual gateway to the varied human and technical resources CIDDE has to offer. Its primary purpose is to provide leadership and support for the application of instructional technologies to teaching and learning at the University. The FIDL provides a centralized multimedia lab facility, develops active-learning courseware in collaborative teams, and implements an advanced instructional technology function to evaluate and to introduce new and emerging technologies for direct application to instruction. FIDL resources directly support faculty using Blackboard and include image, voice, and video capture and editing, video conferencing training and support, and instructional and technical consulting.

- *Technology help desk:* CSSD provides support through their help-desk services. This 24/7 service helps both students and faculty with Blackboard access, including managing user accounts and providing browser and plug-in assistance.

- *Classroom technology:* The increasing faculty adoption of Blackboard seems to coincide with an increased desire to use technology in the classroom. Faculty wish to visit their online course materials, to view web-related content, and to use PowerPoint presentations. Consequently, they need classrooms with such technology as networked computers and data/video projection devices. The University supports a multiyear classroom technology renovation project and has implemented procedures and dedicated resources to keep classroom technology current. In addition, CIDDE's Instructional Media Services group can deliver technology to classrooms that have yet to be renovated. Additional information about the university's classrooms can be viewed at http://www.pitt.edu/~ciddeweb/CLASSROOMS/.

The most important component of the university's support for web-based instruction is the staff resources dedicated to its success. CSSD devotes portions of time from six analysts to running the servers and specifically trains its help-desk staff to deal with Blackboard-related issues. CIDDE devotes time from five analysts and three administrative support staff to running its developmental server, training and supporting faculty, and administering the Blackboard software. Finally, CIDDE staff work closely with designated liaisons to each of the university's academic centers. The liaisons help communicate faculty needs to CIDDE and share information about CIDDE resources and events with faculty.

Future Directions

As faculty continue to use the web and other technologies to enhance instruction, they become more sophisticated in their needs and solutions. For instance, when first using Blackboard, some faculty do little more than post a syllabus and course readings. In subsequent offerings, they often explore additional features, such as online quizzes, chats, and discussion boards. Advanced faculty members are embedding rich content or referencing it as offline content, and exploring application development efforts using technologies, such as Java, Flash, and Authorware.

The capacity to enhance instruction via the web is changing the way faculty teach. Instruction is no longer bound by time and space but can occur in Internet chats (including virtual office hours), threaded discussion boards, mediated presentations, and self-instructional learning materials. CIDDE must anticipate, investigate, plan, and implement solutions to assist faculty in this evolution.

55

USING PBL IN A WEBCT FACULTY DEVELOPMENT SESSION

**Erin F. Sicuranza, Valerie P. Hans,
Karen M. Kral, and George H. Watson**
University of Delaware

In January 2002, Information Technologies-User Services at the University of Delaware teamed up with Institute for Transforming Undergraduate Education (ITUE) fellows to host a series of WebCT classes infused with active-learning strategies. This article describes the WebCT communications class, in which a problem-based learning (PBL) approach was used to teach certain features of the online course-management system. To generate interest, participants were asked to work in groups to address a current, real-world problem as they learned WebCT techniques. This approach was a radical departure from traditional WebCT faculty training sessions that employ minilectures and a lockstep procedure in which participants follow prescribed keystrokes to learn software features.

RATIONALE FOR THE CHANGE

The University of Delaware has established itself as a leader in PBL in undergraduate education. In the PBL approach, students work collaboratively in small groups to solve complex, real-world problems by obtaining, communicating, and incorporating relevant information (Duch, Groh, & Allen, 2001). However, while numerous articles and studies tout the benefits of active-learning strategies, faculty training has not kept pace, and although most University of Delaware faculty training sessions use hands-on techniques and allow experimentation, none had so effectively integrated PBL into the learning process. Many universities continue to use lecture and demonstration methods for training.

Tomei (1999) argues that many adults have accepted the role that technology plays in instruction, yet they perceive a number of limitations that younger people may not. Faculty members, in particular, perceive barriers, such as lack of time and support and limited access to technology. According to Tomei, "proper sequencing of instruction, self-paced learning rates, active hands-on environments and 'learn it now/use it now' strategies aid the adult in overcoming these limitations" (p. 72).

In this age of ubiquitous computing and countless training sessions, a strictly skills-based approach may not be the most effective. Rather, a hierarchical approach that builds a contextual framework may be more appropriate (Sein, Bostrom, & Olfman, 1999). To this end, the facilitators designed a session that would build on the participants' existing knowledge and then move them to more complex, unfamiliar concepts throughout the session. Each of the exercises would provide information or skills necessary to complete subsequent assignments. The facilitators used a compelling real-world problem to provide context for the use of computers instead of simply presenting a tool and the required keystrokes.

THE WORKSHOP SESSION

This new workshop was a collaborative effort among four facilitators: Dr. George Watson, associate dean of arts and sciences and ITUE cofounder; Dr. Valerie Hans, professor of sociology and criminal justice and an ITUE leader; Erin Sicuranza, an instructional designer with user services and an ITUE fellow; and Karen Kral, an information resource consultant in user services and the WebCT administrator for the University of Delaware.

The workshop aimed to introduce participants to three of the four WebCT communication tools (mail, discussions, and chat) and to model how these tools could be used to enhance student communication. The facilitators created a structural framework that began with the mail tool, since all participants were likely to be familiar with it. The session then introduced the discussions tool, building on the work that they started in email. The final section introduced the chat tool, which was unfamiliar to many participants. Each of the tools was introduced and used within the context of an overarching problem.

A great deal of preparation was required of the four facilitators prior to the workshop. Hans developed a compelling real-world problem, which was quite similar to a PBL problem that she might use in her own classes on the courts (Hans, 2001). It took up a timely question for January 2002, asking participants to decide on a trial method for terrorist suspects. Kral and Sicuranza created a WebCT course that included the tools necessary for the workshop, populated the course with all registered participants, and provided designer access to all the facilitators. Watson formed subgroups with four participants per group. He also sent an introductory email message to all registrants, telling them about the workshop's format and confirming their participation. Seating assignments were predetermined so that group members were not sitting near one another, which would ensure that their communication would be computer-mediated rather than face-to-face, thus modeling students' experience of WebCT communication (Sicuranza, Hans, Kral, & Watson, 2002).

Watson began the three-hour session with an overview of PBL and active-learning strategies. Hans continued by describing her use of WebCT and active-learning approaches in her classes at the University of Delaware. After the half-hour overview, the participants were given their first assignment: a group icebreaker. Using the WebCT mail tool, they were asked to introduce themselves to the other members of their group. Each group was then required to devise a group name and to email the information to the instructor. Once all the groups had sent their email messages to the instructor, Sicuranza demonstrated how to open and read email messages within WebCT. She also provided an overview of the discussions tool and demonstrated how to set up private discussion topics for the groups.

The groups experienced difficulty getting started. As noted above, the active-learning approach was a departure from the usual WebCT faculty-training sessions. According to feedback, some participants found it difficult at first to place themselves in the role of students; others were expecting more direction from the facilitators on using the mail tool. The facilitators were also asking participants to communicate using the computer rather than speaking. To overcome some of these initial barriers, the four facilitators monitored the room and assisted participants individually. Once the participants got started, the process went more smoothly.

During the next portion of the workshop, Hans presented the participants with the problem, broken into two stages. For the first stage, she directed them to the discussions tool in WebCT. They were asked to use their private group topics to exchange views about two questions related to the problem for 15 minutes. Following this initial discussion exercise, Kral demonstrated how an instructor can track student progress throughout the WebCT course and how to view student discussion postings. The second stage of the problem asked participants to use the discussions tool to complete three tasks, which included identifying the questions that they had to answer before making any decisions, identifying web resources, and developing questions to ask an expert on terrorism.

The next part of the session introduced WebCT's chat feature and built on the third task that participants had completed in the previous section. The University of Delaware has a resident expert on terrorism, Dr. Mark Miller of the political science and international relations department, and as luck would have it, he was a participant in the WebCT session that day. Hans had contacted him prior to the session and asked if he would be willing to play the role of expert for an online chat session. He enthusiastically agreed. (Even if he were not a participant in the class, Miller could have joined the chat session from anywhere he had access to the Internet.) During the chat, designated participants posed questions, and Miller responded to as many as he could in the time allowed.

For the last ten minutes of the formal session, participants were again directed to the WebCT discussions tool to develop their group's final recommendation about a tribunal for the terrorists. The groups were then asked to post their recommendations along with the most important justifications for their recommendations to the main section of the discussions area, where all the participants could view each group's comments. Even with tight time constraints, two of the three groups managed to complete the final assignment.

The session concluded with an informal, open group discussion. Interestingly, the session generated such enthusiasm that several participants stayed beyond the scheduled time to continue discussing what they had learned about WebCT and about the problem content.

WORKSHOP EVALUATION

Was this an effective way to teach a WebCT workshop? To determine the answer, the facilitators reviewed the class evaluations and sent a follow-up email to the participants. According to the evaluations, most participants felt that the discussions and chat tools would be useful in their teaching; only two felt that way about the mail tool. All of the participants felt that the information was presented clearly, even though facilitators provided less instruction from the front of the room than usual in a training session. Other comments verified that certain participants appreciated seeing the tools from a student's perspective, that the problem was useful for structuring communication, and that some will continue to explore uses of these tools for their own courses.

One person responded that the last part of the class, posting a final recommendation, was unnecessary. However, based on past experience using active-learning approaches in faculty development work, the facilitators felt that asking groups to post a final recommendation provided closure to the problem. It was a good way to end the formal part of the session, especially for those participants who were somewhat uneasy with the problem-based approach at first.

Finally, the email follow-up has proven that participants are indeed using the tools that they experienced in this workshop. Several are using the discussions tool in their classes. Only one is using the chat tool for online meetings, but one respondent said he is thinking about using it to provide extra student assistance. Those participants who are not teaching this semester are planning to incorporate the discussions tool in their courses in the near future. In the words of one participant, "the class was very helpful, and the format was good. I wish more faculty would take advantage of WebCT because students appreciate it."

REFERENCES

Duch, B. J., Groh, S. E., & Allen, D. E. (2001). Why problem-based learning? A case study of institutional change in undergraduate education. In B. J. Duch, S. E. Groh, & D. E. Allen (Eds.), *The power of problem-based learning* (pp. 3-11). Sterling, VA: Stylus Publishing.

Hans, V. P. (2001). Integrating active learning and the use of technology in legal studies courses. In B. J. Duch, S. E. Groh, & D. E. Allen (Eds.), *The power of problem-based learning* (pp. 141-148). Sterling, VA: Stylus Publishing.

Sein, M., Bostrom, R., & Olfman, L. (1999, January/March). Rethinking end-user training strategy: Applying a hierarchical knowledge-level model. *Journal of End User Computing, 11* (1), 2.

Sicuranza, E. F., Hans, V. P., Kral, K. M., & Watson, G. H. (2002). Using PBL in a WebCT faculty development session. *Problem-Based Learning Clearinghouse.* http://www.udel.edu/pblc

Tomei, L. (1999, April). Concentration and infusion—Two approaches for teaching technology for lifelong learners. *T.H.E. Journal, 26* (9), 72.

RESOURCES

The Institute for Transforming Undergraduate Education:http:// www.udel.edu/inst/

The Problem-Based Learning Clearinghouse: http://www.udel.edu/pblc/

56

CREATING TIME AND DESIRE IN AN ANNUAL PROGRAM OF FACULTY FELLOWSHIPS

George H. Watson
University of Delaware

The Institute for Transforming Undergraduate Education (ITUE) has been working with University of Delaware (UD) faculty and other educators from around the world for the past five years. Its extensive program for integrating information technology and real-world problems in the student-centered learning approach known as problem-based learning (PBL) has been successfully matched with the needs of busy members of the higher education community. The ideas we have embraced in designing attractive faculty development programs run the gamut from the obvious to more subtle, from merely mechanical to more overarching. This chapter addresses four general areas and includes the following recommendations:

- Incorporate active engagement and instructional technology.
- Create a safe and collegial environment for learning.
- Recognize and reward successful outcomes.
- Respect and optimize time investments.

INCORPORATE ACTIVE ENGAGEMENT AND INSTRUCTIONAL TECHNOLOGY

In ITUE workshops, we model what we promote by presenting PBL methodology using appropriate technology and web resources. Our workshops also require that we introduce PBL concepts using the same active-learning and student-centered approaches that we advocate. We start each weeklong session with an opportunity for faculty members to work in small groups for a day, solving an engaging PBL problem and working through the process, much like students in a typical PBL course.

Our faculty participants appreciate exploring active-learning techniques through an experiential approach, a hallmark of the successful ITUE experience. We do not simply lecture about the techniques, laying out their underlying educational theory and benefits, but, rather, faculty members experience the power of PBL and other teaching strategies directly. Recently, we have extended this approach to technology-training sessions, where ITUE leaders partner with staff from PRESENT, UD's Center for Teaching, Learning and Technology, to present communication tools in WebCT using a PBL format. Using active-learning strategies in faculty development programs as often as feasible is beneficial, even essential. They not only will benefit the faculty participants' learning, but model new approaches for participants who may not have yet encountered them.

The guiding principles behind our faculty development programs can be paraphrased from "Seven Principles for Good Practice in Education" (Chickering & Gamson, 1987). Good faculty development in our program:

- Encourages contact between fellows and leaders.

- Develops reciprocity and cooperation among fellows.

- Encourages active learning and effective use of technology.

- Gives prompt feedback and sustained mentoring.

- Emphasizes time on task, while respecting the fellows' time.

- Communicates high expectations for all fellows.

- Respects diverse talents and ways of learning among the many disciplines represented.

CREATE A SAFE AND COLLEGIAL ENVIRONMENT FOR LEARNING

ITUE fellowships contributed significantly to creating a community of learners and a sense of belonging to something special. Faculty and teaching staff applied to become fellows through a modest online call for proposals. The application was fairly simple but encouraged faculty to reflect on their teaching and motivation for change. Subsequent participation in the weeklong introductory session and workshops were restricted to those selected to be ITUE fellows. For many sessions, faculty worked together in small groups, solving problems and forming bonds, which is especially beneficial, given that most design their classes or conduct research in relative isolation. Some ITUE members came from departments where they did not feel comfortable discussing reform of their teaching, but ITUE provided a safe and collegial environment for engaging other like-minded individuals. Although the reward of collegiality is not as tangible as new funding, it is nevertheless an integral part of the design of our program.

To sustain the community that was formed in the weeklong session, fellows were offered additional special sessions on emerging topics, which was especially valuable in the early years, as the program was being refined. When time and interest permit, ITUE leaders organize brown-bag luncheons to chat with fellows about their transformation projects and any problems they may be encountering. ITUE leaders are available to consult individually on an as-needed basis or by invitation, particularly on PBL. They are fortunate to have technology partnerships across campus. We now find many ITUE fellows among the staff of our technology partners.

RECOGNIZE AND REWARD SUCCESSFUL OUTCOMES

Attempts to reward faculty often focus on promotion and tenure as well as annual evaluations and merit-pay allocations. Several features of the ITUE program also contribute to recognition and reward for faculty. They include heightened visibility on campus, strengthened external grant proposals, and modest stipends. Finally, some faculty members have elected to pursue the investigation of benefits and outcomes of PBL-based teaching as an active area of scholarship.

The ITUE faculty development program was originally designed to be a yearlong process, an annual cycle of faculty development and course design. Thus, we decided that faculty participating in ITUE would be named ITUE faculty fellows. At the beginning of each cycle, announcements of new fellows were publicized through university public relations and its printed media, via the ITUE web site, and by email. An official letter of appointment was provided to each new fellow, describing our expectations and the benefits of the fellowship. In addition, lists of ITUE fellows and the courses they taught were given high visibility on the ITUE web site. The list of courses became difficult to maintain, but the tradition of listing all fellows' names has continued, including lists of visiting and international fellows in the program.

We knew that the fellowship had become valued when it began to appear in online curriculum vitae and printed résumés under "Honors and Awards." We also discovered that engineering participants were incorporating ITUE-generated ideas about curriculum reform through active learning into proposals submitted to federal funding agencies. Many new funding opportunities for beginning faculty members require an element of education and outreach to complement the research project. Listing the ITUE fellowship on the CV, along with the new ideas for transforming teaching and using technology to assist, has benefited at least a few new faculty members in ITUE in their pursuit of external funding.

Another important form of recognition highlights successful projects by inviting the faculty fellows who conceived them to participate in subsequent programs. The returning fellow is an essential part of our programs. Generally, we invite one or two returning fellows to spend ten to 15 minutes reviewing changes they have made to a course and reflecting on ITUE's role in the process. Occasionally, we also co-host sessions for the entire campus, showcasing successful faculty projects.

Finally, faculty members always welcome financial support, and even a modest stipend or professional-development account can make a significant difference in the motivation and success of a transformation project. Although $1,000 is considered a pittance by science and engineering faculty, we have had good success in enabling positive outcomes with this modest level of support. ITUE fellowships are not disbursed as personal stipends, but they can be used toward hardware or software acquisitions, participation in educational conferences, or almost anything else relevant to the transformation project.

RESPECT AND OPTIMIZE TIME INVESTMENTS

While research and scholarly activities are clearly of importance to university faculty, we believe that most are also interested in doing the best possible teaching. They have a genuine desire to improve student learning, but it can be muted in the interest of preserving the scarce time available for research. Faculty development programs that acknowledge limited faculty time have a better chance of attracting the mainstream members of our faculties and thereby influencing their teaching.

Respect for faculty time is essential when designing and facilitating workshops. As a minor example, workshop participants find it frustrating to sit patiently waiting for the session to start, especially if they have nothing productive to do. Waiting for stragglers discourages those who show up on time and is certainly not a practice we would consider for our undergraduate classrooms. Start on time! As a cushion at the beginning, a brief survey or questionnaire can be made available to early arrivers to help close the gap; see, for example, Preliminary Survey of Institute Fellows, http://www.udel.edu/inst/jun2001/survey.html.

Even worse is the workshop that is delayed because of technological problems, particularly if it is about the use of technology in teaching. Novices contemplating the expansion of their use of technology may be unnerved to witness a workshop delay, because the projector will not properly display the laptop presentation or the presenter cannot expediently log on to or boot up the system of the day. It is prudent to check the equipment and software ahead of time, even if repeating in the same venue as last semester; often something subtle has been changed since the facility's previous use.

Of course, faculty development program design should maximize the learning that takes place in an optimal amount of time, much as we design our undergraduate classroom activities. An hourly agenda should be published in advance. Prior knowledge of the pace and expectations of the program helps smooth its acceptance, as busy faculty members must know when they can break to check their email and adjourn back to their offices. An example of a detailed weeklong program may be found at http://www.udel.edu/inst/jun2001. In addition to the name, synopsis, and facilitator for each part of the program, presentation slides and web resources are included, generally after the presentation, as part of the online agenda.

In our workshops involving classroom technology, we pay particular attention to the ease with which faculty can adopt our recommendations. We steer away from technology solutions that involve inordinate amounts of time and skill to implement; we do not embrace the use of technology for its own sake but rather to further the learning goals that we have for our students. Although an extensive, whiz-bang exhibition of the remarkable array of solutions may feel good to us, we must stay aware of how intimidating it may be to novice users of technology. Keep it simple and relevant! Exciting faculty about a wonderful new technology approach will be of little benefit if it requires too much technical support or a difficult learning curve, leading to frustration and wasted time in a failed implementation.

An example for helping faculty to make the best use of their time in bringing technological solutions to the classroom is the technology-assistance program initiated by PRESENT. Faculty members with teaching ideas requiring technology assistance were solicited through a request for proposals and paired with student technology assistants. The faculty member was expected to contribute ideas that would benefit student learning. Student assistants with expertise in web design or animation creation, for example, were matched to them and managed by PRESENT staff. Faculty members were encouraged to learn the technical skills during the project implementation, but the student assistants did the heavy lifting at the outset. Faculty time is thus optimally used for the project's conception, freeing them to think broadly about learning issues and course objectives without getting bogged down in programming details.

CONCLUSION

By applying elements of our own philosophy, such as active engagement and appropriate use of technology, to the creation and implementation of our workshops, we have engaged faculty members and modeled techniques that promise to transform higher education. Having experienced these techniques firsthand, faculty are better able to incorporate them into their own teaching. By interacting intensely in small groups with their peers, they form relationships that go beyond departmental barriers and provide safe environments for discussing curriculum change. Faculty members gain recognition for participating in the institute and have opportunities to demonstrate what they have learned in public forums. The important insights into active learning that the institute provides have helped some faculty gain external grants. Small stipends motivate them and provide resources that would not have otherwise been available. Finally, by respecting faculty time and scheduling appropriately, we have been able to build workshops that draw enthusiastic participation.

REFERENCES

Chickering, A. & Gamson, Z. (1987). Seven principles for good practice in undergraduate education. *AAHE Bulletin, 39,* 3–7.

RESOURCES

Discussion of technology's role is available at http://www.udel.edu/learn/technology/principles.

Faculty Showcase: Expanding Learning Opportunities by Applying Technology: http://www.udel.edu/inst/2002jan7.html

Institute Fellows and Participants: http://www.udel.edu/inst/overall.html

Institute for Transforming Undergraduate Education: http://www.udel.edu/inst

Preliminary Survey of Institute Fellows: http://www.udel.edu/inst/jun2001/survey.html

PRESENT, a teaching, learning, and technology center at the University of Delaware: http://www.udel.edu/present

Program for 2001 Summer Session: http://www.udel.edu/inst/jun2001

University of Delaware Problem-Based Learning: http://www.udel.edu/pbl

Visiting Institute Fellows and Participants: http://www.udel.edu/inst/visitors.html

Visiting International Fellows: http://www.udel.edu/inst/international.html

Technology Assistance Grant Application: http://www.udel.edu/present/center/grantform.html

57

FACULTY DEVELOPMENT STRATEGIES FOR A MULTIDISCIPLINARY FACULTY IN HEALTH AND REHABILITATION

**Ellen R. Cohn, Diane J. Davis,
Joanne M. Nicoll, and Carol Baker
University of Pittsburgh**

INTRODUCTION

This chapter describes seven faculty development strategies successfully applied between 1997 and 2002 at the University of Pittsburgh's School of Health and Rehabilitation Sciences (SHRS):

1) Articulate the unifying school mission.

2) Establish a school-wide task force.

3) Appoint a director of instructional development.

4) Provide basic tools.

5) Promote ongoing communication and collaboration.

6) Offer school-centered faculty development programs.

7) Conduct needs assessments.

STRATEGY 1: ARTICULATE THE UNIFYING SCHOOL MISSION

The first step was to develop a unifying school mission that emphasized teaching and learning. SHRS is an academic unit within the Schools of the Health Sciences. Faculty members are typically affiliated within one of 11 distinct disciplines, each with a unique professional culture and training requirements, including audiology, clinical dietetics and nutrition, disability studies, emergency medicine, health information management, occupational therapy, physical therapy, rehabilitation counseling, rehabilitation science and technology, speech-language pathology, and sports medicine and athletic training. Each program is a distinct departmental entity, with assigned space, a budget, and a designated chair. While seven of the eight disciplines maintain office space in one location and share classroom space, most of their academic business is conducted within each department. (For further information, see http://www. shrs.pitt.edu.) This diversity created a challenge to identify mutually beneficial, multidisciplinary programming. It also presented opportunities for faculty to learn about each other's disciplines and to combine forces to increase research funding.

The school strives to unite these multiple disciplines to pursue a common mission:

> SHRS, together with the University of Pittsburgh and the UPMC Health System, is a community of students, staff, teachers, researchers, and clinicians who teach and learn from each other. We have a sense of mutual value. We shall strive to do our best and then, to do even better, for ourselves, our colleagues, and those we serve. (School of Health and Rehabilitation Sciences, n.d.)

This mission statement is consistent with the ground-breaking and oft-quoted November 1995 Report of the Pew Health Professions Commission, "Critical Challenges: Revitalizing the Health Professions for the Twenty-First Century." The Pew Commission advanced an interdisciplinary educational imperative for training in healthcare and rehabilitation:

> While legitimate areas of specialized study should remain the domain of individual professional training programs, key areas of pre-clinical and clinical training must be put together as a whole, across professional communities, through increased sharing of clinical training resources, more cross teaching, more exploration of the various roles played by professionals and the active modeling of effective team integration in the delivery of efficient, high quality care.

One of the finest examples of such interaction occurs within a clinical center sponsored by the University of Pittsburgh Medical Center, the Center for Assistive Technology. Here, representatives of various disciplines evaluate patients and train students within the context of a multidisciplinary team (http://www.cat.pitt.edu/). Increasingly, the school is establishing multidisciplinary research centers, such as the National Institute on Disability and Rehabilitation Research (NIDRR), sponsored by the Rehabilitation Engineering Center on Wheeled Mobility (http://www.rerc.pitt.edu/). A recent collaboration with the McGowan Center for Regenerative Medicine represents a stunning opportunity for school researchers to evaluate the outcomes of new therapies, such as spinal cord regeneration. Academic interdisciplinary educational endeavors are also evolving. Recent successes include the SHRS PhD program, an undergraduate introductory course in the rehabilitation professions, and a new undergraduate major in the rehabilitation sciences.

Our faculty development program is therefore mission driven and characterized by two overriding themes: 1) excellence in teaching with technology to enable active learning; and 2) productive interdisciplinary research collaborations. Mastery of these two domains is essential to fulfillment of the school mission: "to advance health and rehabilitation through research, teaching, and professional service." At SHRS, faculty development programming supports service, research, and teaching collaborations.

STRATEGY 2: ESTABLISH A SCHOOL-WIDE TASK FORCE

In September 1997, Dean Clifford Brubaker created the SHRS Task Group on Learning and Support Technologies to "position the School of Health and Rehabilitation Sciences . . . to take full advantage of emerging educational technology and distributed learning paradigms for all levels of academic endeavor including pre-professional through professional, post-professional, doctoral, and continuing education, with the ultimate goal of serving a worldwide community of learners." This description serves as the mission statement for the activities of the SHRS director of instructional development, appointed in 1998.

Four subcommittees formed the strategic planning group: administrative support services, electronic classrooms/labs, faculty and student support services, and information systems. The committees met intensively over a six-month period and drafted a blueprint for the current SHRS instructional technology structure and initiatives.

STRATEGY 3: APPOINT A DIRECTOR OF INSTRUCTIONAL DEVELOPMENT

The SHRS dean identified a director of instructional development from the school's faculty to serve in a part-time (50%) capacity. The director coordinates faculty development programs and school retreats, is an onsite resource to faculty and staff, and serves as a liaison to the university's instructional development and academic computing communities and as an administrative liaison to the school's student bodies. The director also develops new interdisciplinary instructional programming and facilitates instructional planning for web-based and international programming.

STRATEGY 4: PROVIDE BASIC TOOLS

Initially, faculty development efforts offered training in Blackboard software and active-learning strategies. Information concerning active learning was presented at a school retreat and followed up with a program of workshops. Simultaneously, the university offered faculty members multiple opportunities to complete Blackboard training.

SHRS is currently in the fourth year of the five-year plan. Blackboard software combined with increased use of active-learning strategies has transformed teaching and learning at the school. Enhanced multimedia classrooms, a state-of-the-art computer laboratory, a learning-resource center, and course management software are now routine features of the academic experience. Faculty development efforts have stimulated most of the faculty, including the dean and many department chairs, to complete Blackboard training.

Now that faculty members have acquired a common knowledge of active learning and Blackboard, we have diversified our approach to faculty development goals and vehicles. Faculty members develop their skills and enhance their opportunities via participation in formal training programs, web-based modules, school retreats, committee meetings at or outside the school, and one-to-one consultations with peers or content experts or through more passive vehicles, such as web sites, email, libraries, and handouts. The linking of individual faculty members to university-based resources or programs is viewed as an important faculty development activity.

The timing of formal faculty development offerings has also become more variable, ranging from "just-in-time" learning opportunities, presented by a software vendor, to a workshop series. Their content is similarly more varied and flexible. Instructional objectives are based on articulated needs and relate to the school's interrelated mission and business goals. However, all topics usually relate to instructional technology. For example, an upcoming faculty development program will feature a guest speaker engaged in regenerative medical research, who will describe a web-based laboratory notebook and communication strategies.

We believe that even though a faculty member may not find the time to attend a workshop, publicizing the topic may promote interest and behavioral change. For example, prior to the program described above, one instructor emailed his department: "Now that we all subscribe to Reference Manager, why don't we think about electronically sharing datasets?"

STRATEGY 5: PROMOTE ONGOING COMMUNICATION AND COLLABORATION

We strategically foster ongoing opportunities for communication and collaboration, which helps us to share knowledge and to take advantage of existing resources. The Instructional and Information Technology Committee is a school-wide group of technologically engaged faculty and staff convened by the director of instructional development. Extramural committee members include the associate vice chancellor for biomedical informatics in the health sciences and the associate director of the University of Pittsburgh's Center for Instructional Development & Distance Education (CIDDE). The committee's mission is to infuse knowledge and innovative approaches, to exchange information across departments, and to serve as an advisory body to the dean on school uses of instructional technology and web-based vehicles. Typical agenda items are course management software, Internet2 opportunities, classrooms and computing laboratories, tele-rehabilitation, and SHRS computing and telecommunication networks. Technology experts from the University of Pittsburgh and the University of Pittsburgh Medical Center (UPMC) are frequently invited to speak to the group. The committee maintained a Blackboard-sponsored web site.

Additionally, the committee's executive subcommittee meets periodically with the SHRS dean to address information technology policies. The subcommittee consists of the SHRS dean; SHRS directors of information technology, budget and personnel, and instructional development; and a health information sciences faculty member. These meetings are viewed as a faculty development opportunity in that multidisciplinary learning and exchanges occur.

Strong cooperative relationships maximize instructional development and the technology resources available to the school's community of students, staff, and faculty. The SHRS director of instructional development serves as the school's representative to the university committee on academic computing and the University of Pittsburgh CIDDE. She also facilitates SHRS faculty interactions with the liaison to the health sciences library system and the Center for Biomedical Informatics, especially in promoting web-based faculty resources, such as the Faculty Research Inventory Project found at http://www.cbmi.upmc.edu/frip/search.cgi. Our faculty are encouraged to use the electronic resources of the health sciences library system. We held a well-attended, meet-the-librarian, donuts-and-coffee session, during which faculty registered to use proprietary online resources. Faculty are regularly informed about instructionally based programs and relevant instructional grants (for example, for high-speed, network access instructional innovations, and training).

STRATEGY 6: OFFER SCHOOL-CENTERED FACULTY DEVELOPMENT PROGRAMS

SHRS was selected as one of two schools in the university to partner with CIDDE and cosponsor Teaching Excellence Workshops supported by the provost's office. The on-site seminars are relevant to SHRS faculty and attract faculty from throughout the university to our school. Surveys of SHRS faculty, conducted in 2000 and 2001 (described below), provided information concerning their development needs, and subsequent workshop topics included:

- Problem-Based Learning
- Discussion Techniques
- Writing for All Disciplines
- Designing a Web-based Lecture
- Advanced PowerPoint Techniques
- Teaching Portfolios
- Best Practices in Blackboard Use
- Designing Assessment Instruments
- Triple-Jump Technique for Case-Based Assessment
- Unique Teaching Strategies Shared by the University of Pittsburgh's Chancellor's Teaching Award Winners
- Mentoring Students in the Academic Research Setting
- Web-based Global Problem Solving–An Interactive Web Site: http://jurist.law.pitt.edu/
- Classroom Games and Competitions that Promote Active Learning
- The Web-based Research Laboratory Notebook
- Pitt Health Sciences on the Web

STRATEGY 7: CONDUCT NEEDS ASSESSMENTS

Following basic training in Blackboard and active-learning strategies, at the end of the first and second years of faculty development, two types of needs assessments were conducted to identify needs and wisely invest our resources.

- *Faculty surveys:* One strategy directly surveys the faculty. The second iteration of faculty surveys, developed by Nicoll and Cohn (2000), is included in Appendix 57.1.

- *Student feedback:* A second strategy seeks consumer feedback via meetings with students and a formal survey. In a more formal assessment, the director of instructional development collaborated with the director of the University of Pittsburgh office of measurement and evaluation to develop both an undergraduate and graduate student satisfaction survey, included in Appendix 57.2 (Cohn & Baker, 2001). The survey addresses academic advising; academic, clinical, and professional preparation; overall teaching effectiveness; the sense of departmental, school, and university community; and instructional/computing technology. Results are shared with each department via their chairs. Individuals cited by students for exemplary contributions received letters of commendation from the SHRS dean. The survey data also are used to identify faculty development needs.

CONCLUSION

The faculty development program at SHRS is mission centered and multifaceted. Training in teaching with technology initially provided a unifying experience for faculty in multiple disciplines. As faculty development needs evolved, we diversified topics, timing, and delivery vehicles. Close collaborations between school and university resources have greatly enhanced our faculty development efforts.

REFERENCES

Cohn, E., & Baker, E., (2001). *Student satisfaction survey.* Unpublished document.

Nicoll, J., & Cohn, E. (2000). *Faculty needs assessment survey.* Unpublished document.

Pew Health Professions Commission. (1995). *Critical challenges: Revitalizing the health professions for the twenty-first century.* San Francisco, CA: UCSF Center for Health Professions.

School of Health and Rehabilitative Sciences. (n.d.) *Our mission.* Available: http://www.shrs.pitt.edu/about/mission.html

Appendix 57.1

Faculty Survey

School of Health and Rehabilitation Sciences
Faculty Needs Assessment Survey

1) Have you attended faculty development workshops at SHRS in the last year?

Yes ☐ No ☐

2) The following workshops were conducted for SHRS faculty last year. If you feel any of these should be repeated, please indicate by checking the appropriate box.

Creating Web-Based Lectures	☐
Advanced PowerPoint	☐
Case-Based Learning	☐
Blackboard Idea Exchange	☐
Building your Teaching Portfolio	☐
Designing Student Assessment	☐

Comments:

3) Would you attend workshops offered:

a)	during the summer term?	Yes ☐ No ☐
b)	during the early summer session?	Yes ☐ No ☐
c)	during the later summer session?	Yes ☐ No ☐

4) Please identify topics below that you would attend.

a)	Classroom Behavior Management	☐
b)	Managing Teaching Assistants	☐
c)	Cultural Diversity	☐
d)	Academic Integrity	☐
e)	How to Get the Most out of Discussions	☐
f)	Group Tests	☐
g)	Problem-Based Learning	☐

h) Testing for Higher Level Thinking   ☐

i) Matching Course Content, Activities and
Evaluation with Course Goals   ☐

j) Enhancing Traditional Classes with
Web Communication Capabilities   ☐

k) Alternative Student Evaluation Methods   ☐

l) Other _____

_____

5) Please share comments, suggestions, and specific requests below.

Appendix 57.2

Student Survey

SHRS Student Survey

Directions

We are interested in the views of our students with respect to various aspects of your educational experience. For each of the following items, please indicate, **in pencil**, the response that best reflects your opinion.

1) Degree you are currently pursuing:
1=Undergraduate 2=Masters 3=PhD

2) If **undergraduate**, program you are currently enrolled in:
1=AT   2=CDN   3=CSD 4=EM 5=HIM
or
1=OT 2=RS

3) If **masters**, program you are currently enrolled in:
1=MS in CDN 2=MS in CSD 3=MS in HIM 4=MS in RST
or
1=MS in OT   2=MOT   3=MS in PT   4=MPT   5=MS in SM

4) If **PhD**, program you are currently enrolled in:
1=PhD in HRS 2=PhD in CSD

5) How many semesters have you been enrolled in this program?
1=1 semester   2=2   3=3 or 4 4=5 or 6   5=7 or more semesters

Use the following scale to indicate your **satisfaction** with your program's contribution to your **professional development** in each area.

1=Not at All   2=Little   3=Some   4=Mostly   5=Very

  1) Professional knowledge

  2) Clinical/professional skills

  3) Written professional communication

  4) Oral professional communication

  5) Ability to work independently

  6) Ability to work as a member of a team

  7) Use of Internet/computer technology

  8) Commitment to lifelong professional learning

Using the same scale as above, indicate your **satisfaction** with each of the following aspects of your education.

  1) Relevance of learning experiences to your field

  2) Quality of instruction in your program

  3) Breadth of coursework in your program

  4) Quality of academic experiences outside of the classroom

  5) Interaction with faculty outside of the classroom

  6) Class size

  7) Quality of SHRS facilities

  8) Quality of extracurricular/social experiences

  9) Importance of extracurricular/social experiences to your education

Use the following scale to indicate your degree of agreement with each of the following statements about the **academic advising** you are receiving.

1=Strongly Disagree   2=Disagree   3=Neutral   4=Agree   5=Strongly Agree

  1) My academic advisor is easy to talk to.

  2) It is not too difficult to make an appointment with my academic advisor.

  3) My academic advisor helps me identify my educational goals.

  4) My academic advisor provides guidance on the best courses to meet my needs.

  5) My academic advisor helps me develop decision-making skills.

  6) I would consult my academic advisor if I had an academic problem.

7) I would recommend my academic advisor to other students.

8) I intend to keep in touch with my academic advisor after I graduate.

9) My program provides accurate information about requirements within my program.

10) My program provides accurate information about certification/licensure requirements.

11) My program provides necessary guidance about scholarship/financial assistance.

Use the following scale to indicate your degree of agreement with each of the following statements about SHRS in general.

1=Strongly Disagree 2=Disagree 3=Neutral 4=Agree   5=Strongly Agree

1) I feel a part of my departmental community.

2) I feel a part of the SHRS community.

3) I feel a part of the University of Pittsburgh community.

4) If I had to make my school choice again, I would select SHRS.

5) I have found my experience at SHRS to be positive.

Please list below any faculty and/or staff who have been particularly helpful to you.

Please list any comments/suggestions you have related to your experience in SHRS.

Thank you for your participation.

58

FLYING WITHOUT WIRES: HOW A POLITICAL SCIENCE CLASS USED A SET OF TECHNOLOGIES

Andrew Lang
University of North Carolina at Chapel Hill

Once a year, the political science department at the University of North Carolina–Chapel Hill (UNC-CH) offers a course in the statistical analysis of public opinion data. Students in this course obtain a basic knowledge of how public opinion data is collected, how to perform some basic statistical calculations on different types of datasets, and how to interpret the results of those calculations. While the instructor uses a few contrived datasets during the semester to demonstrate how to use the statistical tools, for the most part the class examines actual data, collected and archived from numerous sources. By using actual datasets instead of fabricated ones, the class can also discuss the social and political contexts in play at the time that the data were gathered, thus deepening the course content.

Historically, this class met in a computer lab where the instructor could demonstrate the statistical tools in front of the students at their workstations, but the fixed-seat configuration and the fact that the class size had outgrown its capacity made meeting there impractical. What follows describes how the university's mandatory laptop initiative allowed us to effectively set up a computer lab in an ordinary classroom, using the students' own laptops, wireless networking, Citrix server technology, and the campus Blackboard server.

BACKGROUND ON THE TECHNOLOGIES USED

Wireless connectivity on college campuses has been a boon. It provides an affordable way to extend the wired network to places that are otherwise inaccessible because of building codes, available funds, or structural protection for historical preservation. On many campuses across the country, it provides a way to link faculty and staff offices that are off campus or wherever physical barriers prevent a wired solution. On some campuses, wireless connectivity is part of a larger plan to ensure that the campus network is partially functional in the event of a break in the wired network. While relatively rare on the UNC–CH campus a few years ago, after considerable work to install wireless access points across campus, wireless connectivity is now widespread.

At the same time, the Carolina Computing Initiative (CCI) was also in its early stages of implementation. This university program is designed to enrich the academic environment on campus with robust and ubiquitous computer technology. It requires all freshmen to purchase a laptop computer when they begin studies at UNC and also provides for faculty and staff computers to be replaced on a three-year basis. Although students are not required to buy their computers through the university's agreement with IBM, if they decide to do so, they benefit from a four-year warranty, 24/7 on-campus technical support, and expanded software licensing. Furthermore, the new standard CCI models offer built-in wireless networking, so that the expense of wireless access is factored into their purchase. The CCI is about to begin its third year of full implementation so that every student from the freshman to junior class owns a laptop computer.

Also over the past few years, the College of Arts & Sciences has been experimenting with deploying software through a Citrix server. This software technology works through a Windows server to provide end-users with access to most Windows-based applications. End-users can access these applications either by installing client-side software that communicates with the server or by installing a browser plug-in. Either way, when users launch a supported application from the server, it will look and behave as if it were installed locally on their own computer but will actually be using disk and CPU resources on the server. Without the need to install several applications locally on users' machines, the responsibility of managing software licenses becomes less burdensome; institutions need only purchase as many licenses as will be used concurrently and enforce that limit on the server. Software updates can be kept consistent across users, and the Citrix software will track actual usage on a very granular level so that license agreements can be either augmented or reduced as needed. With our statistics class in particular, students did not have to buy and to install a piece of software that they would not be very likely to use beyond the end of the semester.

APPLICATION OF THE TECHNOLOGY

The class used the campus Blackboard server to store the datasets and exchange results and other information with the instructor and each other. During each class meeting, students were given wireless cards to insert into their laptops, which gave them access to the Blackboard course web site as well as other resources. Once the students logged into their course web site, the instructor typically gave some introductory remarks about the origin of the data and asked them to download it to their laptops. Occasionally, the instructor would also ask them to find archived news articles from Internet sources to provide additional context about the data. When it was time to perform calculations on the data, students were able to launch the statistical application from the Citrix server and perform a multitude of statistical tests. Students who had results to share with the rest of the class could post them on the course web site for the instructor to show on the large display at the front of the room or for others to see later on. Since everything students would need for class was either on their laptops or readily available from servers, they could easily replicate the classroom activities and also complete their individual assignments from anywhere on campus that had network connectivity, such as their dorm rooms. After a few weeks, the students were very comfortable with the technology and becoming quite familiar with some basic exploratory statistical tests.

Having ready access to interesting datasets and news articles about the data being studied and a mechanism for quickly testing hypotheses produced an environment that promoted active discussion and student-generated inquiry. Over time, discussions were less about operating the software and more about the conceptual features of the data and the applicable statistical tests. Students' questions progressed from the level of "How do I find the standard deviation in this program?" to "What happens if we stratify the economic spectrum of those polled?" and the whole class could explore those higher-level questions through different statistical procedures with the instructor's guidance. Furthermore, these questions sparked discussions about the considerations pollsters make when devising a survey, the kinds of statistical tests that are appropriate to certain kinds of data, some of the mathematical properties of various tests, and the political climate that precipitates taking a poll in the first place.

LESSON LEARNED

Although the environment was rich in content, enthusiasm, and meaningful discussion, the overarching lesson was to manage expectations better. Neither the instructor nor the students had used wireless networking or a Citrix server in the past and were disappointed with the occasional technical problems that arose. Such problems included instances when two or three students might have difficulty connecting to the network, when the wireless network traffic was heavy enough to affect performance, or when the course web site was down. While these happened with relative infrequency, classroom activity often stopped until the problems were resolved, which disrupted the flow of the class and disappointed the students and the instructor. Still, in spite of these occasional problems, the class really appeared to benefit from and enjoy the flexibility that these technologies offered, particularly as evidenced by the level of the discussions throughout the semester. In retrospect, the entire experience was a worthwhile experiment—one that we are likely to repeat again in this class and try in others.

59

INFORMATION TECHNOLOGY IN AGRICULTURAL EXTENSION PROGRAMS

Fedro S. Zazueta, Howard W. Beck, and Jiannong Xin
University of Florida

Advances in technology have triggered deep changes. Information technology (IT) is a major strategic player in the successful deployment of new technologies and in the international competitiveness of agricultural producers. This overview of IT use in agriculture focuses on the experiences of the land grant university in Florida.

INFORMATION TECHNOLOGIES IN AGRICULTURE

Up until about ten years ago, nearly all data processing could be summed up in a single word: computers. Today, this term has given way to the broader descriptor *information technology*, which has become generally accepted. It refers to a rapidly expanding range of services, methods, techniques, applications, equipment, and electronic technologies used for the collection, manipulation, processing, classification, storage, and retrieval of recordable information and knowledge. At this time, such technologies include, but are not limited to, computers, software, high-capacity storage, networks, telecommunications, databases, data warehouses, multimedia, the Internet and its World Wide Web, geographic information systems (GIS), computer-aided design (CAD), online services, video conferencing, executive information systems (EIS), electronic mail, and expert systems: in short, all technologies related to the acquisition, storage, recovery, transfer, manipulation, and delivery of data, sound, and graphics, including video.

Nationwide, agriculture's adoption of IT continues to increase. In the early 1980s, less than 0.5% of farms (any establishment from which $1,000 or more of agricultural products were sold or would normally be sold during the year) used computers in agricultural production, including livestock and dairy operations (ECOP, 1980). In 2001, 55% of the 2,165,000 farms in the United States had computer access, and about 43% had Internet access, compared to 12% in 1997. In addition, the percent of ownership, including owned or leased computers, increased from 31% in 1997 to 50% in 2001 (NASS, 2001).

Technology adoption is related to the farm's income level. In 2001, 54% or more of US farms earning $250,000 or more had access to a computer; 55% of them reported using computers for business, and 58% had Internet access. Farms with lower incomes had significantly lower percentages.

During the past few years, most likely because of increasing attention to the Internet, the pace of IT adoption in agriculture was rapid. From 1997 to 1999, computer access on the farm increased by 53%, ownership increased by 75%, use of computers for business increased by 58%, and the number of farms with Internet access increased by 250%.

IT AND AGRICULTURAL EXTENSION PROGRAMS

Extensionists recognized the importance of on-farm, computer-aided management for agricultural production soon after the desktop computer became available. As early as 1982, land grant universities were conducting extension activities at a programmatic level to accelerate computer technology adoption. Early efforts in Florida took the form of state conferences on computers in agriculture, carried through 1992, and typically including a series of seminars, hands-on sessions organized by commodity, and trade shows. In addition, computer applications were incorporated into traditional commodity educational activities, and faculty were given credit towards tenure and promotion for developing and publishing agricultural software. In Florida, this effort was successful enough to staff and to operate a self-sustaining statewide Software Support Office, started in 1982 and absorbed into a newly created Information Technology Office in 1997. Software applications were diverse and included expert systems (ES), computer-aided design (CAD), computer-aided management (CAM), information delivery systems (IDS), simulations, and automated control. In particular, IDS evolved into rich content applications from desktop and mainframe databases into CD-ROM and, eventually, web-based systems.

An important strategy for extension is proactive support for emerging technologies that may give farmers a competitive advantage. Such a strategy was implemented when it became evident that the Internet and World Wide Web were to play important roles in the marketplace. During 1994 and 1995, the UF Florida Cooperative Extension held 50 half-day workshops each year, directed at farmers, on using the Internet for business. Today, Florida ranks at the top in Internet purchases of agricultural inputs and second in marketing over the Internet. In addition, electronic delivery systems have become essential for timely information distribution. The Extension Digital Information Source (EDIS) web page described below delivers more than 20,000 publications per day to Florida Cooperative Extension clients.

As technology allowed faster connections, hardware devices became smarter, and software development tools allowed faster prototyping and development, complex distributed systems emerged. Their application to agriculture exploited fast and reliable communication for the acquisition and delivery of real-time information for tactical management and forecasting for strategic management. The FAWN project described below exemplifies the use of weather data for short-term decision-making and the use of El Niño-based climatic simulation for medium to long-term strategy selection.

EXAMPLES OF SUCCESSFUL IT IMPLEMENTATIONS

Extension Publications System (http://edis.ifas.ufl.edu). UF/IFAS maintains about 5,000 extension publications in electronic format. The EDIS consists of a centralized Document Object Data Base (DODB) from which deliverables, such as CD-ROMs, HTML, and pdf, are generated (Beck, 2001). Rather than using conventional word processing or markup tools, specialists are provided with a tool that creates an interface directly with the DODB. In this way, content is made available immediately upon completion of the authoring and review/approval process. The average time it takes to make documents available to the clients was reduced from 58 days to the time it takes to transmit a *publish* command from the client to the server. Because deliverables are synthetically generated, they become immediately available to the clients. For example, HTML for web pages on EDIS is built on the fly when a user requests a publication.

Florida Automated Weather Network, FAWN (http://fawn.ifas.ufl.edu). In 1996, the National Weather Service discontinued weather programs for agricultural producers and other groups. In January 1997, a freeze that caused a $300 million loss to south Florida's agriculture underlined the need for accurate and timely agricultural weather information. Because of the efforts of the Florida Weather Taskforce, UF/IFAS-IT implemented a *real-time* weather network. Currently, FAWN has evolved from a data collection system to a source of management tools and recommendations. It incorporates the work of the Florida Consortium, a group of climate researchers working internationally, and includes near-term climate prediction as well as crop and disease models. FAWN brought together different groups working on related issues, including individuals from the private sector, academia, extension, and politicians, each with very specific and clearly defined responsibilities.

Distance Diagnostic and Identification System, DDIS (http://
ddis.ifas.ufl.edu). DDIS consists of a Java-based distributed system that provides an environment to identify plant, insect, and disease problems (Xin et
al., 2001). It uses Java Remote Method Invocation (RMI) technology, Java
applications and servlets, object databases, and email. Users in the field capture images using a digital camera or in the laboratory using a digital imaging-
enabled stereoscope or compound microscope. Images are submitted to a central object database from which notification to specialists automatically
occurs. Specialists access the database, perform a diagnosis, and provide recommendations, which are submitted to the object database, which in turn
notifies the user a diagnosis is available.

WHERE ARE WE GOING?

Changes in technology will proceed with organizational and social change.
The rapid evolution of hardware and software devices will increase consumer
demand for timely and accurate information. If current trends in wireless
broadband technologies continue, it is likely that in the medium term,
demands, beyond data, for on-field best management practices will increase
rapidly. These developments, coupled with the rapid advances that are being
made in human computer interfaces, are likely to make IT ubiquitous,
enabling access to dramatically increased amounts of data, tools for analysis,
and decision support systems.

The Extension Service will take advantage of IT developments to
enhance its ability to conduct nonresident education programs. This technology is particularly advantageous to deliver information asynchronously to
widely dispersed clients. However, a full conversion to IT by extension professionals will likely take a generation in most areas of expertise and be driven by
client demands in other areas.

REFERENCES

Beck, H. W. (2001). Agricultural enterprise information management using
object databases, Java and CORBA. *Computers and Electronics in Agriculture, 32,* 19–147.

Extension Committee on Organization and Policy (ECOP). (1980). *Computers in agriculture.* Washington, DC: United States Department of
Agriculture.

National Agricultural Statistics Service (NASS). (2001). *Farm computer usage and ownership.* Washington, DC: Agricultural Statistics Board, United States Department of Agriculture.

Xin, J., Beck, H. W., Halsey, L. A., Fletcher, J. H., Zazueta, F. S., & Momol, T. (2001). Development of a distance diagnostic and identification system for plant, insect, and disease problems. *Applied Engineering in Agriculture, 17* (4), 561–565.

60

THE DEVELOPMENT OF E-TEACHERS FOR E-LEARNING

Judy L. Robinson
University of Florida

The development of an online course or an online module for a course taught face-to-face takes time, technological knowledge, and a team. The team needs the e-teacher as a content expert and implementer and the instructional designer as pedagogical expert and technology adviser. Sometimes the team needs high-level technical expertise that is best provided by a programmer or a person with extensive experience with a particular program, and often the team needs "helping hands" to spend the hours necessary to create interactive exercises and effective multimedia.

Effective university professors in face-to-face classrooms usually have thought a lot about teaching styles and methods of communication and assessment. The same is important for effective e-teaching. Moreover, the knowledge required to create effective e-learning opportunities has increased. Decisions about how an online course is designed and delivered are based on information about how to teach with multimedia and Internet technologies. Effective e-teachers must be informed enough to make those decisions, because they will be teaching the course after the instructional designer has moved on to other projects. Faculty members need not know how to create online courses but to work with instructional designers to realize the range of choices about how the material will be provided to the students.

An interesting phenomenon occurs between potential e-teachers and instructional designers. While it is tempting simply to digitize the textbook, lecture notes, and PowerPoint slides used in a face-to-face class, the downside of such a process is that the online version of the course will be totally linear, without the human interaction that amplifies the classroom experience. If the faculty member is not involved with the designer, they will not discuss how various technologies can be used more creatively and effectively to achieve the same learning objectives. Sometimes, depending on what is to be learned, the linear approach is the best choice; sometimes it is not.

Better utilizing technology and reconceptualizing the materials to be taught takes time and may not be cost-effective at first. However, if discovering what makes effective e-teaching is the goal, then different approaches must be examined. Where possible, effective e-teachers create learning situations that allow choice and self-direction and that show instead of tell. When possible, effective instructional e-designers help faculty members make informed choices about how best to teach online. While the focus is so often on e-learning, we must not forget the development of the e-teacher.

ASSESSMENT OF STUDENT PROGRAMS

61

MEETING ONLINE ASSESSMENT NEEDS THROUGH ELECTRONIC PORTFOLIOS

Barbara B. Lockee, D. Michael Moore, and John K. Burton
Virginia Polytechnic Institute and State University

Since 1998, the Instructional Technology Program at Virginia Tech has offered a distance-delivered master's degree program (ITMA), customized for practicing professional K–12 educators. In its early iteration, ITMA focused specifically on serving the teachers of Virginia through a fixed-sequence, cohort-centered approach. Since then, the online initiative has evolved into a completely asynchronous, self-paced program, enrolling students nationally and internationally. While many aspects of ITMA have changed through the course of its development, the primary assessment strategy remains the same. Electronic portfolios have consistently served a variety of programmatic needs and continue to be the centerpiece of the ITMA student's program-related productivity.

RATIONALE FOR PORTFOLIO-BASED ASSESSMENT

The ITMA online program was created in response to a state mandate for teachers to acquire specific computer technology skills. Educators had few opportunities for related professional development, especially degree-granting opportunities.

The Virginia Tech instructional technology (IT) faculty decided to design the distance program using generative learning strategies with project-based assessment. Courses were transitioned to customized modules that specifically addressed not only the state technology standards but also the IT standards of the Association of Educational Communications and Technology (AECT) and Virginia Tech's own programmatic standards. Each module resulted in the creation of projects, products, or papers that demonstrated the acquisition of relevant skills, knowledge, or attitudes. Therefore, the electronic portfolio served first and foremost as a singular repository for each of the seven faculty to locate and grade all student assignments for each module. As the distance students prepared for program completion, the portfolio then served as the culmination of their work, demonstrating learning and professional growth over time. The faculty formed final examination committees and reviewed the portfolios collectively as a comprehensive learner-assessment mechanism for the entire program.

In light of the current emphasis on teacher accountability, the portfolios also provide evidence to the ITMA students' employers and certifying national organizations that they possess demonstrable skills and knowledge in IT. Furthermore, many of our past students have transitioned to other jobs and/or career paths, using the portfolio as evidence of technology competence. These additional uses for the electronic collections of work were unanticipated but have proven consistent over the past several years.

LESSONS LEARNED

Instructional Issues

The use of electronic portfolios for the evaluation of student progress has provided a more holistic perspective on our learners' abilities. Instead of responding to traditional assessment items, students have to demonstrate skills on a variety of levels, allowing a more accurate indication of achievement and growth. The use of web-based multimedia to demonstrate concept and skill attainment has afforded the learners a wider range of possibilities for representing new knowledge.

However, the exclusive use of electronic media to instruct and to assess has elicited some deeper pedagogical and philosophical issues that must be addressed. First, we must consider how the learners' messages are changed by the need to communicate through a delivery channel that is sometimes foreign to them. Altering the communication mechanism from a traditional, text-based format to an unfamiliar and, thus, more potentially challenging tool has surely influenced both the content and the form of learner responses. Some students have found that making their IT abilities visible through the portfolios communicates them more powerfully, while others who struggle with the technical issues cannot communicate at all.

We must also resolve the tension between communicating specific portfolio expectations and maintaining the portfolio's role as an opportunity to synthesize and analyze. While some learners can specifically address the outcome criteria in creative and effective ways, others may include components that do not clearly target the predetermined instructional goals. Although we want to encourage creativity and individualized outcomes, we must also work to ensure that the distance students are working toward and completing the specified program goals.

Logistical Issues

Most challenges associated with the implementation of the portfolio approach were logistical. At first, the IT program was responsible for the establishment and maintenance of the server system to manage the portfolio space and access privileges for more than 70 students. Since then, the university has created an institution-wide filebox system, providing electronic storage space to all Virginia Tech students. The new, centralized system is accessible through file-transfer protocol (FTP) or the web, and learners must acquire the skills necessary to move their files and maintain their sites very early in the program. Sometimes this skill requirement presents challenges for those teachers with little computer experience. The IT program continues to facilitate the learning of basic computing skills early to begin the process of portfolio development.

Socio-Psychological Issues

The portfolio-based assessment strategy has changed the face of student evaluation, since it personifies individual learning achievement, eliciting the learner's strong sense of ownership. For our students, the portfolio has become a representation of self in a globally accessible environment. This medium makes publicly available student talents, personal philosophies, accomplishments, and future goals. Conversely, it can demonstrate less than optimal skills and content that may be relevant to program participation but not appropriate for public consumption. For example, the exposure of work that does not meet instructional criteria and standards can be harmful. Even though work may be under revision, it remains continuously accessible. While most learners find public access to their work positive, some are reluctant to have personal information available on the web in any form. Future iterations of the portfolio development experience will most likely include mechanisms for accessing certain web pages via password or some other regulated process.

CONCLUSION

The electronic portfolio has already played a number of vital and evolving roles in its realization. First, it has served as a focal point for course development. The need for learners to demonstrate mandated competencies naturally led to production-oriented modules, the deliverables of which integrate easily into the portfolio schema. In terms of assessment, the web-based tool has provided us with a creative means to evaluate attainment of outcomes that are largely media-based. Logistically, the management of student work has been streamlined by the establishment of a personal web framework for each student, readily accessible by all instructors. Finally, the electronic portfolio has afforded our learners opportunities for synthesis, analysis, and reflection through media that can visualize their ideas in new and exciting ways.

62

ASSESSING INSTRUCTIONAL USES OF ONLINE SYNCHRONOUS MESSAGING IN A HYBRID COURSE

Carol DeArment
University of Pittsburgh

Computer technologies increasingly are being used to enhance traditional face-to-face instruction in higher education. Internet-based, or online, interactive text-messaging tools provide opportunities for instructor/student and student/student dialogue for purposes ranging from administrative housekeeping to reflective knowledge building. The increasing number of college courses that blend computer communication technologies with traditional instruction and learning practices has created a need to understand how to use these technologies effectively.

A qualitative case study was conducted in the summer of 2001 in a graduate course at the University of Pittsburgh. The study used faculty and student perceptions to gain insight into how computer-mediated, text-based messaging tools can enhance learning when they are integrated with traditional face-to-face instruction in a hybrid course. The instructor used asynchronous threaded discussion, synchronous (real time) virtual classroom discussion, email, and group tools provided by course management software. Her rationale was based on learning theories that support active engagement with course content through student dialogue; the online text-messaging tools provided a way to compensate for her inability to devote class time to discussion because of the number of students (60), classroom constraints, and the content-heavy curriculum.

The researcher interviewed the course instructor and selected eight students for in-depth interviews and focus groups throughout the semester. The researcher, as observer/participant, also attended face-to-face class meetings, collected course documents, and surveyed the entire class of 60 students at the end of the semester. The study indicated that online, text-based communication integrated with a face-to-face class can provide more opportunities for active engagement with course content. However, computer-mediated communication raises critical questions about instructional design. A discussion of findings related to synchronous discussion tools follows. While the synchronous discussion tool is comparable to a virtual chat room, that term has recreational connotations that do not apply to the instructional rationale that guided use of the synchronous discussion addressed by this study.

INSTRUCTOR'S PERCEPTIONS

The instructor required students to participate in at least one of several synchronous sessions that she scheduled to review for tests and to converse with a guest expert. She felt that this discussion tool closely "replicated the informal give-and-take of a real-time conversation and allowed students a chance to bounce ideas off one another." She believed students would feel more comfortable asking questions and getting clarification in the synchronous mode than they would with the asynchronous communication tools.

More than 20 students participated in the first session, which was held to review for a test, and the instructor had difficulty keeping up with the flow of their questions. While the instructor was working on her response to one, students would enter the virtual space, exchange informal remarks with each other, and ask new questions. The screen space became incoherent or, in the words of study participants, "chaotic," due to the number of superfluous messages. The instructor found the synchronous session was not effective with more than 12 students. Although she valued the informality and immediacy of this tool, she noted that in face-to-face sessions, "students ask one question at a time," making it easier to respond and to maintain a coherent dialogue. In succeeding sessions, the instructor learned to explicitly mention the student's name and the question to which she was replying, and she scheduled more than one study session in an attempt to limit the number of participants at any one time. She also encouraged students to refer to archives for her follow-up answers to their questions.

STUDENTS' PERCEPTIONS

Because of the synchronous online study sessions' informality, students generally said they felt more comfortable asking questions than they would have felt sending an individual message to the instructor. They appreciated the instructor's explicit information on what they needed to know for upcoming tests; the spontaneity of the synchronous sessions prompted the instructor to share some hints that she probably would not have had an opportunity to provide otherwise. While students might not have been able to attend a face-to-face study session, anyone could print out the archives of these discussions, and students found this capability invaluable. Synchronous text-messaging also allowed students to interact with a distant guest expert, who provided immediate information about a timely topic. Students appreciated this unique opportunity.

However, students' overall perceptions of the virtual classroom were clouded by their frustration with superfluous banter. They said that unnecessary comments took up too much screen space and, whether as real-time participants or readers of archives, distracted them from the meat of the textual exchanges. Two sources of fluff (a term frequently used by study participants) were the salutations that students extended each time a participant entered or left the virtual space. Other unnecessary comments seemed to derive from a desire to keep the sessions informal and friendly, as illustrated in this excerpt:

Figure 62.1

Example of Comments

ANN:	Well, Karla, there's a lot of content in Module 3, and it is all important, I think, but I tried to pull out the really, really, really important!
MATT:	Hello Ann how are you?
ANN:	Hi Tami!
TAMI:	Hello everyone, Ann!
KARLA:	Yes, you have narrowed it -- some!!!!
	JIM has entered. [03:58:15 PM]
ANN:	Hi Jim!
JIM:	Hey all. Not signed up, but just lurking...
	MARY has entered. [03:58:45 PM]
DAN:	Ann, on quiz 2, will you have the fill in the blank on the quiz?
KARLA:	To me, cataloging and indexing seem to be the most important.
	MARY has left. [03:58:57 PM]
	AMY has entered. [03:59:22 PM]

In the class survey at the end of the semester, 71% of participants said the textual exchanges in the synchronous medium could have been transacted just as well without online technology. This tool was the only one that some students (9%) considered potentially "harmful," because a session might end before the instructor had an opportunity to review and to clarify student messages that contained misinformation or misperceptions. Furthermore, since participation in the virtual classroom was required only once, students did not have an opportunity to adjust to this communication tool, which contributed to a common perception that it was significantly less effective than the asynchronous threaded discussion board for engagement, interaction, and thinking.

Students pointed out at the end of the semester that they were least accustomed to using this synchronous type of communication tool. They compared it to a recreational chat room, with which most had some experience, and the difference between that and the instructional context of the asynchronous messaging tool disoriented both students who had used the recreational tool and those who were simply anecdotally familiar with it. Students speculated that, as virtual technologies became more prevalent in college courses, instructors and students would adapt their interactions to use synchronous text messaging tools more effectively.

Student perceptions, more than faculty perceptions, were influenced by complex contextual factors, which included course content, assignments, instructor style, classroom constraints, and attributes of the technologies. In addition, students' past experiences and incoming attitudes were intrinsic factors in their perceptions. Their comments especially showed that negative experiences with a technology were difficult to overcome and affected their perceptions.

Thus, synchronous messaging offered some instructional benefits by providing opportunities for interaction and engagement as follows:

- Synchronous dialogue provided a sense of immediacy and informality that simulated the face-to-face discussion valued by most of the participants.

- Because of its informality, some students felt more comfortable asking questions than they would have in an email message to the instructor or during a face-to-face session.

- The printed archives, a visual record of the dialogue, gave students a way to scan for useful information after the synchronous session, which was useful for both students who had participated in the session and those who had not.

- The spontaneity of synchronous online discussion prompted the instructor to share some hints for the exams during study sessions that she might not have had an opportunity to provide otherwise.

- Synchronous text-messaging gave students a means of interacting from a distance with a guest expert who provided a sense of immediacy about an important topic.

RECOMMENDATIONS

While synchronous text-based messaging in this class did not permit the kinds of reflective discussion associated with higher-level thinking skills, it was highly useful in providing a means of dialogue from a distance with a guest expert who had specialized knowledge and experience in a critical field. This mode of communication was also useful in scheduling virtual study sessions; most of these graduate students, many of whom lived at a distance from campus, could participate in at least one without having to travel. However, with each succeeding virtual session, the instructor learned lessons that would help to cut down on messages that some students found to be distracting, if not downright annoying. Lessons learned by the instructor, along with others compiled by the researcher after analyzing the data, follow.

The instructional usefulness of these sessions might improve if the instructor would:

- assume the role of moderator or leader or appoint someone else to serve this function

- provide students with directions, training, and practice before the first session

- plan a general direction for the session, including goals and instructional objectives

- provide guidelines on netiquette (online etiquette) in an attempt to eliminate messages that some students might perceive as rude, for example:

  - require students to enter the virtual space by a particular time and to avoid logging off until the session has ended to decrease the amount of screen space taken up by announcements of arrivals and departures

  - require students to wait for the instructor to answer one question before posting a new question

  - require those posting a message to indicate which previous message they are responding to by using the name of the previous sender

  - encourage students to forego greetings and salutations

    ~ ask students to abstain from other superficial comments that clutter the screen

- find ways to regularly assess student perceptions of the online tools and use the results to try out modifications during the semester
- limit participation to groups of ten or fewer students

63

THE MATH EMPORIUM: THE CHANGING ACADEMY OR CHANGING THE ACADEMY?

Michael Williams
Virginia Polytechnic Institute and State University

Very few institutions have been as seemingly impervious to change as those of higher learning. With a history measured by millennia, who can blame higher education's faculty and guardians for feeling that the current invasive wave of technological intrusions is but another passing fancy?

To date, not very much has changed inside our institutions. Sure, there have been lots of activities around the edges, using resources like email and web pages. Some wonderful and effective programs have been created, typically at great expense. Nevertheless, these efforts have largely been on the margin. Have we collectively become more effective? Probably. Have we become more efficient? Hardly. Any real gains from economies of scale or scope are still missing.

I would like to discuss an example of what we can do to better prepare ourselves for whatever does come along. In particular, I'll describe the Math Emporium project at Virginia Tech.

The Math Emporium, a 60,000-square-foot, 24/7 facility with 500+ workstations arranged in an array of well-spaced hexagonal pods, opened its doors in the fall of 1997. We have learned much along the way and adapt our offerings each year. I'll describe the way we currently handle a particular course, which will illustrate many of our principles.

MATH 1015

Math 1015 is a one-semester, precalculus course covering college algebra and trigonometry. It's not very exciting stuff and well within the curriculum of high schools. About 1,600 students use the course to satisfy mathematics distributional requirements each year. Student backgrounds vary widely. We offer this course as one large block that meets together exactly once at the outset for an orientation. At the orientation, we make the students aware of resources that are available to them, which include a "home", office hours from 9 a.m. to midnight five days a week, a walk-in tutoring lab, online course materials, online videos, a course advisor, a fully detailed course schedule, and a testing system. Student progress is monitored, but they may go faster if they like. All the goals, expectations, procedures, and rules are precisely prescribed a priori. Aside from keeping up, students' schedules are their own concern.

During operating hours, faculty, graduate students, and advanced undergraduate math students staff the floor of the Math Emporium. Faculty assignments are made on the basis of two hours of floor service for each course credit assignment (a three-credit course = six support hours). Important economies of scope and scale are gained by using this staff to support all Math Emporium courses, not just Math 1015. The structure of *a course/an instructor/many students has been reconfigured into many courses/many instructors/many students.* In this model, the faculty mindset moves from "my student" to "our student", which has been difficult for some. Since floor schedules are regular, associations between students and faculty do form, however.

ASSESSMENT OR LEARNING TOOL?

From time immemorial, faculty have complained about the way students interrupt their lectures to ask, "Will this be on the test?" The nerve of students to think that anything we say is not a pearl worthy of an honored and permanent place in their minds and available at any time henceforth; for example, during the upcoming hourly exam!

For students, of course, what more natural question could they ask? The test is how they will be judged. It's a reality that we should try to put to work for us. If we let them know something about the test early on, their objectives will become more sharply defined. A possible danger would be to drift into a kind of teach-to-the-test mode. We feel the model we are developing drives the student to spend more time working many, many more problems, while keeping them broadly aware of the full spectrum of the subject matter, all relatively painlessly.

Therefore, we built an online testing system with the following properties:

- An unlimited supply of practice tests and quizzes is available anytime, anywhere to enrolled students.

- Practice tests and quizzes are constructed from the same pool of questions as the tests and exams that count.

- Each question is selected from an infinite collection of questions generated by a problem program or stem. Each is unique, and, moreover, its nature and random selection mean that students must know how to solve it and not simply rely on rote memory of a set example.

- Every individual learning goal for the course is tested by one or more questions.

- There are enough question stems that practice tests significantly differ.

- Tests (practice or the real thing) are graded immediately, and corrected answers are marked.

- All previously taken tests are available for online review at any time during the semester.

- Students' current standings in the course are available to them at all times.

By stating the goals and expectations explicitly at the outset, all mystery as to how to succeed in the course is removed. The students have the responsibility and the authority to manage their individual learning experiences. This last point is crucial; to repair the current situation, we must restore the understanding that, ultimately, the students' success in learning rests squarely in their own hands.

The instructors available for support are naturally separated from the testing mechanisms and, therefore, are free from the usual adversarial conflict of the student/teacher relationship. The students feel freer to approach faculty as coaches who are on their side.

As for results, the two principal observations are that 1) the students are performing better in downstream courses; and 2) our costs per student credit hour have decreased (in one course, from $78 to $26). Further details are available upon request.

What Is Gained?

The Math Emporium project permits us to examine the viability of an alternative model, to find ways to address fundamental problems in distance education, and to leverage our faculty to advantage (i.e., save money). As many faculty find financial matters distasteful, new methods are held to a standard that insists on provably superior results. Well, what if the students do just as well, but the costs are much less? We can argue that small classes and lots of professorial interaction give the best results, but who can afford such luxuries across the board in the face of shrinking budgets and faculties?

Resource

Math Emporium home page: http://www.emporium.vt.edu/

64

USING ASSESSMENT TO
IMPROVE TEACHER EDUCATION

Susan P. Giancola
University of Delaware

No other profession is more important to the future of our young people than teaching. However, teachers are often criticized and undervalued by the popular media. Frequently glib statements about how the use of technology will fix the problem are made with no supporting data. How can teacher education programs show the public that they are producing high-quality, well-trained teachers? Evidence is what matters.

The University of Delaware's School of Education is launching an ambitious assessment program. The program applies to core components of teacher education courses. Included in the program are measures to assess the effectiveness of technology in learning and the importance of teachers learning how to use technology. By highlighting assessments related to technology, we will be able to respond to another need: specifically, to demonstrate to accreditors and others the value of technology-enhanced teaching.

Our approach to assessment is based upon three simple principles: 1) core components of teacher education courses should be assessed, 2) they should be assessed against professional criteria and standards, and 3) all instructors should participate in the rating of all components. We are calling our pilot program a course-embedded assessment system. All assessments are currently performance-based; that is, they are projects valued in their own right and not simply paper-and-pencil examinations. Because consistency in scoring is critical to the assessment process, the instructors who regularly teach each course are participating in an "inter-rater" reliability study: that is, each instructor scores the same set of performance tasks. When inconsistencies appear, either the items being scored will be clarified, or all instructors will be brought to a common understanding of their meaning. Approximately 15 courses, involving over 30 sections, are participating in the pilot program and reliability study. One course project involves the development of a resource for teachers that includes a critique of selected children's literature.

The student is required to publish the resource on the web and provide several links to additional online resources. Another course project requires teacher education majors to choose a unit of instruction and construct their own summative test. A third course project requires students to integrate technology into a lesson plan and to publish the lesson plan on the web. The participating instructors for each of these three projects are developing evaluative criteria and rating scales that apply to all course sections and all aspects of the course project.

The implications for such an assessment system are many and varied. As planned, the system will allow university administrators to measure student performance and monitor course quality. Deficiencies can be recognized and improved; outliers can be identified and examined.

While these practices are crucial, the ability to experiment within such a system is especially exciting. With indicators identified and routinely tracked, experimental modifications of teaching methods can be studied with minimal effort. The course-embedded assessment system will enable systematic study of the impact of technology upon teaching and learning as instructors experiment with technologically advanced and innovative teaching methods. Assessment of the impact of technology upon learning will be mainstreamed. As a consequence, the impact of technological innovations can be compared with the impact of other types of learning enhancements. We expect that accreditors, the general public, and the teachers themselves can gain a better understanding of what is and what is not working.

65

THE JOY OF DISTANCE LEARNING: RECIPES FOR SUCCESS (WITH APOLOGIES TO IRMA S. ROMBAUER ET AL.)

David Potenziani
University of North Carolina at Chapel Hill

BUILDING AN ONLINE COURSE: MAKES ONE COURSE

While not certain of success, here's an approach you can try. Approach the process with plenty of time.

Combine in one development team:
1 faculty member (discipline open) with no online experience
1 instructional designer
1/2 graphics developer
1/2 web developer
1/2 project manager

Beginnings are fragile times. When we started developing our first web-based course in 1997, we had no idea what we were doing. While no one had created such a course at UNC before, we charged into the process as though we knew what we were doing. Our hope was to create a five-course core curriculum in public health. Like all pioneers, we were lost most of the time, but we still knew where we were heading.

The development team was like a Hollywood World War II bomber crew; we had one of everything. We found that an instructional designer who can work with faculty and not confront them with jargon is gold. Faculty members generally want to know how to solve specific technical and logistical problems, giving a savvy team a chance to slip in instructional design concepts disguised as answers to questions. The other members of the team were needed for the technical bits that no faculty member could be expected to know how to do. Finally, we recognized that project management was necessary if we were to succeed.

Primary Goals

Begin by meeting with the entire team to identify the primary goals:

- the educational goals the faculty member wants students to attain

- the deadline for when the course enters the classroom

- the type of online course site (freeform web site or a course management system)

Be consistent across all the courses developed.

Getting faculty to identify their curricular goals was harder than we anticipated. We spent weeks in discussions about those goals and tried to knit them to make a cohesive whole across the five courses we were developing. The terms of our funding were to start the courses online within 12 months. That deadline provided the necessary spur to keep everyone, mostly, on the task. It ended up taking 14 months. We decided to use a course management system, since we were already conversant with one—WebCT. It allowed us to concentrate on the development of materials and provided a standardized interface for the students to use. Once students mastered the navigation for one course, they had mastered it for all of them. We recognized that these students would have few opportunities to ask the faculty for guidance in finding and using course materials. To simplify that task, we created a path through the course materials that always showed the next task students had to take. We organized the materials so that they could find readings, help files, exercises, tutorials, and assessments easily within each part of a course.

Establish Ground Rules and Roles

- The faculty member is the content expert but has to learn a few things about online instruction. For example, lectures that last 45 minutes online are four times too long; online lectures need authentic tasks at periodic intervals to keep students engaged.

- The development team is the final authority, with the faculty member having a veto on how content is expressed.

- If necessary, bring in an outside consultant to express the same ideas and advocate for the same approaches as the local team. Set aside technical discussions until the faculty members identify their instructional goals.

The importance of spending time working through the instructional design cannot be overstated. Our hope was to transform the courses into an interrelated body of work that provided students with the best science, authentic tasks, and a holistic approach to public health. The faculty decided to use a case study to knit the courses together: an outbreak of cryptosporidium in Milwaukee during 1993. Each course approached the outbreak from its disciplinary perspective and with the tools of that discipline. The courses required the students to integrate what they learned about the outbreak from each of these perspectives into a unified whole.

The approach also focused faculty efforts on the instructional questions and avoided the distractions of instructional technology. The technical staff refused to discuss technology until the faculty had worked through the pedagogy. Faculty members did not initially agree with that position; however, the approach afforded the technical staff the time to research appropriate technologies and organize for the production of online materials.

Identify the Technical Approaches

- Determine what kind of technology students are likely to have.

- Identify the required technical standards in bandwidth and software, taking care to choose free ones.

- Provide training for faculty in minimal technology. Remember that they are faculty and not web developers.

We identified the technology that the students needed and mandated that all the materials and interactions had to work under those constraints. We specified that all web materials had to be deliverable over a dial-up Internet connection using a 28.8 kbps modem. We also mandated that none of the software could cost the student any money but had to be freely available for downloading.

Let the Faculty See an Example of a Finished Piece

The technical team was helping the faculty to understand what was possible with the staff and production facilities we had put in place. We decided that the best approach was to develop a tutorial and interactive exercise apart from any of the courses. We developed a multimedia presentation that explored John Snow's seminal analysis of an outbreak of cholera in London in the 1850s. We wrote a script, developed graphics, devised a navigation system, and recorded music and narration. It took about six weeks to complete and stretched our capacities to the limit. We wanted to use John Snow's own words from his treatise on the subject to inform the presentation and found a volunteer drama student, who read the narrative while we manipulated the images to be synchronized with the text. A team member composed a musical theme that provided the right touches of haunting menace that we believed Londoners felt as the epidemic threatened the metropolis. We also created exercises that asked students what they might do at a critical juncture. We offered them an opportunity to type their answers in a text box and then presented a model answer, asking them to compare the two. The result was a presentation that at times was compelling in its drama but expensive and difficult to produce.

Evaluate, Evaluate, Evaluate!

From the beginning, we worked tirelessly to develop evaluation instruments to measure the effectiveness of our courses. We all intended to develop courses that had the same academic rigor as our traditional core courses, and we wanted to demonstrate that fact. Every course went through a battery of online surveys and telephone focus groups during both the formative and delivery stages. We wanted to understand how students and faculty perceived the course's quality. The discussions with faculty have evolved into monthly meetings of the Teaching Guild, where faculty and staff involved in online instruction gather to discuss developments in the field. Our instructional designers have published several articles in peer-reviewed journals discussing and evaluating the effectiveness of our courses.

Recognize That Online Course Development is Messy

Of course, the process was not nearly as smooth as presented here. We all had misunderstandings and confusion over how we were going to produce the courses online. At times, faculty members became frustrated (I'm being polite) with the constraints of the technology or the approaches the technical teams developed. The instructional designers labored hard to preserve what they perceived as the educational quality of the materials and interactions, when the faculty and technical staff members just wanted to get the job done. Everyone else, who questioned why we needed to use that technology when another approach was clearly better, yelled at the technical staff. Everyone took a turn feeling threatened, frustrated, or worn out (more polite terms) by the perspectives and actions of others. We ran into major scheduling problems as deadlines slipped, and we were all tempted to blame each other. Some faculty members chafed at the technical staff's insistence that materials continue to come at a steady pace so we would not miss the ultimate deadline. Unaccustomed to working on such a tight schedule in a medium not well understood, at one point we had to find a different faculty member to finish the development of one of the courses.

BUILDING A CURRICULUM: MAKES MANY COURSES

As with a meal, one course does not suffice. Repeat the steps above for as many courses as desired. The following steps help in building a curriculum.

Prepare for Ongoing Responsibilities in Online Teaching

The result of our experience helped our faculty better understand how to teach online. Every offering of the core courses has prompted each faculty member to request technical assistance for improvement or to add a new feature. Online core-course faculty members have become quite expert in teaching over the web. They have mastered the art of keeping contacts with students alive and lively, while never meeting them in the flesh. They have seen the importance of the presentation quality of their tutorials so that they accept the need to use professional-quality audio equipment. They have adjusted the student-to-instructor ratio to find the best balance for optimum effect (currently about 20 to 1). They have learned that setting reasonable expectations for communicating with students is of paramount importance.

Set Student Expectations to the Reasonable End of the Spectrum

The faculty found that they were on call for student questions round the clock, seven days a week. Students began to expect immediate responses to their email questions and discussion group postings, especially when they were scattered across the globe and did not recognize that they were several time zones away. Faculty members developed procedures to have teaching assistants screen routine questions and built up a stockpile of standard answers to common questions. In short, faculty members have built up the same types of approaches and expertise they have used in their face-to-face courses. The job is still not easy and does require more time and effort to teach than a traditional course.

Anticipate the Technical Problems Students Will Have by Using Technology to Assess Their Skills

The project allowed our technical staff to understand faculty and student needs—and limits. It led directly to the development of an online skill building application that tests the student's computer system and connection to see that it has the capacity and software to run all the applications in any online course. At the same time, it shows the student how to navigate through course materials and teaches them how to do some seemingly basic, but vital, operations, such as cutting and pasting or entering a URL. Teaching these basic capabilities has reduced the need for initial technical support to a fraction of what it was originally.

Online Programs Need a Human Being to Serve as Coordinator, Helper, and Friend to Students

The core-course development along with the experience gained in other online courses and programs has demonstrated the need for ongoing distance-learning support services for students. Successful online programs have a visible and consistent coordinator who provides the essential function of keeping in touch with all the students. The students come to rely on these coordinators as a personal connection with the life of the school. They serve as academic advisor, cheerleader, confidant, and even disciplinarian. Without the glue of such a role, students tend to drop out of courses when they begin to feel the weight of graduate work and the lack of physical connection to the school.

Make Sure Technical Support is Always Available

We have learned the necessity of providing 24-hour-a-day technical support to all students via the telephone, email, and web pages. Students learn quickly that they are just a phone call away from technicians versed in the types of technology they are using and specifically trained to address problems over the phone. If a student presents a problem that indicates a systems failure, the issue is escalated to the responsible agency and tagged so it will not be forgotten. The system can even send messages to pagers and wireless email devices that alert systems staff to the problem. These steps may seem extraordinary, but in the online context, they are necessary and prudent. Students who take online courses are most often working professionals who have little time to waste waiting for a system to respond to their request. They need a solution, and they need it immediately. With our students on every continent, we cannot just close our eyes. For good or ill, online courses mean responsibility round the clock.

Some Questions for the Future

So, where are we headed? Clearly, the next step for the school is to recognize that the gap between online and face-to-face courses is going to close. Faculty members in traditional courses are starting to use the same technologies that their online counterparts use, especially as the core-course faculty work in both worlds and provide living, talking examples for their peers. Faculty members in traditional courses are hearing requests from their students via email and are beginning to post course materials on the web.

Are online courses for everyone? Probably not. Curricula that involve laboratory work, professional socialization, or professional mentoring are probably not suitable. In our experience, online courses work best for practitioners who have already identified themselves as public health professionals, have significant experience in the field, and want advanced training and education to meet their career goals. They are highly focused students who bring the wealth of their experience to the courses and do as much to teach each other as faculty.

Does online course development really need so many people? You bet. Faculty members' jobs are built on research and teaching, but teaching online requires specialized skills that are pointless for faculty to master. Of course they can learn such skills; it's just a waste of their time. Where faculty members do advance their skills is in gaining insights into teaching from confronting instructional issues in the crucible of online course development and beginning to glimpse the possibilities for communication and collaboration inherent in information technology.

PART VII
ASSESSING THE EFFECT OF TECHNOLOGY ON LEARNING

66

USING BENCHMARKING TO MEASURE THE IMPACT OF WEB-BASED COURSES IN NURSING

Diane Billings
Indiana University

INTRODUCTION

As faculty begin to use educational technology, such as the Internet and course management tools, to support effective teaching and learning, it is important to measure the impact and outcomes of their use. This essay describes a project conducted at three schools of nursing in collaboration with the Flashlight Project of the Teaching Learning Technology Group of the American Association for Higher Education. It uses benchmarking to set standards for teaching and learning in web courses and assess outcomes. The project developed a framework for assessing educational practices and outcomes in web courses, adapted the Flashlight Project Current Student Inventory (Ehrmann & Zuniga, 1997) for a specific discipline, and then gathered data from students about their perceptions of the best practices in the web courses. The project started in 1998 by developing the framework and establishing reliability and validity of the instrument. In 2002, the project became available nationally for use at other schools of nursing, and the benchmarking processes are being disseminated to other disciplines at the project partners' universities.

THE BENCHMARKING PROCESS

Benchmarking is a process-improvement technique that allows performance comparison. While commonly used in business and industry, benchmarking is also appropriate for universities, academic units, or even individual faculty to measure their practices against national norms and to use the results to stimulate dialogue and improve practices locally.

The benchmarking process involves several steps. The first is to determine what to benchmark. In the project described here, the benchmarks were derived from the *outcomes* particular to a health discipline with a clinical practice component: access, convenience, improved learning, recruitment, computer proficiency, preparation for real-world work, socialization to the profession, and satisfaction with the web's teaching and learning environment. We also identified the *educational practices* that are essential to success in teaching and learning in web courses based on Chickering and Gamson's (1987) principles of best practices in education: time on task, high expectations, rich and rapid feedback, active learning, interaction with faculty, interaction with peers, and respect for diversity. The *use of technology* was defined as having an effective technology infrastructure that promoted effective use of time.

We found it helpful to put these benchmarks in a framework (Billings, Conners, & Skiba, 2001) to more easily test our hypotheses and understand our findings. The model indicates that technology plus the use of educational practices will produce the desired outcomes.

The second step of the benchmarking process involves developing a survey instrument to gather data from the students. The items for the instrument were derived from the Flashlight Program's Current Student Inventory (Ehrmann & Zuniga, 1997) and adapted for nursing. The instrument has 52 items; 40 five-point Likert-type items gather information about students' perceptions of the outcomes, use of the educational practices, and the use of the technology; ten items are used to gather demographic data.

The third step is to gather the performance data to establish the norms. Our first study had 219 students, who were enrolled in primarily full-web BSN or MSN level courses at three different universities. The survey was linked into each web course, and students had the option of participating in the study according to Institutional Review Board (IRB) protocols at the three participating universities.

Once the data are collected, the fourth step is to compare data from courses or institutions. Comparisons can be made across all of the benchmarks (variables); the data can also be aggregated for a collective look at trends within the profession. At this time, we are increasing the numbers of the participating schools and refining the benchmarking reports.

The fifth step, of course, is to use the results for course and program improvement. We believe this application is best done within individual faculty groups at the level at which change can be made. The dialogue should include all members of the course development team, including the instructional support staff. Having an external facilitator is one way to discuss findings and to strategize improvement.

Results

Results indicated that students found the courses accessible and convenient. In fact, there were positive correlations between convenience and satisfaction, preparation for real-world work, and socialization. Students were also satisfied with the web courses, and their computer proficiency improved by the end of the course. Students also reported being moderately socialized to the profession, an outcome of significance to health disciplines. The one outcome of concern was that students felt isolated, or "disconnected," from the faculty and their classmates. For these students, the course tends to be less satisfying.

In this study, students reported that the educational practices were essential to attaining outcomes. For example, the perception of active learning correlated strongly with satisfaction, but students indicated they were somewhat less likely to interact with the faculty and their classmates. Students reported spending about six to ten hours per week participating in the course but did not think this time was either more or less than they would devote to an on-campus course.

Students did not find the technology (hardware, software) and the accessibility and reliability of the infrastructure supported productive use of time. However, for most of the students, faculty, and the institution, this web course was one of the first.

Lessons Learned

The findings from our study were helpful and led to discussion among the stakeholders at each campus. For individual faculty, the findings gave concrete data about performance gaps and areas needing improvement. For example, they realized that they should make the learning activities more active and require group work to promote greater collaboration among the students. The qualitative comments also provided direction about the need for feedback and clear directions about assignments. Faculty also appreciated that the students were, in fact, spending sufficient time with the course.

The findings also provided direction for the course's educational technology team. Faculty development programs can be designed around problem areas and courses designed to facilitate how students navigate through them. Often, the educational technologists can most directly advise faculty about course activities to increase the use of effective teaching and learning practices in web courses.

The findings are also useful to administrators. The technology infrastructure is clearly central to student satisfaction and productive use of time. Investment in the technology must continue, to assure usable course management tools, help desks, etc., but also to maintain personnel to assist faculty in redesigning courses once specific direction is provided from the benchmark studies. The need for faculty development is ongoing, and all three schools continue to offer workshops and seminars to assist faculty in designing their courses around the best practices.

Finally, the findings have proved useful in conducting program evaluation and providing data for accreditation reports. Because the findings are not just satisfaction indices or use counts but, rather, provide information about educational practices and to what extent specific educational outcomes have been met, actual programmatic changes can be initiated based on the assessment data.

USE OF BENCHMARKING IN OTHER SETTINGS

Benchmarking is a universal process that can provide direction to a variety of disciplines. However, it is essential for a discipline, an academic unit, or an entire campus to identify its own benchmarks. What are the desired outcomes? How will educational practices contribute to those outcomes? What are the benchmarks that this group seeks to attain and will hold as the gold standard for its practice? What technology is necessary to support both the outcomes and the educational practices? Developing a model or framework, selecting relevant questions for a reliable and valid survey, analyzing data for performance indicators, and checking against benchmarks will assist any group in discovering the impact of the use of technology on its teaching and student learning.

ACKNOWLEDGMENTS

This chapter is based on the work of the author; of Helen Connors, PhD, RN, FAAN, Associate Dean, University of Kansas School of Nursing, Kansas City; of Diane J. Skiba, PhD, FAAN, Associate Professor, University of Colorado Health Sciences Center; and of Robin Zuniga, Associate Director, Flashlight Program.

REFERENCES

Billings, D., Connors, H., & Skiba, D. (2001). Benchmarking best practices in web-based nursing courses. *Advances in Nursing Science, 23* (3), 41–52.

Chickering, W. W., & Gamson, Z. F. (1987). Seven principles for good practice in undergraduate education. *AAHE Bulletin, 39* (7), 3–7.

Ehrmann, S., & Zuniga, R., (1997). *The Flashlight evaluation handbook.* Washington, DC: Corporation for Public Broadcasting.

RESOURCES

The Flashlight Program: http://tltgroup.org

The use of Flashlight at Indiana University: http://kb.iu.edu use key word "Flashlight"

Kobs, A. E. J. (1998). Benchmarking: A data-oriented look at improving health care performance. *Journal of Nurse Care Quality, 10* (3), 1–6.

67

A CASE FOR AUTHENTIC ASSESSMENT: NUTRITION AND DIETETICS INTERNSHIP PROGRAM

Erin F. Sicuranza and Ann Rucinski
University of Delaware

In 1995, the University of Delaware instituted a Nutrition and Dietetics Internship Program in partnership with the Delaware Division of Public Health. Although it began as a local program, it has recently expanded to include a national distance education component and relies heavily on innovative technologies for the delivery of content and experience.

The program is designed to provide a minimum of 900 supervised practice hours, equipping dietetic students with the knowledge and skills necessary for an entry level generalist. It seeks to produce trained practitioners with an emphasis in community nutrition, particularly public health. The program also prepares graduates in the use and application of innovative technology. The distance education option was created to reach students in remote, underserved areas. Upon successful completion, graduates are eligible to sit for an examination and become registered dietitians (RD).

In an effort to meet the stated objectives, which are heavily skills based, the faculty created assignments that mimic field experiences. They adopted a case study method that incorporates problem-based learning techniques, which enable interns to sharpen their professional development skills, leading to success in future careers. This approach helps the interns learn how to learn.

The case studies fall into three broad categories that are required in the supervised practice programs (dietetic internships): clinical dietetics, food service management, and community nutrition. Currently, each of six case studies focuses on a different dimension. Using digital video and WebCT, an online course management system, the case studies are interactive experiences, rather than traditional and text based, and provide interns, to a certain extent, the benefits afforded by face-to-face communication. The faculty are using technology to simulate an environment that is as close to real life as possible. Each case study centers on a fictional client, portrayed by an actor, filmed in digital video, and displayed through a series of web pages.

The following section focuses on one of the six interactive, web-based case studies in the internship program. It will demonstrate how the faculty have tried to create realistic assignments and to measure student success with authentic assessment techniques. According to Grant Wiggins (1990), "Assessment is authentic when we directly examine student performance on worthy intellectual tasks. Traditional assessment, by contrast, relies on indirect or proxy 'items'—efficient, simplistic substitutes from which we think valid inferences can be made about the student's performance at those valued challenges." Each case study follows a pattern similar to the one outlined in this article. When developing these cases, the faculty focused on the critical tasks required of a dietitian and the best ways to assess student competency in these identified areas.

Clara Hayes: A Clinical Dietetics Case Study

This case study begins with a brief narrative on Clara Hayes, a 69-year-old woman who drives herself to the local hospital. She complains of shortness of breath, swollen ankles, and "just feeling poorly." Upon admission, the nurse conducts a health history, nutrition screen, blood tests, and an EKG. Our students, serving as dietetic interns, are given additional background information in the overview and are provided with questions to prepare them for the remainder of the case study exercises.

In addition to the narrative overview, interns have access to Clara's health history, her laboratory results, and the notes taken by the admitting nurse. The idea was to create a medical chart similar to those a student would face in the hospital. For more authenticity, the faculty secured permission to use actual forms from a regional healthcare management company. The forms were completed in longhand and scanned for students to access via the web (see Figure 67.1).

The interns are then asked to answer two questions and submit them via WebCT:

1) What do you know about this patient before entering her room? Be specific.

2) Is Clara at nutritional risk? If yes, explain why. If no, defend your position!

Faculty then assess whether or not the students are getting off to a good start.

Figure 67.1

Portion of Health History, Page 1 of 3

HEALTH HISTORY

NAME: Clara Hayes DATE OF BIRTH 6/14/32 DATE ____

I. CHIEF COMPLAINT (MAJOR REASON FOR OBTAINING PHYSICAL)
SOB "just feeling poorly"
Ankle edema

II. PAST MEDICAL HISTORY
SURGERIES: (IE: APPENDECTOMY, HYSTERECTOMY, HEART BY PASS, GALLBLADDER, ETC.)

Appendectomy	YEAR 1950
Hysterectomy	YEAR 1996
	YEAR
	YEAR
	YEAR

HAVE YOU EVER HAD A BLOOD TRANSFUSION? ____ YES __X__ NO

CHRONIC MEDICAL PROBLEMS: (IE: LUNG DISEASE, HIGH BLOOD PRESSURE, HEART DISEASE, DIABETES, CANCER, ETC.)

NIDDM	YEAR 1990
CRI	YEAR 1998
HTN	YEAR 1995
Osteoporosis	YEAR 1985
	YEAR

SIGNIFICANT ILLNESSES: (IE: PNEUMONIA, TUBERCULOSIS, RHEUMATIC FEVER, ETC.)

Pneumonia	YEAR 1992
Mono	YEAR 1988
	YEAR
	YEAR

Interns are also asked to complete several assignments prior to conducting the virtual consultation with Clara. For example, given Clara's height and weight, interns must calculate her body-mass index (BMI) using an online calculator. They must identify the mechanism of action and any potential drug/nutrient interactions from a list of her current medications. These assignments are also submitted via WebCT to the program coordinators.

The compilation of these formative authentic exercises and assessments help to prepare interns for the next phase of the case study, the virtual consultation. Reviewing the submissions enables the faculty to determine whether or not the interns are on the right track at several points, thereby providing opportunities for critical intervention, if necessary.

Once students begin the consultation with Clara, they experience more self-reflective formative assessments, while progressing through the case. First, the intern is presented with two ways to begin the consultation. Based on that decision, a short video clip will reveal a reaction from the client. At its conclusion, the intern is given critical commentary about the selected choice. The interns may return to the decision point and revise their choice based on the commentary from the first attempt.

Throughout the consultation, interns are given many choices about how to proceed. Following their decisions, interns will see Clara's reactions on video and receive critical commentaries and summaries to help them gauge the appropriateness of their choices. At certain times in the case study, interns can access additional information, such as laboratory results, nurses' notes, and questions.

As a summative assessment, interns are asked to complete and print out a Nutrition Progress Report page while they are on campus during the one-week orientation. Again, this page is an actual form used by a regional healthcare management company, scanned in portable document format (.pdf). To complete this progress report, interns must take into account all the information gathered from supporting materials and the virtual consultation. They are expected to discern which information is most appropriate for the report. According to the program faculty, students new to the field tend to provide too much information, and the coordinators help them winnow it down. In the end, interns present and discuss their completed reports in class.

ASSESSMENT

Is this an effective way to prepare future dietitians? To answer this critical question, the program faculty conducted an evaluation of the six case studies with a group of 25 interns. They were asked to evaluate certain items using a Likert scale of 1–5 (1 = most positive; 5 = least positive). The questions evaluated the case studies based on ease of use, level of independence from the instructor, applicability to practice, reality-based orientation, scientific accuracy, and usefulness and adequacy of resources. Most students rated these items in the 1–2 response category, with very few responses of a 3 or more. Additionally, students were asked to rate their increase in confidence, ability to apply theory [in] to practice, and overall satisfaction. Again, the majority of the responses were in the 1–2 range.

Students also provided some qualitative feedback on the case study system that was generally very positive. They made comments, such as "Very realistic and pertinent to what we will be doing in the internship" and "As close to reality as you can get while being on a computer." One student commented, "More videos and choices would make the cases more realistic." As a result, the faculty are developing four new virtual case studies that will be available this summer.

To continue our investigation into the effectiveness of this instructional model, the intern survey is being improved for the next session. The instrument will be broken into two parts: One focuses on case study questions; the other will evaluate the consultations. This redesign will provide the interns with opportunities to give more in-depth feedback relating to the two distinct segments of the case studies.

The program faculty have also created a peer review survey that was sent to over 200 nutrition and dietetic internship directors around the country. These directors were invited to take a tour of one case study and provide feedback via a web-based survey. The directors were asked to comment not only on the use of WebCT and video but the authenticity of the case and assignments as well. This study is ongoing, and results will be available in summer 2002.

The faculty also observed the "entertainment" value of the interactive case studies. As the technology became more complex, interns were disappointed when they were presented cases with less complex and involved technologies. The faculty noted that the interns working in groups would approach the consultation several times, because they were interested to hear the clients' various responses. Overall, the faculty found the virtual case study approach a useful tool in a dietetic internship orientation.

REFERENCE

Wiggins, G. (1990). The case for authentic assessment. *Eric Digest.* Available: http://ericae.net/edo/ED328611.htm

SUGGESTED READINGS

Duch, B. J., Groh, S. E., & Allen, D. E. (2001). Why problem-based learning? A case study of institutional change in undergraduate education. In B. J. Duch, S. E. Groh, & D. E. Allen (Eds.), *The power of problem-based learning.* Sterling, VA: Stylus.

Hamilton, C., Rucinski, A., & Schakelman, J. (2001, June). Innovating professional development for future health care practitioners. *T.H.E. Journal, 28* (11), 79–87.

68

ASSESSMENT: MEASURING THE IMPACT OF TECHNOLOGY-BASED TEACHING ON LEARNING

Ross A. Griffith, Wake Forest University

ASSESSMENT METHODS

The instruments being used to measure the effectiveness of the computing initiative implemented at Wake Forest in 1996 include the following: College Student Experiences Questionnaire (CSEQ), freshman/senior essay, College Student Survey (CSS), Higher Education Data Sharing (HEDS) Consortium Senior Survey, Wake Forest faculty survey, Higher Education Research Institute (HERI) Faculty Survey, in-house faculty computer survey, and in-house student computer survey.

CHANGES AMONG STUDENTS AND FACULTY

The CSEQ, HEDS Senior Survey, Wake Forest faculty survey, in-house faculty computer survey, and in-house student computer survey were administered to faculty and students before and after the computing initiative was implemented.

Administration of the CSEQ to freshmen, sophomores, and juniors in 1998 and 2000 indicated that our students' computer use in a number of areas has increased significantly. Certainly, such increases are expected, but ours are also significantly higher than other institutions nationally. Figure 68.1 depicts the sum of nine different computer items representing *quality of effort* for the 2000 Wake Forest students as compared to 1998 Wake Forest students but also as compared to national norm groups, including undergraduate students at research universities (RU), doctoral universities (DU), comprehensive colleges and universities (CCU), selective liberal arts colleges (SLA) and general liberal arts colleges (GLA).

The Wake Forest faculty survey results also indicated significant increases in their use of computers in a number of ways in 2001 as compared to both 1998 and 1995 (see Figure 68.2). Like the CSEQ results for students, the faculty results on both the 2001 and 1998 HERI Faculty Surveys' computer use items were higher overall than at other, comparable institutions nationally.

Figure 68.1

College Student Experiences Questionnaire (CSEQ) — Quality of Effort: Computer and Information Technology Scale

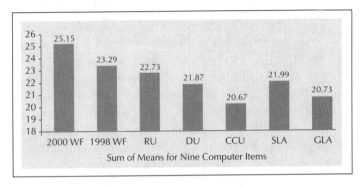

Figure 68.2

Wake Forest Faculty Survey — Means

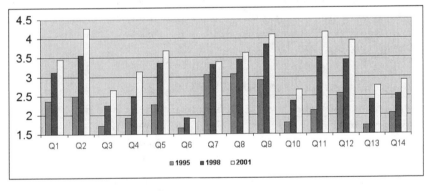

Q1 Computers in teaching
Q2 Computers in communication
Q3 Computers in individual instruction
Q4 Computers for presentations
Q5 Computers with information gathering
Q6 Computers for modeling/simulation
Q7 Computer knowledge compared to colleagues
Q8 Computer training and assistance
Q9 Students proficient with computers

Q10 Technology changed effectiveness of teaching
Q11 Effect of computers on communication
Q12 Effect of computers on resource material
Q13 Effect of computers on teaching/presentations
Q14 Effect of computers on teaching approach

ARE STUDENTS LEARNING MORE WITH TECHNOLOGY?

The question of learning outcomes as a result of technology use is being asked universally. While more research in this area is needed, it is very challenging, labor intensive, and potentially frustrating. For example, one institution examined a physics class. The investigator was fortunate in being able to assess two sections of the same course in one of which the instructor used technology and in the other did not. After much work, the investigator was dismayed to learn that the instructor awarded A's to all students in both sections. Even though this assessment was inconclusive, studies to determine the effectiveness of classroom technology use should continue.

The 2001 College Student Survey (CSS), administered to Wake Forest graduating seniors, asked, "To what degree did the use of technology in your classes add to your mastery of the course material?" A total of 33% of the seniors indicated "a great deal," and 53% answered "somewhat." This self-reported information from the 2001 seniors is certainly positive regarding the use of technology and its improvement of learning. Obviously, faculty must be asked the same question.

CONCLUSION

Survey results on Wake Forest students and faculty have demonstrated that both constituencies use technology significantly more than in the past and significantly more than their counterparts at institutions of higher education nationally. Recent results from Wake Forest seniors suggest, too, that students are learning more as a result of technology in the classroom.

RESOURCES

A tale of two HEDS with ubiquitous computing.

Assessment of the impact of ubiquitous computing.

Connecting students and faculty through technology, globalization, and collaboration at Wake Forest University.

The above readings can be accessed at: http://www.wfu.edu/administration/ir/presentations/index.html

69

FORMATIVE EVALUATION THROUGH ONLINE FOCUS GROUPS

Barbara A. Frey and Susan W. Alman
University of Pittsburgh

Web-based courses in higher education require renewed attention to the ways faculty teach and students learn. One strategy used to assess students' satisfaction with their distance education courses is the online focus group—group interviews, posted over the web, to gather descriptive, exploratory insight through the participants' detailed opinions and feelings.

In May 2001, the University of Pittsburgh began an online FastTrack program leading to a Master's Degree in Library and Information Science (MLIS). The program responds to the growing need for library and information science education in the Pennsylvania region and beyond. In order to monitor the students' satisfaction, to solicit input and recommendations, and to identify problems, online focus groups were used as one method of formative evaluation.

Focus group research, commonly used in face-to-face environments, was effective in this web-based environment, because all the students were experienced online communicators; these skills are essential to their success in the program. They are typical adult learners, balancing many roles, and prefer the flexibility of asynchronous discussions to synchronous chats. The focus group and web-based communication literature plus our experience in distance education guided the online focus group process.

With careful attention to their design, online focus groups can produce valuable results for faculty. Our first recommendation is to establish a clear goal for conducting the focus groups and communicate it to the participants. Our goal was to monitor student satisfaction, to solicit input and recommendations, and to identify problems with the new online program. Students have to know that their time and participation are needed and valued. They also need a secure environment that encourages honest, direct postings. We created such an environment by establishing a temporary course with our course management system. Its software allows teams to have private discussion forums to which only members and the instructor/facilitator had access; instructors and administrators did not. We randomly assigned eight or nine students to each focus group. Participation was optional, and students could post anonymously.

In addition, we suggest that the focus groups be held for a limited time. We limited our focus groups to ten days, which seemed to give students enough time to read and to respond several times to one another's comments. To begin the discussions, we posted six clear, open-ended discussion questions in each forum. The questions had an informal tone and dealt with students' expectations, the technology, interaction with the instructor, interaction among learners, and comparisons with traditional classes. Each question was a different thread of discussion. In traditional focus groups, student responses trigger a network of additional, spontaneous responses. We wanted to provide a similarly open environment.

We found that the rapport between the facilitator and the participants was an important consideration that should be addressed early in the focus-group planning process. The facilitator of these groups was an instructional designer from the university's Center for Instructional Development & Distance Education (CIDDE). An experienced online facilitator, she was not involved in the development or teaching of the courses. Trust is an important component of focus groups' dialogue and especially difficult to achieve in a ten-day online experience. Therefore, we incorporated a brief, face-to-face presentation by the instructional designer into the students' on-campus experiences prior to launching the focus groups. She explained their purpose and process and assured the participants of confidentiality and copies of the final report. She also joined students for two of their other on-campus activities. We believe that establishing a sense of trust with the facilitator was extremely beneficial to the focus groups' communication.

We had a total of 140 postings from our 35 students. Only seven postings were anonymous. Analyzing all the information we collected was the biggest challenge. Analyzing the results by replicating themes both within and across the focus groups was the format that worked best. An advantage of discussion boards was that the participants' online postings served as a transcript for examination.

In our case, most of the feedback focused on the online delivery format rather than the course content. For example, participants repeatedly noted the benefits of their cohort's support and the accessibility of their instructors. They wanted and appreciated feedback from their instructors. The challenging and time-consuming aspects of web-based courses were often mentioned but not necessarily from a negative standpoint. These learners expected a graduate course from a high-quality institution to be demanding. Group work had both advantages and disadvantages. Students appreciated collaborative learning opportunities but found scheduling synchronous planning sessions and completing assignments as a group to be difficult.

We struggled with the anonymous postings, because they made it impossible to calculate the exact number of focus-group participants. One student, seven students, or a student who had previously posted by name could have submitted the seven anonymous postings. We determined that student participation was between 51% and 71%. Only 5% of the postings were anonymous, yet the option promoted security and confidentiality. To address this problem in the future, we will ask students posting anonymously to self-select and use a three-digit signature number, which will allow us to track the number of participants more accurately, without revealing their identity.

Focus-group research is one of several strategies used to determine learner satisfaction with this MLIS program and to identify needed improvements; for example, additional instructor feedback on discussions, clear course expectations, more course options, and a netiquette guide. Instructors also use suggestion boxes and "water cooler" discussion forums and midterm evaluations to assess learner satisfaction. The course management system also provides user statistics that faculty can monitor. The focus group feedback resulting from specific questions provides instructors with valuable suggestions for immediate application as well as future revisions. In the final analysis, students know when they are learning and can offer a wealth of information if given the opportunity.

RESOURCES

Ohio State University. (n.d.). *Electronic class discussion.* Retrieved October 24, 2000, from http://www.osu.edu/education/ftad/Publications/elecdisc/pages/found.htm

Indiana University. (n.d.). *Focus groups.* Retrieved January 22, 2002, from http://universe.indiana.edu/clp/rf/focusg.htm

Krueger, R. A., & Casey, M. A. (2002). *Focus groups: A practical guide for applied research.* Thousand Oaks, CA: Sage.

70

Assessment as the Lever

Kevin Barry
University of Notre Dame

In "Implementing the Seven Principles: Technology as Lever," Chickering and Ehrmann (1996) examine the seven principles of effective practice in higher education and discuss ways in which various technologies might be used to enhance practice in each area. Faculty interest in technology and its use for teaching and learning has provided an opportunity to examine courses and teaching strategies to see if they align with known best practice. The same strategy can be used to assess the effectiveness of a teaching strategy or an entire course.

At the University of Notre Dame, the assessment activities that are part of Scholarship of Teaching and Learning (SoTL) projects have been the lever that has prompted faculty members to examine their courses and teaching strategies. The Kaneb Center for Teaching and Learning initiated the campus SoTL (Boyer, 1990) project in 1999 as part of the Carnegie Academy for the Scholarship of Teaching and Learning (CASTL) program. The campus SoTL project called for faculty to submit proposals for projects in which existing practice would be examined or new initiatives would be attempted and assessed. A SoTL support team comprised of two staff members from the Kaneb Center, one person from institutional research, and a national Carnegie Scholar from the chemistry department was formed. It selected nine campus projects and worked with the faculty involved to devise assessment methods for the questions that were being asked. Details on the projects are available at http://kaneb.nd.edu/sotl.html.

It was also necessary to ensure that student learning goals were clearly identified for each teaching strategy to be assessed. Developing clear goals in the form of student outcomes often led to discussions of the importance of writing goals in a way that would allow measurement based on observable student behaviors. In another effort of the Kaneb Center, we developed the Teaching Well Using Technology workshop, in which technology is discussed only after goals have been clearly stated. In many cases, course goals had previously been defined in more general terms or using passive language that focuses on instructor behaviors rather than student learning outcomes; for example, "This course will cover..." The opportunity for faculty to reflect on their courses in a new way frequently results in many questions beyond the original plan to assess a new strategy. Questions that arise are often much broader and may involve rethinking what the most important goals of the course are; what pedagogical strategies would be most effective in realizing them; and what assessments would truly measure their achievement.

In a recent meeting of SoTL project participants, one of the faculty members said, "Though I started out thinking about a very specific question relating to the teaching of this course, I'm now asking questions about the entire nature of the course, what its goals should be, and how it should be taught." That statement provides an excellent indication of the impact that is possible when faculty begin to assess even a very specific part of their teaching. There is now an opportunity to use the current interest in assessment, as evidenced by movements like the Carnegie program on the Scholarship of Teaching, as the lever that gets faculty to consider their teaching in light of desired student outcomes and to help them identify best practices that will facilitate student achievement.

REFERENCES

Boyer, E. L. (1990). *Scholarship reconsidered: Priorities of the professoriate.* Princeton, NJ: The Carnegie Foundation for the Advancement of Teaching.

Chickering, A., & Ehrmann, S. C. (1996, October). Implementing the seven principles: Technology as lever. *AAHE Bulletin,* 3–6.

71

STUDENT PERCEPTIONS ON THE VALUE OF POWERPOINT

Barbara A. Frey and Daria C. Kirby
University of Pittsburgh

Classroom lectures with PowerPoint presentations are an everyday occurrence in the Katz Business School at the University of Pittsburgh. Many MBA faculty members post PowerPoint slides on their web sites for students to print and bring to class. Well-developed slides provide a valuable outline that assists professors with their delivery and organizes the lecture material for students.

Literature is available on the graphic design of PowerPoint presentations, but relatively few articles have been written on the instructional considerations. In this particular case, the professor developed PowerPoint slides for her Organizational Behavior class based on her class notes and the textbook's instructor's manual. Her purpose in using PowerPoint was to engage the students' interest and facilitate their understanding of the course material. The slides consisted of text, graphs, charts, and images. An instructional designer reviewed them for organization and clarity. In order to examine student perceptions on the value of these PowerPoint slides, we developed and administered a survey to three sections of Organizational Behavior (95 students).

These 95 students are quite familiar with PowerPoint presentations. Not only had PowerPoint been used in most of their MBA courses, but also they had participated in an advanced PowerPoint workshop at the beginning of the MBA program. They collaborated on team projects involving PowerPoint presentations. Therefore, at the time of our survey, they are well aware of the benefits and challenges of designing effective PowerPoint presentations.

Our 12-item Likert scale survey examined student perceptions of how PowerPoint presentations affect their attention, behavior, motivation, and recall of lecture material. It also addressed the value of PowerPoint for note taking, studying, and participating in class. In addition to the Likert scale items, the survey included two open-ended questions that addressed 1) why students would like to see or not see PowerPoint presentations and 2) suggestions for improving PowerPoint presentations. In a pilot study, the Cronbach's alpha for survey reliability is .80 (.80 or higher is considered acceptable).

The 5-point Likert scale ranges from strongly disagree (1) to strongly agree (5). Most of the learners reported positive attitudes toward the use of PowerPoint in this course. The two highest mean responses were for "PowerPoint helps me take better notes" and "PowerPoint helps to emphasize key points." Students also agreed that PowerPoint helped to hold their attention. Interestingly, they agreed that "professors who use PowerPoint presentations are more organized during their presentations." This professor was interested to know whether posting slides on the web prior to class had an impact on student attendance. In this case, students disagreed; they were "less likely to attend class when PowerPoint handouts are posted on the web."

The open-ended questions also provided valuable information. Several students commented that PowerPoint was easier to read than the chalkboard. It aided them in taking notes and allowed them to focus on what the instructor was saying rather than "frantically writing." The most common student suggestion for using PowerPoint was to keep the slides simple. In other words, avoid putting too much information on one slide. One student suggested that background designs be removed to simplify printing.

This survey is a formative evaluation instrument that provides us with important information in designing PowerPoint presentations. For example, one strategy the professor used was including slides with specific discussion questions. Students agreed that PowerPoint used in this way increased their class participation. As a result, the professor now plans to use this strategy more and to explore more active-learning strategies. She is considering slides that require students to vote on an issue, put several behaviors into sequence, or match statistics with management behaviors. Another strategy she used was to supplement the text slides with graphics. Students agreed that visual images helped them to recall content during exams. In addition to implementing some of the student recommendations, the professor plans to experiment with a portable mouse that will allow her to move around the room during the presentations.

Ultimately, the instructor, not the computer, is the most important component of effective PowerPoint presentations. With careful attention to the instructional purpose and design, presentation software like PowerPoint can be a valuable supplement to effective instruction.

INDEX